THE ETHICAL THOUGHT
OF HANS URS VON BALTHASAR

THE ETHICAL THOUGHT
OF
HANS URS VON BALTHASAR

CHRISTOPHER W. STECK, S.J.

A Herder and Herder Book
The Crossroad Publishing Company
New York

The Crossroad Publishing Company
481 Eighth Avenue, New York, NY 10001

Printed in the United States of America

Library of Congress Cataloging-in-Publication Data

Steck, Christopher W.
    The ethical thought of Hans Urs von Balthasar / Christopher W. Steck.
        p. cm.
    "A Herder and Herder book."
    Includes bibliographical references and index.
    ISBN 0-8245-1915-9 (alk. paper)
    1. Balthasar, Hans Urs von, 1905-   .—Ethics.   I. Title.
BX4705.B163 S74 2001
170—dc21

                                        2001004059

    1   2   3   4   5   6   7   8   9   10   05   04   03   02   01

To my parents

JOHN W. STECK (1921–1999)
and
SARAH LANG STECK (1926–1978)

Contents

ABBREVIATIONS	ix
ACKNOWLEDGMENTS	xi
INTRODUCTION	1

CHAPTER

1 Aesthetics and Human Response   7
The Place of Beauty in von Balthasar's Theological Reflection   9
The Beautiful Form   14
Beauty and Human Agency   20
The Interpersonal Encounter   28

2 The Trinitarian Horizon of Human Action   34
The Triune Personal God   36
The Relation of the Son to the Father   39
Christological Incorporation   43
The Dramatic Form   50
Divine Command Ethics—Initial Considerations   58

3 Divine Commands and Human Fulfillment   62
Christian Obedience   64
The Question of Fulfillment   72
Obedience and Fulfillment   80
Conclusion   91

4 Creation and Covenant   93
Christian Particularism   95

The Presuppositions of the Covenant   102
For the Greater Glory of God   107
Neighbor Love within the I/Thou Encounter   112
Conclusion   121

5 Contemplation and Action   123
An Aesthetic Ethics: Iris Murdoch and the Vision of the Good 124
Christian Perception   128
Christian Attunement   145

CONCLUSION: In Praise of Glory   150

NOTES   161

BIBLIOGRAPHY   207

INDEX   219

Abbreviations

━━━━━━◆◆◆◆◆━━━━━━

GL1–GL7   *The Glory of the Lord: A Theological Aesthetics* in seven
volumes
Vol. 1 *Seeing the Form*
Vol. 2 *Studies in Theological Style: Clerical Styles*
Vol. 3 *Studies in Theological Styles: Lay Styles*
Vol. 4 *The Realm of Metaphysics in Antiquity*
Vol. 5 *The Realm of Metaphysics in the Modern Age*
Vol. 6 *Theology: The Old Covenant*
Vol. 7 *Theology: The New Covenant*

TD1–TD5   *Theo-Drama: Theological Dramatic Theory* in five vol-
umes
Vol. 1 *Prolegomena*
Vol. 2 *The Dramatis Personae: Man in God*
Vol. 3 *The Dramatis Personae: The Person in Christ*
Vol. 4 *The Action*
Vol. 5 *The Last Act*

TL1–TL3   *Theologik* in three volumes
Vol. 1 *Wahrheit der Welt*
Vol. 2 *Wahrheit Gottes*
Vol. 3 *Der Geist der Wahrheit*

Acknowledgments

————◆━◆◆◆━◆————

T HIS BOOK IS A REVISION and development of my dissertation. In writing the dissertation, I was blessed with two (co-)directors, Professors Margaret A. Farley and Cyril O'Regan, different in many ways but sharing a common learned love of the Catholic, Christian tradition. I was first introduced to von Balthasar in a course on his thought offered by Professor O'Regan, and throughout the research and writing of the dissertation Professor O'Regan helped me see the spirit of von Balthasar's thought. Professor Farley's help extended far beyond the dissertation. I was the (very grateful) beneficiary of her ready ear and ever apt response throughout my studies at Yale. To both Margaret and Cyril I owe an enormous debt of gratitude.

To my Jesuit brothers I offer my fond and prayerful thanks. In my studies at Yale I received the support and encouragement of the leadership of the New Orleans Province of the Society of Jesus. The Jesuits at the Fairfield and Georgetown communities have been welcome companions at the different stages of this book's development. Several Jesuits of the Georgetown community (John Langan, S.J., Otto Hentz, S.J., and Scott Pilarz, S.J.) were helpful in different ways in the endeavor to turn the dissertation into a book. The companionship and patience of Jesuit friends were important during the ups and downs of the project.

To the editors at Crossroad: my thanks to John Jones for his early encouragement and to Alison Donohue and Michael Parker for their very helpful advice. Early feedback on the project from Gene Outka and Thomas Ogletree of Yale University helped me clarify the book's argument. Many others made the project bearable and often enjoyable: colleagues at Yale, good friends, and a very loving family.

For the gifts of life and love, given many years ago and continuing in the present, I express my profound gratitude to my parents, John W. Steck and Sarah Lang Steck. It was from them that I first learned what Christian generosity and love were all about. I hope it will prove someday to be a lesson well learned and well lived.

Finally, for the aforementioned gifts, for the many not noted or known, and for whatever goodness appears in what follows: *Deo Gratia*.

Introduction

————◆•◆•◆————

IN THE CHAPTERS THAT FOLLOW, I attempt to construct the ethical theory implicit in the writings of Hans Urs von Balthasar, especially *The Glory of the Lord* and *Theo-Drama*.[1] While a number of ideas and claims in these works provide important bases for his ethical theory, I offer the following as central: God's glory appears. It has appeared within human history in the person of Jesus Christ and continues to appear before us, foremost in the testimony of Scripture and the ministry of the church, but also in the labor of the Spirit in all of creation. "God's glory appears"—the simple phrase signals two important claims. First, *God's* glory appears. God's own being, and not just some new fact about the divine nature, manifests itself to human perception. Second, God's *glory* appears. The manifestation is glorious and thus commanding, attractive, and transformative to the beholder. God's glory, divine beauty, draws the beholder, ek-statically, out of his or her previous existence into a participation in the continuing mission of Christ.

Because of the christological foundation of his ethics, von Balthasar, I believe, offers an important contribution to the reform effort of the last several decades to articulate an ethics that is both rooted in the vocation of the Christian and broadly "catholic." That reform, called for by Vatican II,[2] was anticipated in Gérard Gilleman's *The Primacy of Charity* and reached an early milestone in Bernard Häring's *Free and Faithful in Christ*.[3] But at least in one regard von Balthasar's ethics runs counter to the general trend in Catholic ethics in that it moves nearer a divine command ethics, traditionally viewed as antithetical to Catholic moral commitments. However, von Balthasar's theological aesthetics ("God's glory *appears*") lays a foundation for reshaping the

1

motifs of divine command theory (e.g., divine sovereignty, divine freedom, interpersonal encounter) into a form that addresses at least some
of the concerns raised by critics of divine command ethics (e.g., an
emphasis on the opposition between the divine and the human; a
nominalistic view of the created order; a moral obligation that is heteronomous and a-rational). Because of this aesthetic reshaping, his
ethics, in the best of the Catholic tradition, witnesses to the possibility
of the Catholic "and." That is, it is an approach to the moral life that
preserves some point of contact between the human and the divine
(between reason and faith, experience and Scripture, nature and grace).
And it does so while simultaneously embracing other themes that
resound in the Catholic spiritual tradition but are typically kept on the
margins of its strictly natural law reflection: the living presence and
sovereignty of God in one's life; the Christian life as the intentional
response to God's work in salvation history; the covenantal encounter,
which stakes a particular claim on the human agent; the vocational call,
which comes in the prayerful consideration of what God wants for
oneself. Ultimately, I want to go beyond a descriptive claim about von
Balthasar's ethics (i.e., it is a form of divine command ethics) to a specific, normative claim: the central commitment of divine command
ethics—that the moral obligation confronting the individual depends
in a substantive way on the divine will—can and should be part of
Catholic theological ethics.

The great theologians of our time, Karl Barth, Karl Rahner, and, of
course, Hans Urs von Balthasar, all sound the note of theological voluntarism. That fact in itself might argue that Catholic ethicists should
attend to the theme. But additionally, there is a shared theological
commitment which drives each of these thinkers to incorporate volun-
tarist elements (albeit in vastly different ways): God desires to relate to
each of us covenantally, that is, personally, and that relationship constitutes, at least partially, our identity. Many Christians generally share
this commitment. Unfortunately, it is also one of those theological
ideas (one thinks of eschatology and pneumatology as well) that has
been treated as irrelevant to ethics. However, insofar as our interpersonal relationship with God is central to the ethical theories found in
Barth, Rahner, and von Balthasar, their approaches offer examples of
how this theological idea can have ethical implications.

For Karl Barth, the Christ-event does not so much add a new
attribute of human existence (e.g., a covenantal quality) to a nature
which is otherwise indifferent to Christ. Rather the form and shape of

that existence are now "covenantal" from the ground up and are thus defined by historical and personal encounters with God. No neutral identity exists apart from that encounter. This total, christological transformation means that there can be no true knowledge of who the person is and, correspondingly, no true knowledge of how one is to live apart from Jesus Christ. Moreover, because our true identity is found only in the event-filled, historical relationship with God—a relation filled with the new and unexpected, each person precisely *is* (i.e., exists, achieves self-hood, etc.) through her daily responses to God.[4] An ethical system of universal moral norms threatens to squeeze human activity, and thus human identity, into a uniform mold that hides the existential quality of human activity—that is, its capacity to manifest an identity-shaped response to a grace that is always concrete, historical, personal, and ultimately determinative of our being.

For Karl Rahner, the human person is engaged in a fundamental project of freedom, borne and sustained by God, in which the individual determines *who* he or she will become before God. The agent shapes the project in his or her response to the (divine) horizon of freedom through particular acts of love, whose trajectory transcends the concrete particularity of their objects. As this fundamental project of self-determination moves to completion and fulfillment, the individual's freedom is increasingly stamped through these concrete acts with a fundamental yes or no to God.

Yet this project of freedom is more than one of shaping our lives according to a simple binary choice of yes or no. It is the project to "realize *self*," to determine the identity of our existence. Thus, in the achievement of *self*-realization, there must be something individuating about one's yes or no, something beyond a generic answer to God, reflective of the individual's unique personhood. One could argue that such an individuation is grounded in a person's autonomous choice about who he or she will become. But Rahner argues that the source of the *entire* project of *self*-realization, and not just the binary decision to say yes or no to God, must lie in the Absolute if that project is to achieve its radical depth and finality. The absolute ground of human freedom, then, is not only the sustainer of human freedom; it is also the giver and sustainer of *uniquely personal* freedom. God opens up human transcendence in the concrete by leading it along a particular path within the domain of universal laws and norms.[5] That path is comprised of a unique ethical law which is the individual's way of realizing self.[6]

> We are dealing with the unique . . . individual, who in faith and love is
> not . . . to [hand over to God] a universal human nature which is the
> same in everybody . . . Rather each individual is to entrust *himself* in the
> uniqueness which belongs inalienably and inseparably to him as a his-
> torical and free being. But [this implies] basically that there must be a
> unique and quite personal relationship between Jesus Christ . . . and
> each individual . . . which is not exhausted by abstract norms and uni-
> versal laws. . . . [and which is] *ultimately identical with the destiny and*
> *with the deed which is required of every person in his whole life, and for*
> *which he is responsible.*[7]

The uniqueness of the individual is not only the object of God's *creating* will, Rahner states, but also the object of God's "morally binding will."[8] Though rarely commented on by Catholic ethicists
influenced by Rahner's thought, this ethically binding, theological voluntarism is integral to Rahner's thought. He introduces it as part of a
comprehensive argument about the dignity of the person and the manner in which that dignity is brought to its full realization in one's relationship with God. The dignity of the person does not simply *allow* the
element of voluntarism; it positively demands it. And thus in different
ways, we find in both Barth and Rahner a connection between self-
identity and God's personal and binding will for the individual.

Another instance of this linkage between command and identity
occurs in the work of Hans Urs von Balthasar. Like Barth, but unlike
Rahner, von Balthasar articulates this link in a christologically specified
way. For von Balthasar, just as the Father "missions" the Son to a specific task which defines his existence, so also the Father missions each
Christian to a particular christological and life-defining project. The
Christian, through the gift of the Spirit, is fully incorporated into the
risen life of Christ. From this christological location, he or she enters
into the Son's relationship with the Father in a radical way that is
scarcely imaginable in Barth's thought.

In introducing an element of theological voluntarism into their
thought, both Rahner and von Balthasar reveal the influence of
Ignatius of Loyola.[9] Both von Balthasar and Rahner believed that the
theology and spirituality of Ignatius represented an important advance
in the history of Christian thought. And both similarly believed that
the church's theology and ethics had not yet "caught up with the
unconscious theology underlying" Ignatius's *Spiritual Exercises*.[10]
Ignatius effected a "revolution" in the understanding of Christian life
that "has not yet been fully recognized."[11] Toward the end of his life,
Rahner wrote:

Ignatius was not simply a very holy man—after all, that much applies to every saint. With him, a new theology begins to be lived out, and the task of articulating this theology reflectively has not yet really been tackled. And the success of this enterprise will be a very substantial factor among those deciding the fate of future Catholic theology.[12]

The deep grammar of von Balthasar's ethics and theology resonates powerfully with the *Spiritual Exercises*. Therefore, his project might be understood as a contribution to this task of articulating an Ignatian theology and ethics for the Christian community. Indeed, I believe that in at least one regard his contribution is superior to Rahner's: because von Balthasar's thought is less structurally indebted to one particular theological system (i.e., that of Thomas Aquinas), he can and does allow Ignatius a more comprehensive influence in shaping his theology, and in particular his ethics. Because of this influence, we can appropriately describe von Balthasar's ethics as an "Ignatian reconfiguration" of divine command ethics.

The fact that his writings offer little in the way of an explicit reflection on theological ethics makes the task of examining von Balthasar's ethics difficult. While it is true that he did write one essay on ethics, "Nine Propositions of Christian Ethics,"[13] this does not adequately reflect the moral theory implied in the seven volumes of *The Glory of the Lord* and the five volumes of *Theo-Drama*. His theological aesthetics is almost completely absent from the essay. In particular, the essay glosses over how Christian action is a response to the *perceived* (i.e., aesthetically) appearance of divine glory. Thus, while I will refer to the essay, the focus in this book will be on *The Glory of the Lord* and *Theo-Drama*. Since von Balthasar provides no systematic treatment of ethics, we must attempt to assemble a coherent theory of ethics out of his approaches to related concepts—e.g., human agency, anthropology, and freedom. The theory I present below is indicated in his writings, though never made explicit. Given the richness and depth of von Balthasar's ideas and their unsystematic presentation, however, there probably can be no definitive interpretation of his ethics. In addition to this expository and developmental effort, the book, as I indicated above, reaches toward the normative—that is, a claim about what can and should be part of a Christian, Catholic moral theory.

In the first of five chapters, I sketch out the basic features of the theological aesthetics of *The Glory of the Lord*. It offers a way of "seeing" the world and the Christ-event that illuminates certain elements: creation's radiance as propaedeutic to God's revelation, the convergence

of freedom and surrender, the glory of the Christ-*form*, and the obediential decentering which that form awakens in the human subject. In
Theo-Drama, von Balthasar expands and develops his "iconic aesthetics" into a "dramatic aesthetics": he views human action in light of the
salvific drama, one whose form invites the beholder's lived and storied
response. In the second chapter, I explore this dramatic form and show
how it leads to an ethics that shares some key emphases with divine
command theory. Chapters 3 and 4 explore the difficulties this approach
presents to many Christian ethicists, particularly those in the Catholic
tradition. Chapter 3 takes up the issue of whether obedience to a commanding God is antithetical to the traditional Catholic idea of an
intrinsic connection between the moral life and human fulfillment. It
suggests that with his Ignatian idea of the Christian's "mission," von
Balthasar can argue that God's commanding address to the person
draws to fulfillment the deep movements of the human spirit and, particularly, its desires for self-identity. Chapter 4 addresses the concern
that an ethics of divine command necessarily forces Christian ethics
into an esotericism. I show that von Balthasar advocates the integrity
and relative autonomy of creation because the covenant requires that
the "otherness" of creation be preserved precisely so that God can
enter into a relationship with it. Finally, I return to the aesthetics of
The Glory of the Lord in light of *Theo-Drama* to argue that for von
Balthasar Christians' ethical existence is a response to the appearance
of God's work in the world before them.

1

Aesthetics and Human Response

———◆◆◆◆———

I N *THE GLORY OF THE LORD*, Hans Urs von Balthasar makes a connection, fundamental to his theory, between perception and response. The connection, in turn, provides the ground for a further link, implicit in von Balthasar's thought, between perception and ethics. This chapter explores how von Balthasar uses the idea of "beauty" and its theological analogate, divine glory, to establish this connection. The aesthetics, or theory of perception, that von Balthasar develops is based on the idea that the appearing form of Christ relativizes all worldly measures of beauty. Yet because Christ's form truly appears in the world, as a form *of* the world, God's communication does not overwhelm the created order but rather refashions it in order to serve divine glory. The ethical significance of this becomes clearer in the second part of the chapter, where I examine how this appearing glory unlocks a particular type of moral agency in the human person. In Jesus Christ, God's glory manifests itself to the human perceiver, commanding total submission, and yet it also engages human freedom and autonomy. By interpreting the moral act through the lens of the beautiful form and the response it evokes, von Balthasar draws together these two currents, the divine command and the free human response.

Two observations, one about the methodology of this chapter and the other about von Balthasar's concept of "beauty," should be made at the outset. Much of this chapter follows von Balthasar's philosophical reflection "from below"—that is, we move *from* a reflection on general moral experiences in the world *to* the particularity of Christian moral existence. For von Balthasar, the danger with such an approach is that it could distort what Christ has revealed by force-fitting it into a preconceived, earthly mold. For this reason, von Balthasar's aesthetic argument is ultimately Christian (both in its source and content). Still, he approaches it on both philosophical and Christian levels—a "stereo-scopic view," if you will. Although a philosophical examination has as its formal object the same created reality that is used by God to express his absolute Word, it must be a tentative one. For in any adequate the-ological (or Christian moral) reflection, one cannot bracket the ultimate christological end point. We proceed then with intentional awareness of how our analysis "from below" is influenced by and culminates in an explicitly christological (and ultimately trinitarian) account.

In regard to von Balthasar's understanding of beauty we can note that the specific valence of beauty that configures von Balthasar's the-ory of perception (and thus his ethics) is not earthly beauty but its the-ological analogate, divine glory. Even so, "earthly" beauty receives close examination in von Balthasar's thought because it is the site where the earthly becomes theophanous (i.e., where it manifests God). In the beautiful form creation already offers a reflection of divine glory and thus the beautiful form shows creation's availability to be made the bearer of divine communication.

Von Balthasar provides examples of experiences of beauty (e.g., works of art). Yet these are more exemplary for him than paradigmatic. All realities (objects, activities, etc.) participate in beauty, but do so according to the nature of the reality being perceived. However, so much of what we experience in our daily lives can scarcely be called "beautiful." Indeed, we are continually confronted with "the shrillness of all that is ugly, that is warped, that is hopelessly mediocre and vul-gar" (*GL4* 20). Wherein then lies the beautiful? Von Balthasar pro-poses that creaturely realities have the power to express themselves in meaningful forms. We experience this power in our response to the wondrous eyes of an infant or to the frailty of an elderly person. These creaturely forms manifest the created entity's worth and dignity and, in doing so, command our loving reverence. The expressive, com-manding power of the object to draw forth a response of love is at the heart of what von Balthasar means by "beauty."

"Glory" for von Balthasar refers to divine beauty. Glory—*kābôd* in Hebrew, *doxa* in Greek—is the term used most frequently by biblical writers to express the appearance of divine splendor in and through the forms of the world.[1] Since reality is always charged with divine presence, it is always possible for graced eyes to find in worldly forms the reflection of the absolute. The decisive appearance of divine beauty, glory, in earthly form is reserved for the Christ-form. Here the absolute does not appear in such a way that the form points *beyond* itself to the divine; rather Christ is himself absolute truth, goodness, and beauty in concrete form. He makes visible that to which every other instance of truth, goodness, and beauty can only point.

The second part of this chapter illustrates that there are different levels of human response corresponding to the different expressions of beauty. The beautiful form that is simply attractive to behold (e.g., a beautiful painting) evokes a psychological response; our affection is moved toward the object. But there are also forms of worldly beauty that radiate the divine presence, the principal case being the human neighbor. Such forms elicit a moral response. Finally, the beauty of earthly glory, Christ, evokes a response in the human person that is total. The person gives herself over in the surrender of faith.

The Place of Beauty
in von Balthasar's Theological Reflection

The link that von Balthasar makes between the Christian moral response and a perception of divine *beauty* might seem at first glance to sentimentalize and even trivialize the harsh demands that the path of the cross can entail. By grounding ethics in a response to the beautiful form, we effectively introduce a principle—pleasure-seeking—that is foreign to Christian ethics. The corresponding image of the Christian agent would appear uncomfortably similar to Kierkegaard's aesthete: an identity-less individual, drifting from one moment of pleasure to the next, forgoing the self-denying discipline that the moral life requires. Von Balthasar attempts to distance beauty and aesthetics from these false associations in the "Introduction" to volume 1 of *The Glory of the Lord*. For von Balthasar the beautiful form awakens the moral response in the first place by decentering the individual, drawing her obediently beyond herself. The beauty of Christ, as the glory of God appearing in the world, pierces and transforms the individual, drawing forth an obediential response that is not so much sensual, as happens in the case of Kierkegaard's aesthete, but affective, rational, and expressive of the new creation she has become.

Despite this Christ-tutored understanding of beauty, one can still question the helpfulness and appropriateness of constructing theology, and derivatively ethics, around the idea that the gospel is not only true and good but also beautiful. Moreover, once we recognize the analogy that von Balthasar makes between beauty and divine glory, we begin to suspect that he is asserting something still stronger: divine *beauty*—the glory of the Lord—is *the* primary lens for interpreting God's work in Christ. We can glean two supports for this focus on beauty/glory from von Balthasar's writings. First, such a focus has been an important part of the tradition, and the shift away from a theology of divine beauty or glory raises at least a prima facie concern that theological discourse has undergone a distortion. Second, beauty is necessary if we are to preserve the connection between contemplation and action, or between truth perceived and truth done.

The two arguments are mutually supportive. The first argument has two parts. Initially von Balthasar makes the general claim that a theology of glory can be found at the center of the most important and creative theologies in Christian history. He pursues this argument in the second and third volumes of *The Glory of the Lord*. In this series of monographs dealing with diverse individuals (some are theologians, others literary figures), von Balthasar shows how a theology of glory formed the "middle point" of texts produced by such individuals as Irenaeus, Augustine, Anselm, Dante, Pascal, and Hopkins. He finds indicators of this theology in the themes that reappear in the works of these great thinkers: the ever-greaterness of God, the *eros* of human longing which Christ awakens, the orientation of nature to the advent of grace, the sacramentality of the world's images, the shattering of human understanding before the "whylessness" of God's love as revealed in Christ. That key figures in the Christian intellectual tradition have espoused themes central to a theology of glory argues in favor of such a theology.

The second part of this first argument for the focus on beauty lies in the particular conceptual framework von Balthasar uses to pursue his own theology of glory. In addition to the general appeal to key theologies of glory, von Balthasar also appropriates the ideas of one instance of that tradition, authoritative in the Catholic tradition because of its association with Thomas Aquinas: the scholastic idea of the transcendentals. This framework is important inasmuch as it allows him to argue for some analogous ties between beauty and glory.[2]

A brief overview of this tradition can help us understand von

Balthasar's particular appropriation of it. The doctrine of the transcendentals arose in response to the newly translated writings of Aristotle, which challenged Christian thinkers to develop their own, Christian interpretation of reality.[3] Aristotle presented a world in which everything could be classified in terms of ten exhaustive categories (e.g., species, genera, accidents), all of which shared in the common trait of describing beings. "Being," for Aristotle and for the Thomistic tradition that followed him, is not just the most inclusive of categories; it transcends the very notion of category. It is the most general and universally predictable feature of reality, transcending yet including all of them.[4] In addition, being can be viewed under different aspects (as one, true, good, and beautiful), which are distinguished not as different realities but as different ways of perceiving being. Insofar as being is undivided in an existent, it is "one." Insofar as it is knowable, it is "true." Insofar as it is lovable, it is "good." Insofar as it is both knowable and lovable (at once), it is "beautiful." And all beings are, as being, undivided, knowable, lovable, and beautiful. Hence, like being itself, these transcendentals transcend any category and are attributable to all beings.

While some debate whether Thomas ever held beauty to be a distinct transcendental,[5] he did make an important distinction that, for von Balthasar, provides Aquinas's thought with an adequate philosophical basis for a theology of glory. God is the one whose very essence is to exist; every other creature has its existence (the principle whereby it *is*) as something additional to its essence (the principle whereby it is *what* it is). This distinction between the *being* of God (who exists in "purity," to use Etienne Gilson's term,[6] since his act of being is his "essence") and the *being* of the creature (whose existence is always limited, contingent, "borrowed") allowed Thomas to use a common language (e.g., "being") in his examination of both universal being (*ens commune*) and absolute being (God) without equating the two.[7] Creation participates in the perfection of God, while remaining radically distinct from God (as seen in the "real distinction" between God's being and the being of creation).

We can speak then of an "analogy of being" between God and creation. Words that express perfections we experience in ourselves and in our world (truth, goodness, beauty, existence) can be attributed to God once we recognize that the perfection is found in God in a supereminent manner, that is, in a way that exceeds what human imaginings can grasp.[8] Like "being" itself, earthly perfections are participations in qualities that exist in God in an infinitely supereminent fashion. Thus, divine beauty, glory, has its analogue in earthly beauty. Von Balthasar underscores the christological basis of this analogical tie. The created order reflects God's goodness and beauty because the Father always intended creation to have its exemplar and goal in the Son.

We have therefore in von Balthasar, as one support for his focus on beauty, a twofold retrieval of the tradition. First, he derives from the tradition a normative claim for a theology of glory. Second, he makes use of a specific form of that tradition, the scholastic transcendentals, as a framework for arguing the analogous tie between earthly beauty and divine glory. Thus, beauty is important because it assists in a theological reflection on divine glory.

But, even if we grant that one can establish an analogous connection between beauty and glory, we might still wonder why von Balthasar continues to appeal to the beautiful form when it is clear that glory is the proper focus of theological reflection. Here a second support for the focus on beauty becomes important. For von Balthasar, some notion of earthly beauty and the beautiful form must be part of our theological reflection as a ground for the themes associated with a theology of glory. Two themes are important here. First, preserving the link between truth perceived and truth performed requires beauty. Second, beauty is the location where creation can be made to reveal God. Ultimately for von Balthasar, no genuine theology of glory—and thus, no adequate Christian theology—can be achieved without the inclusion of beauty as a part of the philosophical substratum of theological reflection.

First, beauty is necessary because it alone can preserve the connection between truth and goodness, as we shall see in the chapter's second part. For von Balthasar, once beauty no longer merits the serious attention of philosophical reflection, truth and goodness will undergo a certain deformation and become isolated realms of human knowledge. Truth will be equated with scientific conclusions, and goodness will be reduced to utilitarian calculations. Thus, fairly consistently, von Balthasar characterizes truth and goodness apart from beauty as "cold," "bare," "naked," or "pragmatic"—qualities that point to the absence of any existential link between truth and goodness. The themes surrounding the idea of beauty (e.g., dynamic movement, attractiveness, desire, ek-stasy) make this connection possible: insofar as it is also beautiful, truth can awaken our moral response. The link between truth and goodness (or, action) which beauty preserves is the natural foundation which, in a theology of glory, is transformed into a link between the objective revelation in Christ and the subjective response of faith.[9] Excluding the idea of the beautiful form distorts the response of faith into a mere submission to divine power.

But more importantly, beauty is essential for theology because it acts as the guardian of the depth of creation and ultimately of its "openness" to a revelation from above. As we will see later, creation is more than what is visible on the surface or what can be discovered in its component parts. That something "more" about creation is essential if the God who is ever greater than creation is to reveal the divine self within the forms of creation. For von Balthasar, the weakening of our aesthetic perception (i.e., our capacity or willingness to "see" the beautiful form) has dimmed or even blinded us to the glory of God by removing from sight the location where that glory appears. Retrieving beauty is thus necessary not simply to restore the aesthetic appeal of Christianity but to enable us to speak meaningfully of the revelation of what is essentially more than creaturely in the forms of creation.[10] It is necessary to preserve the *thickness* of creation lest the conditions for a genuine self-revelation of God be undermined.[11] Moreover, allowing our perceptions of the world to be tutored by a consideration of the beautiful form assists in that preservation. For beauty indicates that the world is already more than simple facts and that its goodness is more than the determination of cost and benefits.

We can detect in this notion of creation's depth the influence of Erich Przywara, who introduced von Balthasar to the doctrine of the analogy of being.[12] Particularly important for the development of von Balthasar's thought was Przywara's idea that the God world relationship is one of dynamic "polarity": creation is oriented toward God's revelation in Christ in such a way that revelation does not violate the world's integrity, but neither are the structures of the world a rigid mold to which revelation must then conform itself. The world is autonomously and dynamically open to the advent of grace; thus, Przywara describes creation in terms of a "limitless openness" to becoming and "restless potentiality."[13] For von Balthasar, the beautiful form heralds creation's openness to "something more."

We can add one further argument for beauty's role in theology to von Balthasar's two. Contemporary ethicists call our attention to the importance of metaphors and images in our moral imagination and, consequently, in how we perceive our moral horizon. Ethical reflection requires more than getting the facts straight and more than arguing

from premises to conclusions. It also involves a complex process of seeing, experiencing, and interpreting by means of adequate images and
concepts. These same thinkers introduce alternative images that correct what they perceive to be an impoverished or distorted moral
vision.[14] The endeavor to discern the good act requires that we also
attend to the ways in which our concepts, ideas, and images veil or
disclose the world to our moral perception. Describing objects and situations through appropriate metaphors and images helps in determining the appropriate moral response. In addition, these scholars have
made us aware that some images act as root metaphors or basic concepts that ethicists knowingly and unknowingly use in their construction of moral theories. For example, Iris Murdoch believes that much
of contemporary ethics is tainted, in often unrecognized ways, by a
notion of the person as existential chooser. In place of this view, she
offers the image of the agent as obedient perceiver and goodness as
true vision.[15] Von Balthasar's notion of "beauty" serves both as a kind
of description of the objects within our moral horizon and as a basic
concept that shapes a particular understanding of the moral life.[16] I
believe the view of the moral life that emerges in his thought shows the
soundness of his appeal to beauty.

Von Balthasar states that "theological aesthetics must properly be
developed in two phases," a theory of vision and a theory of rapture
(*GL1* 125). I will follow this lead by first examining the objective side
of the beautiful form and then turning to its human response.

THE BEAUTIFUL FORM

Form and Splendor

A faithful attending to the world reveals its *depth* and *mystery*. The
object before us is never simply known in a comprehensive sense, and
thus we can speak of a "hiddenness" in the object. In the case of one's
encounter with a free subject, this hiddenness relates to the mystery of
what it is and what it will choose to become. But von Balthasar suggests that there is a deeper mystery about the object before us: What
is this reality around us, this mystery of existence itself, that it can serve
as a medium that allows things to appear for us? What makes it possible that things can express themselves to us and that we can know
those expressions? Or, what is that "light," to use von Balthasar's lan-

guage, which illuminates objects of the world? But ultimately, the hiddenness of the object relates to the simple but unanswerable mystery of *why* something is. It is this last question in particular that opens every manifestation of the finite form, every "epiphany," to becoming a "theophany." In the *contingency* of the beautiful object, we perceive a freedom (it does not have to be). In the *beauty* of the finite object, we perceive a giftedness (its presence to us is not only freely bestowed, but attractive and thus experienced as gift).[17] The epiphany of the finite form directs us to the Giver who is self-grounded freedom.

Von Balthasar recasts the Platonic metaphor "light" to describe and interpret this communication of what is "other." All objects of our perception are made visible by a light that shines forth in them and illuminates them. Like shadows on the wall, objects indicate this luminous horizon without presenting the light itself as an object of perception. Every appearance of beauty evidences this bipolar quality of outer form and inner light—the perceptible, comprehensible expression of the object, on the one hand, and a sheen of mystery revealed in the outward appearance but not reducible to that appearance, on the other.[18] Von Balthasar refers to this polarity as form and splendor. *Form* is the external manifestation of a being's "inwardness," or what von Balthasar often refers to as its "intimacy." It is what first draws our conscious attention when encountering the object. The object's visible shape and harmony, the convergence of its component elements and dynamic "life" as a whole, allow us to see it as form. *Splendor* is the radiation of the inner depths of the object out of which the form appears.

The language von Balthasar uses here may seem odd to the contemporary ear, but the reality he is describing is not. Examples, he believes, can be found in our daily lives.

> In a flower, a certain interior reality opens its eye and reveals something beyond and more profound than a form which delights us by its proportion and colour. In the rhythm of the form of plants—from seed to full growth, from bud to fruit—there is manifested an essence, and to reduce the laws of this essence to mere utilitarian principles would be blasphemous. (*GL1* 444)

Similarly, we can observe that in the visible expression of the human person lie hidden depths (e.g., subjectivity, freedom, and personal uniqueness) which we cannot grasp or possess but which provide the "splendor" in which the "form" of the person comes to be seen. The individual's acts are precisely expressive of a *personal freedom* and not those of an automaton (i.e., something that can simply be explained and thus transparently known). But because the acts are truly expressive, they reveal to us this person, or her "form," if you will. In short, we do not read a natural form without perceiving something "invisible" as well, something "beyond and more profound." This is "perhaps the central Balthasarian doctrine of aesthetics: that form is so constituted as to be able to irradiate *from within itself* the light that illuminates its beauty."[19]

Because concrete instances of beauty indicate the "mystery" of a deeper ground, they present veiled glimpses not only of the deeper structures of reality but ultimately of absolute being itself. The splendor of the beautiful form testifies that in *this* form can be found the choice, the will, and the freedom of the Creator, and thus that in *this* form truth and goodness can be found.[20] Already in the gratuitousness of a flower's appearance, in the lovableness of a mother's smile, in the provocativeness of a martyr's witness to the truth, we find some initial indicators of the basic nature of our existence. Deputized by grace, these can become representatives of the divine.

> If it is true that the divine revelation of grace perfects created natures
> . . . revealing the transparence of all being in the world to the absolute
> ground of being—then everything of beauty found in the world (and
> with it too the true and the good) is drawn up into a relationship to this
> inexhaustible standard. (*GL2* 11–12)

Here we find the foundation for the Ignatian ideal, *hallar Dios en todas cosas* ("finding God in all things"), which, we will see in chapter 3, is central to von Balthasar's ethical theory.

Aesthetics

"Form" and "splendor" are not so much properties of an object's appearance. Rather they together provide an image that helps us interpret our experiences of the world and indicates how that world discloses itself to us. They form one part of von Balthasar's theory of perception. In referring to his theory of *theological* perception as a theological *aesthetics*, von Balthasar intentionally plays on the two meanings of "aesthetics" (*Ästhetik*), that is, a theory of beauty (its common usage), and a theory of perception (its etymological root). Aesthetics is a way of perceiving that is instructed by the beautiful form; *theological* aesthetics is perception tutored by the appearing glory of God. The former has its own relative autonomy but is also the condition and possibility of the latter. A theory of perception instructed by beauty yields several insights that are tentative and yet bear on how we perceive the Christ-form.

First, the world is *expressive*, not just lying there, inert, unveiled only with an illuminating gaze. This expressivist theme has much in common with Martin Heidegger's idea of truth as disclosure (*a-lētheia*).[21] Truth for von Balthasar, as for Heidegger, is not primarily the correspondence between the object and what one believes to be the case about that object. Rather truth is an event; it occurs in the object's self-expression to the knowing subject.[22] Von Balthasar desires to correct what he considers to be the excessive contemporary emphasis on the *subject* in the subject/object encounter. He attributes that unfortunate imbalance to the erasure of beauty and mystery in the modern world, qualities he believes important to the biblical tradition. In his effort to restore a native, expressive radiance to worldly forms, von Balthasar turns to the Old Testament concept of the *kābôd* (glory) of God (*GL4*) and its New Testament counterpart, *doxa* (glory) (*GL 7*). For both Testaments, von Balthasar argues, God's glory is manifested in earthly garments. Building on this biblical view, he suggests that all creatures

> possess the never wholly comprehensible power of appearing before one another and manifesting themselves, not only in their naked existence, but also in their potency, which casts a spell around itself, either to keep others away from the sphere of its own life or to keep them in its power. (*GL6* 32)[23]

The object not only communicates itself, but in doing so, it manifests a power, or "spell," that affects the perceiver with wonder before the free gift of that which appears. Not just the human, but all appearing forms in nature can effect such wonder in those who have not lost their vision for mystery.[24] Ultimately, the world is expressive because God, its creator, is triune expression (*GL2* 282–308). All creatures have a *conatus* toward becoming imitative of the Son, that is, becoming expressive words of the Father.[25]

Second, a true knowing of the world requires an *engaged* relation between knower and the object. It involves an affective and *affected* perceiving of the world. Such a mode of perception stands in contrast to what Charles Taylor calls the "disengaged self," a type of knowing that requires an emotional distancing of oneself from the world.[26] The knower reverences the object by recognizing a certain initiative on the part of the object in expressing itself. This in turn requires a receptive "stepping back" on the part of the knower, to allow the space for the object's disclosedness.[27] The subject, for example, does not truly perceive a work of art by imposing her own idea upon it, but by allowing herself to be affected by its beauty.[28] Of course, not all earthly forms compel our responses in the same way. The more the light of divine freedom illuminates the form, the more deeply will the perceiver be affected. The human person is created as uniquely expressive of God. More than any other worldly form, *this* form can be called glorious and, more than any other form, *this* form requires our "stepping back" to attend to its self-expression.

Finally, von Balthasar's aesthetic interpretation of the object's expression leads to one further insight, one that he shares with the phenomenological tradition: a suspicion of all forms of reductionism. The mode of perception called forth by the beautiful form focuses the beholder on the "life form" of the object. The primary object of one's perception of a great work of art is not its component dimensions and color schemes, but its organic whole. Against certain forms of modern empiricism, von Balthasar believes this mode of perception to be basic to all human knowing. We "see" the world in wholes: as life forms, as narrative histories, as dramas encompassing a variety of actor-agents: "Wholeness streams and shines through the fragments."[29] Von Balthasar desires to "combine the cool precision of scientific research with a constant awareness of the totality apparent only to the eye of reverence, the poetic-religious eye, the ancient sense for the cosmos."[30] Positivistic science does, of course, contribute to our perception of the world, but it must be made to serve the knower's reverent grasping of the whole. Only in the form, the "whole" of the object, do we find its full expression. Only here does it make its claim on us and grant us the self-evident appeal to its beauty, goodness, and truth.

"Christian perception" (i.e., perception empowered in grace to perceive "the whole form of revelation as it appears within the whole of the created world" [*GL1*, 297]) shares these same three emphases. First, the object of Christian faith, the Christ-form, cannot be subjected to human fashioning. Rather it expresses something that in and through itself makes a claim on us. Second, it is only in faith's "engagement" (surrender, obedience, love) with what God has done in Christ that the believer can see that revelation. Finally, the Christ-form gives a priority to an aesthetic holism over analytic judgments. Studying the "pieces" of God's revelation in Christ (e.g., the differences between the four Gospels, the historical influences on the various biblical authors, the literary genres of the time) must always serve to make the whole *form* of the Christ-event more visible in its coherent unity.[31]

The Christ-Form

The ultimate justification for using the aesthetic categories of form and splendor and the idea of beauty is that through them something genuine and true about Christian revelation is made evident. We will examine the Christ-form further in the next chapter, but a sketch seems appropriate at this point in order to give a better indication of how beauty serves von Balthasar's project and how it is that the Christ-form can be called at once beautiful and glorious, earthly and divine.

According to von Balthasar, we can speak appropriately enough of the "beauty of Christ," but only as one whose form and visibility are established by God precisely where human eyes can find only an ugly formlessness: the death of crucified one (*GL7* 23). The beauty that is disclosed to us in Christ is the glory of an absolute and free divine love. *Not* "love" that is "glorious" simply in that it is *love* or even love *for us* but rather because in it appear the lordliness and splendor of divine, intratrinitarian love. The particularities that compose the form—Jesus' birth into the Jewish faith with its history of encounters with God, his teachings, the power and authority displayed in his miracles, the different images and emphases conveyed in the four Gospel portraits, his association with the marginalized, the rejection by his own and his bloody death, the unanticipated resurrection and the repeated assurance of divine love for sinful humanity—are all illumined by the mystery to which they all in turn converge and point: this *kābôd-doxa,* this ever-greater weight and mystery of divine love. Von Balthasar underscores that the Christ-form is no simply beautiful form. Since Christ entered into complete solidarity with sinful humanity, the form of salvation includes the "monstrous form [*Ungestalt*] of sin, suffering and Cross" (*TD3* 55). Von Balthasar maintains that on the cross there is an exchange between the wrath of the Father and sinful humanity as represented by Christ, and through this exchange, the absurdity of sinful rejection enters into God's triune life. He further believes that normal human logic cannot make sense of this exchange or what it represents for God's triune life. Yet all understanding is not left behind at this point for an apophatic denial. The "form" that appears out of this formlessness (i.e., out of the unfathomable inclusion of sin in the life of the Godhead) can be seen, but only *as glorious.* We do not, cannot, perceive it with neutral objectivity, but only through the ek-static faith that lets us see in this formlessness the display of lordly, unfathomable love. And solely "the sight of this love and its attractiveness" compels us to faith (*GL7* 207).

The incomprehensibility of this Christ-form then is no "mere deficiency in knowledge, but the positive manner in which God determines the knowledge of faith" (*GL1* 461). Here we see the interplay of form and light, of meaningful content that appears only in the light of a greater mystery, and, I believe, a confirmation of von Balthasar's use of the lens of beauty. What appears in the beauty of Christ is not a puzzle that lies as yet unknown next to what *is* known about Christ, but rather, the tragedy of Good Friday illumined by the even deeper mystery of a why-less, self-giving love.

> To be sure, if God is to become manifest in his nature as God, then a necessary part of this manifestation is his eternal incomprehensibility: *si comprehendis, non est Deus*. But here "incomprehensibility" does not mean a negative determination of what one does not know, but rather a positive and almost "seen" and understood property of him whom one knows. The more a great work of art is known and grasped, the more concretely are we dazzled by its "ungraspable" genius. We never outgrow something which we acknowledge to stand above us by its very nature. And this will in no way be different for us even when we contemplate God in the beatific vision, since then we will *see* that God is forever the greater. (*GL1* 186)

To return to aesthetic categories, the ugly formlessness of Christ is bathed in a radiant mystery of triune love. We see now not ugliness but boundless love for the human creature.

BEAUTY AND HUMAN AGENCY

In his aesthetics, von Balthasar is concerned not only about the *visibility* of the Christ-form, but also with how this visibility is tied to a certain form of response. By restoring the expressiveness of the object, his aesthetics indicates dimensions of human agency that would otherwise be lost to view. In this aesthetic view, the paradigm of human action has little to do with an individualistic or aggressive pursuit of self-fashioned goals. Rather, human action is the active receiving of and response to the address of the other. *Moral* action, we will see, rests on a responsibility grounded in the gift and claim of the other.

There is an artificiality in our examining separately first the object and then the subject-response, especially given von Balthasar's stress on the relation that binds the two, subject and object, together. However, the approach helps isolate and explore von Balthasar's understanding of human agency, principally how for him the world before us empowers certain moral responses.

Beauty as Address

For von Balthasar, relationality is basic to human existence. The human person does not exist primarily in herself, and only occasionally and accidentally in the act of communication (i.e., offering herself, revealing herself) to a subject. Only through expressing oneself to the other does the person exist. Sheer inwardness in itself—that is, the person apart from self-expression within relationships—achieves no form. Such an individual would be existence without essence, freedom without determination. Thus we have von Balthasar's repeated claim that the person realizes herself only in the other.[32] This realization has its partial moments in "encounters" with the nonhuman other, but reaches its inner-worldly perfection in the encounter with one's fellow human beings. We are directed toward others, and this directionality is fundamental to our sense of self; our identities are constructed through relationships with others. The ultimate ground for this self-expressive relationality is the Trinity: "The finite *person* bears the stamp of the *imago trinitatis*, which means that it can only be and become a person by relating to the other persons it encounters on its way through life" (*TD5* 302).[33] We wait for the advent of the other's address and to be welcomed by it into our personhood.

Interpreting the worldly encounter through the idea of the beautiful form means, once again, shifting the balance in the engagement away from the subject to the object, the "thou," and attending to the other's integrity or "weight." Von Balthasar describes the disclosure of the other as language and address: "spoken words" in the case of plants, "speaking words" in the case of animals, and freely chosen language in the case of the human person (*TL1* 94–98). The introduction of this additional sense (i.e., hearing in addition to seeing) is important as von Balthasar wants to argue that the subject's perception of the object is neither a matter of an active and controlling glance at it (vision), nor a passive receiving of its self-statement (hearing). Rather it is an *active receiving* (vision and hearing) in which the agent freely allows herself to be claimed by the object and receive the gift of its self-expression. In order to experience the object, the agent must freely, *actively*, enter into "its spell and radiant space." This idea of active receptivity is key to von Balthasar's understanding of human agency. We attune ourselves to the object and in so doing experience its claim and our responsiveness. And in *receiving*, and thus also *responding to* the other (the two moments cannot be separated from one another), we express ourselves and thereby achieve our own identities.

Consider the case of being drawn out of a prejudice. When an individual encounters another whom she prejudges and values according to stereotypes, there is an important sense in which the individual has not yet heard this other. Her prior map of the world is already colored with certain values and lived truths that dampen the words of the other and blur the other's appearance. Truly seeing and hearing this other means becoming a different person through receiving the new address of this other. In hearing this other, she now sees a different world, one textured with perceptions and values that for the first time allow this other to be.

Beauty, Gift, and Gratitude

There is nothing mechanical about the exchange between two individuals.[34] On the contrary, the genuine encounter involves an engagement of freedoms wherein the free self-disclosure of one is greeted and returned by the free self-offering of the other—mutual gift and self-expression joined in an intertwined emergence of the "We." The other grants the agent freedom by opening a moral stage upon which she can act. The response that the other calls forth allows the agent to witness to who she is, to communicate *her*-self in receiving the claim of the other. However, two elements in the above are in tension with one another: a subject desiring to express herself to another and, at the same time, the other who makes a prior (and independent) claim on that subject's response. The human exchange should be mutual, and yet it seems innately inclined toward conflict. For von Balthasar, what encourages mutuality in human relationships is the testimony of beauty in the exchange.

The key here is a proper understanding of human relationships. Every genuine relationship with the other involves a type of bond that is more than the product of autonomous choice. Some form of value appears in every expression of another, in every manifestation of form.

If the object before the agent merely relayed information about itself, it would appear "as a cold light," unable to evoke in the onlooker "the lure of the discovery of the other." What arises in the communication is the establishment of a bond between the subject and the object, one whose contours reflect a natural, albeit rudimentary, love. The good, the object of moral action, is not something that we strive after for the sake of possession but rather a dialogue we enter into, that is, through giving and receiving.[35] The dialogical dimension of the good reflects the triune creator: the "good" takes place in encounter and mutuality.[36] Apart from this mutuality in the earthly realm, the worth of the other modulates into what is simply good about the other *for me*. Goodness would then be made relative to the needs and wants of the perceiving subject instead of indicating the intrinsic worth manifested in the expression.

This is where beauty can lend its testimony to the object and "cement" the bond that holds the relationship together in freedom. In the natural grace of earthly beauty two elements shine forth inseparably: the giftedness of the appearing form and its attractiveness (two elements that also reflect the twofold meaning of the word "grace").[37] Because of these two elements, beauty overcomes two different one-sided approaches. On the one hand, the object is not simply an objective truth of bare fact lacking existential import, for the beautiful form is attractive to the beholder. On the other hand, the object is not simply a malleable thing to be refashioned into some benefit by an evaluating subject, for the beautiful form is objective gift. The beautiful form draws together objective truthfulness with the striving of the beholder toward fulfillment in relationality. The agent's intentionality is directed away from worth as domestication of the other for my sake to worth as spontaneous pouring forth of a gift.[38] Truth and goodness, apart from beauty, threaten to condense, respectively, around the (now *dis*engaged) objective and subjective poles of worldly encounter.[39] Truth gets reduced to what is "out there," removed from the agent (i.e., correct laws and right ideas), while goodness becomes preoccupied with what satisfies the agent. As long as these two poles are disengaged, there can be no true encounter or harmony of freedoms. The truth of the other (the "object") would have nothing to do with the agent's desires and, ultimately, her identity. However, with the inclusion of beauty, the two poles are bridged through the deep, ontological eros—a love that is established between the why-lessness of every appearance (its giftedness) and the rapturous response of the beholder.

The quality of the object that evokes our action is this giftedness. It offers its beauty to us without being called forth by us. The primal experience of being awakened to self in the love of the Thou immediately modulates into a primal experience of gratitude.[40] "The gift" of the other "implies a task" (*TD3* 458). Ethical behavior takes shape as grateful response.

Von Balthasar is not alone in interpreting Christian ethics in light of the dynamics of gift and grateful response. Enda McDonagh, for example, observes that divine revelation can be "understood in terms of God's gift of himself to his people," first in creation, then in a more personal giving in Jesus Christ. In this gift, a call is implied.[41] But remaining on the phenomenological level for the moment, we might ask what it is about the "giftedness" of the beautiful object, its "address," that grounds a response or makes a claim on us. The answer is not readily self-evident. For while we sense that a gift "should" be greeted with an appropriately positive response, the introduction of moral terms to characterize the exchange seems to distort its gift/response dynamic, turning it into one of gift/obligation. If a gift is given freely, as *gift*, it cannot have such moral strings attached.

Von Balthasar's aesthetics helps to negotiate this tension between gift and obligation. The creativity, spontaneity, and freedom that appear in a work of art are consonant with the ordered harmony that is evidenced in the work. Its beauty reflects obedience to a law in which freedom finds expression, and thus freedom and lawfulness are not contradictory. Von Balthasar frequently appeals to Mozart's *Magic Flute* as an example of a beautiful form that is a free creation and yet also displays a "rightness"—it *should* be so and not otherwise. In the gift/gratitude exchange, there likewise appears an aesthetic "rightness," now in the form of human action. Both agents in this form express themselves in freedom; the fruitful joining of their freedom reveals itself to us in the harmony of that form embracing their mutual actions.

An aesthetic evaluation (i.e., judging the rightness of the form) is a way of making a moral evaluation. The exchange between free, gracious gift and free, joyful reception is beautiful, and this beauty indicates the divine "law" of human freedom. In the beauty of gift given and received lies the event to which all human action must be oriented: the good of interpersonal love. The "wrongness" we sense in the act of ingratitude is not only an aesthetic wrongness, but a genuine moral wrongness. But it is more a visible deformation of freedom's expression than a failure of some moral principle—for example, justice or beneficence. Like Kant, von Balthasar connects the realization of human freedom to submission to the moral law, but von Balthasar adds two un-Kantian emphases. First, the law that freedom embodies is universal but not simply uniform. That is, it subsists in the engaged, interpersonal actions of unique individuals in which personal particularity, creativity, and spontaneity so shape the course of their encounters that aesthetic rightness more aptly describes the embodiment of the moral law than conformity to universalizable maxims, where the particularities tend to be viewed as accidentals accruing to an isolable, moral core. Second, the moral law has an epiphanic dimension.[42] It is *aesthetically perceived*, not just judged to be the law through an objective application of rational principles. At the heart of what we sense to be the "wrongness" of refusing the gift is an intuition that what should have been glorious—free, creative, loving—is instead "marred."

An appeal to something like the first (i.e., the aesthetic lawfulness of morality) can be found in some writings of narrative ethicists. An action is the right choice for a particular agent because it "fits" with the narrative patterns of her life and developments within it. But the criterion for von Balthasar of what is aesthetically fitting is not merely immanent. The moral law that is embodied is not simply horizontal coherence and consistency, but the interpersonal "law" of divine freedom, which radiates in the loving exchange. Thus, the first (un-Kantian) emphasis must be read in close connection with the second, the *radiant* beauty of the morally good act.

The second element, however, is more important for our concerns and merits further attention. It relates to how God appears in the Christ-event and sets the stage for the particular kind of obligation that Christ's life imposes upon its beholder. Von Balthasar finds in the beautiful form a kind of joining of lawfulness and freedom. The gifted painter, for example, creates neither through "brute freedom" (e.g., through randomly chosen brush strokes) nor through a rigid obedience to pattern and symmetry. Rather the painter follows some guiding inspiration—perhaps, for example, some loosely conceived idea—that gives a creative form to the work. The "rightness" of Mozart's *Magic Flute* is not a constraint on Mozart's freedom but an expression of it. Something analogous holds in the free event of divine revelation:

The beauty of God incarnate can never be determined in advance by theological *a priori*. It appears as a phenomenon whose necessity is internal to itself, and thus as a manifestation of freedom. No outer dition or plastic force dictates the form of beauty: it cannot be other than it is, simply because of the logic of its own inner balance and inner adequacy, even "comprehensiveness."[43]

The self-evidence and absoluteness of the Christ-form is a consequence of the fact that this form is a visible expression of a higher, divine law. The object of graced human perception is codetermined by the visible form and divine freedom which appear in it (form and splendor). The visible form itself opens human perception to this radiant higher law of divine life, while this higher law witnesses to the authority of the form. The appropriateness found in the Christ-form is the recognition that in the seemingly contingent events of salvation history "there is also revealed the rightness" of God's work (*GL1* 163). Thus the divine "necessity" expressed in this form, which von Balthasar believes is indicated by the Lukan δεῖ and Anselm's *rectitude*,[44] is not a constraint imposed by the structures of the world but a visible faithfulness to the divine nature which comes to perfect expression in Jesus Christ.

We can likewise describe the "ought" that the interpersonal encounter establishes as "aesthetic," because in both the case of our response to the human other and that of the graced response to the Christ-form what is at stake is our completion of a "moral" form. And this (potential) moral form is radiantly beautiful for the reasons just given: it is the creative expression of freedom, and it casts a ray of divine lawfulness. The necessity of this aesthetic ought is softer than the binding inflexibility of logical consistency. It invites and attracts; it does not at all cajole with the threat of reprisals.[45] The truth of this is hinted at in every interpersonal relation, but achieves its full earthly clarity in Christ. In Christ, God sets aside the divine right to command obedience through power and, we might even say, through what is justly due. Rather in humility, powerlessness, and poverty, God invites a response, one that "matches" the divine gift in its freedom and totality.

We will see in chapters 4 and 5 that von Balthasar does not leave us with an amorphous intuition that some action merely "looks" good. The Christian community can establish norms, or "signposts," that guide our judgments of "rightness." Ultimately, however, our aesthetic judgment of an act's "fittingness" can be traced to the fact that in the epiphany of the gift/response interchange, the divine law of being breaks through and offers us an earthly reflection of the trinitarian life: that is, it reflects the eternal gift of the Father to the Son, the Son's joyful surrender of all to the Father, and the joining and confirming of that free, mutual exchange in the presence of the Spirit.

Love as Free and Obedient

This gift/response exchange is important to von Balthasar's understanding of freedom, for it shows how moral action can be both obedient and free (and thus commanded and autonomous). Two poles characterize von Balthasar's approach to human freedom. They parallel the bipolarity of human existence we saw above (inwardness and relationality). First, freedom includes the most basic sense of autonomy (what von Balthasar calls *autoexousios*). I *will* myself to be, posit myself as a responsible agent. Second, freedom is expressed in and through an "outside" world that calls forth the agent's response. This second pole underscores the fact that autonomy emerges not in isolation from the other but only in an engagement with the other. We take possession of ourselves in the creative, self-expressive replies we fashion to the gift and call of our world. The Christian must, I think, be committed to some form of this bipolarity. On the one hand, we decide ourselves in free acts. On the other, these decisions take place in a normative horizon which enables our free self-determination by providing us possible forms in which it can become embodied. For von Balthasar, the normative, moral framework for freedom, at least on the intramundane level, lies in the contours and dynamics of the subject/object encounter viewed aesthetically. Our self-expressiveness only becomes *expression*, visible as beautiful and free human form, through obedience to the normative forms of human action.

Beautiful objects and finite goods, as they appear in the persons, events, even things in the world, offer us a "stage" on which to act. We fashion our identity in the very recognition we give them through decision and action. Thus, the good, beautiful objects of our horizon do not merely form an extrinsic platform for human action. Through our acceptance of their beckoning, we are given the freedom to express identities formed by them. Beauty is thus not only free, but freedom-granting. In the "seeing" of beauty, the subject breaks out of the self-enclosed sphere of nonfreedom into the expansive horizon of love.[46] Freedom, therefore, is not only just deciding autonomously who we will be, but also deciding how to perceive and relate to the world. And the only way truly to perceive the world, and thus be able to respond in freedom to its beauty, is through obedient love. Love alone, von

Balthasar tells us, grants epistemic access to the truth of the world.[47] It does so because it withholds limitless judgment and surrenders itself in "trusting devotion" to the goodness and beauty of what is revealed (*TL1* 100).

While similar ideas about the moment of receptivity can be found in other thinkers,[48] von Balthasar underscores the subjective realignment that takes place toward the object in perceiving reality and gives it existential weight. We are affected by what is perceived through love. In keeping with his commitment to interpreting the lower in terms of the higher, the gift/response exchange in terms of the I/Thou encounter, von Balthasar makes interpersonal love the standard for understanding the nature of true perception of the world. In interpersonal exchange, truth ceases to be a "fact" and comes into its own as a "free, personal reality" (*TL1* 97). The *perception* of such truth of the other is always a "*wahr-nehmen*," a taking of truth to oneself and living in accord with its exigencies (*GL1* 120).

The active receptivity demanded here is a type of obedience, because it requires a suspension of one's own self-assertion. In the alien realm of the "not-I," the individual encounters creatures whose immanent dignity and "weight" prohibit their unilateral appropriation by her in service to her cause. The beauty that appears in them calls forth an obedient response wherein the agent lets *them* be: lets them be what or who they are before her. In a sense, the agent obeys their claim to her attention and in doing so surrenders her claim to mastery of all. She lets herself be formed and molded by this object's claim to intrinsic worth and value.[49] Yet this renunciation is not self-annihilation. The giftedness of the other awakens love. The movement to express self to the other now unfolds in the context of mutual love. Only in the act where freedom and obedience converge does an adequate, inner-worldly manifestation (i.e., a form) of the dialogue of human freedoms appear. This form represents an obedience to the other's claim and a free expression of the agent's own identity.

THE INTERPERSONAL ENCOUNTER

In the discussion above, we have begun to see how von Balthasar's aesthetics illuminates the interpersonal encounter among human beings and ultimately the encounter between the human person and God. *If* there is some telos toward which everything in creation is striving, an "omega point," for von Balthasar it is this: the gracious encounter of personal freedoms. A more complete exposition of this encounter of freedoms must wait until after we have introduced von Balthasar's interpretation of the Trinity (chapter 2). However, some initial points about the interpersonal encounter can be noted here.

For von Balthasar, the manifestation of God's glory appears in the realm of the human person in two ways. First, the human creature is made, prior to and apart from the establishment of the covenant, an image of God. All creation reflects God's glory, and, in that sense, images God. Von Balthasar, however, is aware that Scripture makes a different kind of claim about the human person. God has "set an image of himself over against himself," which, because it resembles the archetype, has "certain traits of glory . . . intrinsically . . . proper to it (Ps 8)" (*GL6* 15). God's glory is "proper" to the human person in two ways. First, like absolute being, the person has the capacity for free self-expression.[50] Second, following Genesis 1–2, the human creature is a *steward* of God's creation, "a representative of God and of God's power as ruler" (*GL6* 91). In both attributes, God has granted the human person a type of lordship that represents the glory proper to human existence. This sphere of lordship allows the human person to be other before God without ever being absolute other.[51] It is the nature of stewardship that as we grow in it, we become more responsible to the one who made us stewards. And, the development of genuine freedom occurs, we will see in chapter 3, only through receiving our identity from God.

The theological beauty that appears in the human person is available to all persons, Christian and non-Christian. The cosmos perhaps has lost its divinity, and the contemporary person is no longer able to find glory within that horizon. However, for von Balthasar, the human other survives the dimming of creation's radiance and offers a possible site of glory's appearance.

> The metaphysical question, which seemed to be buried for me as far as the cosmos is concerned—to such an extent that what Paul presupposes, viz., that we would "see" God plainly in his works . . . simply seems no longer to be the case, and Karl Barth therefore holds that he can deny the natural knowledge of God—is always ready to break open in the encounter with the "Thou."[52]

The human other can be stripped of beauty and thinned along reductionistic lines like any other part of creation. Her life form is then fractured into an aggregate of spacial dimensions, genetic type, psychological profile, and so on. This *can* be done, but here, in the case of the human, its validity as an enterprise becomes most suspect. In the human person we are confronted with a depth that we cannot, even in our desacralized time, dismiss.

The second mode in which glory manifests itself in the human realm, the "I-Thou" encounter, develops out of the first. For von Balthasar, the human person is always a being-in-relationship; in being *what* we are, we are being *with* others. I have suggested that this relationality attains an inner-worldly perfection in the interpersonal encounter.[53] Within the genuine encounter, a self-renunciating receptivity (of the subject) coincides with self-giving, self-communication (of the object, or "thou"). Indeed, in its perfect form, this mutuality leads to a real union of freedoms. The self-communication of the "thou" is received as part of the developing identity of the agent, and vice versa. This joining of freedoms reflects the glory of its paradigm, the triune life of the Godhead.

We can speak then of two forms that mediate God's glory in the human realm—the human person herself and the person in relationship. But for von Balthasar, the "I-Thou" event, both in its inter-human and divine-human manifestations, is the privileged moment of the manifestation of God's glory. Even the "lordship" which God grants humanity (its stewardship and freedom) is given as preparation for the "I-Thou" relationship of the covenant.

In anticipation of chapter 3, we can note here how von Balthasar believes this relationship is brought to perfection in the New Testament encounter with God. In Christ, God brings the individual into trinitarian mutuality. There the Christian surrenders to the address of the Father and in doing so receives her personhood, that is, her christological mission. The mission, gained through self-surrender, shapes her life, gives it beauty, transforms the particularities of her existence into a life form uniquely her own and makes her existence ever more transparent to divine glory. Divine glory "finds a receptacle," a receptacle that stands "out clearly as the real glory of the Lord, the manifestation of absolute sovereignty" (*GL5* 107). It is a glory that appears not in the person in isolation, but in her covenantal encounter with the absolute Thou.

God's Glory and Human Response

Nonetheless, the divine–human engagement cannot be conceived of simply along the lines of an interhuman encounter, now with a divine

"Thou." God is neither simply "Other" or "non-Other," as von Balthasar repeatedly emphasizes.[54] There are, however, helpful ways in which the aesthetic themes of this chapter, which have led to an aesthetic interpretation of the I/Thou encounter, can also open up our understanding of the event of God's address without constraining that event within human categories. Three dimensions of human agency discussed above—obedience, eros/love, and freedom—are not overturned but find their perfection in the faith response.

First, we have seen that an encounter with the beautiful form, one that involves a true seeing and responding to the form, always effects a moment of obedience. This, too, finds an analogy in the act of faith where the believer responds with a perfect *fiat* and *"lets God be* what he wills to be" (*GL7* 161). The demand that

> the beautiful itself makes to be allowed to be what it is, the demand, therefore, that we renounce our attempts to control and manipulate it, in order truly to be able to be happy by enjoying it: all of this is, in the natural realm, the foundation and foreshadowing of what in the realm of revelation and grace will be the attitude of faith. (*GL1* 153)

In responding to the object of love, we allow it to mold and shape us. Likewise, faith is the attuning and adaptation of our whole existence to God so that "we could just as well call faith obedience" (*GL1* 220).

Second, the erotic, decentering move away from self to the other effected by beauty is elevated through grace and reoriented toward its appropriate terminus: the glory of God manifested in the Christ-form. If the glory of that form awoke no "familiar echo" in the heart of the human person, von Balthasar tells us, it would remain "absolutely incomprehensible and thereby a matter of indifference" (*GL4* 14). Instead of indifference, however, we are drawn by a connatural desire for the divine life offered in Christ.

> And if God, in anticipation, infused into me a longing for true love, so as to draw me to it (Jn 6.44), he did this only that I might recognise it when it emerges before my eyes in corporeal form. The light of faith is an echo of God's love. . . . (*GL1* 218)

Finally, the freedom awakened before the beautiful form is preserved and perfected within the horizon of grace. God's summons is not a "power that does violence but rather one which summons insistently" (*GL6* 59). The persuasive power of the Christ-form is not like that of "mathematical proofs and evidences, in which personal freedom and decision have no place." Rather, it is a form that witnesses to itself precisely because it makes Christ's followers free through "the evidential power of love" (*GL1* 482).

This reshaping of subjective features is not simply the effect of the inner workings of grace, but rather occurs in one's encounter with the divine. The subject's graced transformation requires its transformative object, that is, Jesus Christ. But there is an important sense in which *this* object, the divine revelation in Jesus Christ, does *not* represent a continuation of the subject/object polarity described above.

> It is God himself who illuminates us, who indeed marks us with his word and places his image in us, and it is only in this grammatical reversal (in which the object becomes the active subject) that Christian seeing is attained. *What* is finally perceived depends on the initiative of the object. (*GL7* 287)

Our response to God is never simply an "autonomous word existing alongside Christ's word." We are rather "enacted" by God (*GL1* 191). The response of the believer to the Christ-form is deeper than both the psychological impression evoked by worldly beauty and the moral claim established by the appearing form. The active receptivity of the human person attains its fulfillment in the Christian's perfect identification with Christ: "yet I live, no longer I, but Christ lives in me" (Gal 2:20).

The Interpersonal Encounter and the Dramatic Form

The aesthetic theory introduced in this chapter suggests that we *see* the world in a different light once we attend to the beautiful form and the ecstatic response it evokes. Von Balthasar's aesthetics has indicated one earthly foundation of what becomes in grace our participation in the trinitarian life: the *openness* of both the appearing form (it manifests a "something more") and the perceiving spirit (it "receives" in perceiving). The human other manifests an impenetrable mystery of freedom. That is, the other is object before us, not closed in itself, but posited gift to us by an ultimate, absolute freedom, for what else could explain the incomprehensible grace of the object's revelation to us? The overflowing mystery of the object stirs in the subject her own form of openness: she receives the gift of its self-expression. This open, theophanic dimension of the object becomes the location of divine revelation in Jesus Christ. His life manifests the mystery of divine freedom in its self-determination as endless love for humanity. In turn, the Christ-form opens the individual to a new receptivity, the surrender of faith. Thus in the twofold openness of the subject (i.e., its receptivity) and of the object (i.e., its mystery), we find the conditions for the encounter with God.[55] Vis-à-vis God, this response is one that is both obedient to the form (i.e., Jesus Christ) and grateful for its gift.

Nonetheless, the gift/response exchange, however helpful in illuminating key features of human action, is too one-dimensional to provide a model for the interplay that occurs in the dialogical encounter of freedom. We have sought in this chapter to follow von Balthasar's use of beauty as a heuristic lens to accentuate a perspective on our existence that he believes is often lost in contemporary life. In the "Introduction," I referred to this approach as an "iconic aesthetics." However, the aesthetics that we have followed in this chapter must be expanded, so that the "picture of Christ" does not "ossify into an icon" (*TD2* 21). For we now turn to consider in more depth the divine–human encounter, which is an encounter of *freedoms*. The model that has guided much of our reflections in this chapter, that is, the single ek-static response to the appearance of beauty, is inadequate to represent this dynamic encounter. A new aesthetic category must be deployed to make this drama of freedoms visible. Visibility requires form, a meaningful whole. The encounter between God and humanity is no different. There must, therefore, be a form that expresses the organic whole of this dynamic encounter. Early in the pages of *The Glory of the Lord,* von Balthasar alludes to such an aesthetic form, a "primal form that is beyond 'I' and 'Thou' (since it, and it alone, encompasses both)," that will help make visible this encounter (*GL1* 25): the dramatic form. We turn now to examine that aesthetic, dramatic form and the trinitarian horizon that gives it its theological shape.[56]

2

The Trinitarian Horizon
of Human Action

———◆◆◆◆◆———

I N THE LAST CHAPTER, we introduced the link between perception and action, between beauty seen and ecstatic response. However, the world that the agent perceives is not a static object, but
—as seen in free, interpersonal encounters—dynamic, and even dramatic. And thus the "iconic" aesthetics of the last chapter, which
focused on the perception of and the response to the beautiful form,
must be further developed. But in turning now to examine the dramatic interchange of freedoms in salvation history, we do not discard
the aesthetics of *The Glory of the Lord*. We rather redeploy von Balthasar's aesthetic ideas with a view to how they apply to dramatic form. In
Theo-Drama, von Balthasar argues that the Christian beholds the drama
of Christ's story aesthetically: the Christian truly *perceives* the drama
and finds it *beautiful* and *glorious*. We can, therefore, speak of a "dramatic aesthetics," or, more accurately, of a "theo-dramatic aesthetics."

Nevertheless, there is a certain kind of subject–object complexity
about the dramatic form as von Balthasar develops it in his *Theo-
Drama*, which distinguishes it from the aesthetics of *The Glory of the
Lord*. The distinction between the two is greater or lesser depending
on how von Balthasar employs his concept of the dramatic form.
Sometimes in von Balthasar's writings, the dramatic form is simply
another version of the aesthetic form we saw in chapter 1, only now
instead of perceiving a single object, the individual encounters a dramatic story, but one whose meaning for him coalesces around a single
insight, idea, or teaching. More frequently, the perceived form is such
that in complex ways its dramatic meaning addresses various parts of

our lives (e.g., temporal, personal, vocational, social), illuminating different features and aspects in a manner that cannot be summed up as a single interchange. Most important, however, and most distinct from the aesthetics of our first chapter, is the deployment of the dramatic form that might be called "trinitarian." What is perceived has something to do with the agent. He cannot refuse to respond to it as he could a piece of art. He beholds not just a dynamic "Thou," but a dramatic "We."[1] The poles of subject and object become more open-ended as the beholder (the subject) sees himself as part of this freely developing form (the object). All three of these deployments appear in von Balthasar's interpretation of the theo-dramatic form. The beholder sees in the drama of the Christ-event the simple, glorious message, "You are beloved of God." The economic narrative illuminates his struggles with sin and doubts, his efforts to be loving, his discouragement at life's limitations. And finally, the believer steps back (or, better, steps forward) and sees that his freedom has a place in this large, complex drama, that is, his christomorphic task.

In this chapter we will examine how the drama of the economic narrative frames and shapes the Christian's moral existence. But before proceeding to that point, we must first clarify von Balthasar's understanding of the Trinity. I will not attempt to give a full justification of von Balthasar's trinitarian theology. Doing so would require a systematic exploration of his *Theologik* and an analysis of his interpretation of conciliar teachings. It will serve our purpose enough, I believe, to examine his interpretation in *Theo-Drama* of the Godhead's triune countenance as revealed to us in Christ (i.e., the economic Trinity), and how this dramatic, trinitarian horizon illuminates the Christian life.

Nonetheless, a certain understanding of the immanent Godhead—one consonant with Scripture and building on the Christian's community's subsequent reflections—is presumed in *Theo-Drama*. In the first section I sketch this and situate it within contemporary discussion. We will see that von Balthasar develops the Greek emphasis on the tri-personal nature of the Trinity. Though such language is not without its problems (susceptible as it is to tritheistic misunderstandings), it nevertheless illuminates an essential relational and even dialogical dimension of the mystery of the Godhead. Next we turn to the particular understanding that von Balthasar has of Jesus' relationship to the Father. Without separating it from the absolute love and communion between the Father and the Son, von Balthasar highlights the obediential aspect of that relationship. It is not, however, simply a formless obedience to a sovereign will. Rather it is shaped in the mission, the task that the Father assigns to the Son. This mission constitutes Jesus' person and identity but also allows Jesus something like an earthly autonomy and freedom. In the third section of this chapter we will see how the Christian comes to share in this relationship of Jesus to the Father. Through the work of the Spirit, human action is incorporated into the very tripersonal dynamics of the Trinity. The Christian's participation in the stream of this triune exchange is specifically "in Christ" and turned to the Father. Every command and task given to the human creature is a continuation of and a sharing in the dialogue between Father and Son as revealed in the mission of Jesus Christ. But how can our earthbound stories—with their daily micro-dramas of making friends, earning a living, raising children, dealing with loss and death, and so on—become part of this eternal, dramatic dialogue? In our fourth section we look at von Balthasar's answer to this question. He expands his aesthetics of the beautiful form into a theory of the dramatic form. The theo-dramatic form which appears in the economy of salvation casts a light on the drama of our own lives and gives to them a christological meaning.

THE TRIUNE PERSONAL GOD

Karl Rahner's axiom that the economic trinity truly reveals, *is*, the immanent trinity has become a widely accepted starting point for much of the contemporary exploration of the doctrine of the Trinity.[2] Von Balthasar's thought reflects a resolute commitment to the noetic point of the axiom—that is, that the "economic Trinity assuredly appears as the interpretation of the immanent Trinity" (*TD3* 508). More specifically, for von Balthasar, as for Rahner, this axiom means that the form of the Son's earthly relationship with the Father is itself a revelation of the Eternal Word's procession from the Father.

Von Balthasar begins with God's existence as triune love and pushes to the limit the analogous language of "persons" as applied to the three hypostases. Von Balthasar gives the hypostases individual subjectivities so that they "face" each other as "Thou."[3] Thus, for von Balthasar the relationship between Christ and the Father was not an anthropomorphic mask assumed for a time and later discarded in the course of salvation history.[4] And while Scripture does not apply the language of "persons" to the relations of the Trinity, the Christian community has done so for fifteen hundred years. The problem in present usage of the term "person" is that it connotes the idea of an isolated and completely autonomous, psychological center of will and action, features that, if embraced, would make tritheism unavoidable. Yet the language of "personhood" need not be held hostage to contemporary biases. In addition, forgoing the language of person could cause a loss of meaning in our understanding of God.[5] Instead, we can continue to think through the images that our language provides and offer correctives to their tendencies to mislead.

We cannot attribute all qualities of personhood (e.g., that of separate centers of willing) to the persons of the Godhead, or "hypostases" (to use the more neutral language of early Greek theologians). However, von Balthasar believes we can make a more modest claim: the hypostases can be described as subject-centers of free acts. God's freedom is not merely the freedom vis-à-vis the world but something more related to God's triune nature: "God is not only by nature free in his self-possession . . . he is also free to do what he will with his own nature. That is, he can surrender himself: as Father, he can share his Godhead with the Son, and, as Father and Son, he can share the same Godhead with the Spirit" (*TD2* 256). Since God is absolute *and* triune freedom (and does not become so only in the movement *ad extra*), there must be in the relations within the Godhead "*areas of infinite freedom* that are *already there* and do not allow everything to be compressed into an airless unity and identity."

> The Father's act of surrender calls for its own area of freedom; the Son's act, whereby he receives himself from and acknowledges his indebtedness to the Father, requires its own area; and the act whereby the Spirit proceeds, illuminating the most intimate love of Father and Son, testifying to it and fanning it into flame, demands its area of freedom. (*TD2* 257)

Von Balthasar does not, of course, mean by this that there are three separate agents. But while each divine person shares perfectly in, *is* fully one with, the one existence of God, each person also shares in the one consciousness of God in that person's own way.[6] Similarly, each of the persons of the Trinity has that person's own mode of participating in the one freedom and subjectivity of the Godhead.

We cannot protect divine unity by cordoning off a particular qual-

ity (e.g., consciousness or subjectivity) and proposing it as absolutely
"free" of all triune plurality, interpreting God's knowledge and love
"in a monadic fashion."

> If we take [the doctrine of the Trinity] seriously, it will be impossible to
> engage in the kind of reflection upon the "divine attributes" that, start-
> ing only from the divine essence or absolute Being, excludes from con-
> sideration the internal processions within the Godhead (as commonly
> happens in treatises *De Deo Uno*). For example, with regard to the cre-
> ation of the universe, . . . [God] wishes to be almighty not solely by cre-
> ating [but also] by begetting and breathing forth, and allowing himself
> to be begotten and breathed forth, he hands over his power to the
> Other—whoever that Other may be—without seeking to take it back.
> (*TD5* 66)

The biblical portrayal of Christ's relationship with the Father can appropriately, albeit imperfectly, be described as "interpersonal."[7] If we are
to avoid the "anti-trinitarian timidity" which Rahner finds common
among theologians, we must allow the revelation of this interpersonal
encounter to feed our imagination about the immanent life of the triune God.[8] And thus, von Balthasar introduces, by way of analogy, all
those qualities of human intersubjectivity associated with the mutual
encounter of finite freedoms into the heart of the intra-trinitarian relationships: spontaneity, word and response, dialogue, drama. Even the
"fundamental philosophical act, wonder, need not be banished from
the realm of the Absolute" (*TD2* 257–58).

Von Balthasar realizes, of course, that our experiences of free interpersonal relationships are shaped by their necessary finitude and temporality and that such creaturely qualities cannot be attributed to the
eternal Godhead.[9] However, banishing some qualities (e.g., interper-
sonhood) from the Godhead can be as distorting of our image of God
as applying literally these same qualities. And not only the image of
God is at stake. Certain images of intra-trinitarian love prejudice us
toward some "ideals" of human love (and vice versa). If intradivine
love is *a* or even *the* formative image for our understanding of the ethical life, we do well to reflect on what images might serve it best. Von
Balthasar wants to complement the (appropriate) image of triune love
as restful, contemplative enjoyment of the divine self with other images:
exchange, gift, surprise, newness, creativity.

The key problem with the above, of course, is that it seems to
threaten the *unity* of the Godhead. The image of a communion of love
offers us a way to begin to conceive how the triune multiplicity of the

Godhead can be harmonized with the equally important claim of God's unity, and von Balthasar joins other contemporary figures in making use of the image.[10] Nonetheless, this model by itself is not adequate to indicate the unity that exists in the vibrant dynamism of triune exchange, and von Balthasar supplements it with another, as we will see below.

THE RELATION OF THE SON TO THE FATHER

According to the Christian doctrine of the Trinity, the earthly work of the Son is an expression in time of the eternal procession of the Son from the Father. His earthly labor for human salvation and liberation represents the will and purpose of the Father. Doing the will of the Father is not a work peripheral to his identity, but rather is the expression of his identity. And thus his labor on earth continues his eternal procession as the Word of the Father. The difficulty for von Balthasar's readers lies in his particular portrayal of the Son's relationship to the Father. And since von Balthasar understands the Christian moral life as a participation in the relationship between the Father and Son, it is important to examine its dynamics carefully. Two parts of his interpretation of this relationship are key for his ethics and should be highlighted: the Son's obediential relation to the Father and the tie between the mission of Christ and his personhood.

"Not My Will but Yours"

The question is whether Jesus' earthly deference to the Father is a feature of his earthly existence or something more essential of intradivine life. Out of fear of subordinationism (i.e., the Son is inferior to the Father), the tradition has generally resisted ascribing Christ's earthly submission to the immanent life of the Trinity. Thomas Aquinas, for example, maintained that the Son cannot be "subjected" to the Father in his divine nature since such subjection is inconsonant with divine equality.[11] On the contemporary front, the *implications* of the doctrine of the Trinity for the Christian life are as much a matter of discussion as the doctrine itself. The way in which we image God "implicitly represents" what we take to be "the highest good, the profoundest truth, the most appealing beauty."[12] One reason to question ascribing doctrinal importance to the earthly deference of Jesus to the Father's will is that such a view may encourage patriarchal interpretations of human relationships, a concern raised by feminist theologians.[13] Thus the argument against attributing any kind of hierarchical pattern to the processions based on the equality of the triune persons is supplemented by an additional argument: such an attribution would present the Christian with a paradigm for human relationships that is harmful and even destructive. This is not necessarily a case of refashioning the doctrine of the Trinity to fit with contemporary ethical sensibilities. Our language of God expresses the constant and formative religious experience of the Christian community. And insofar as that community has experienced God as nurturing, liberating, and salvific, our language should express the same.

Nonetheless, the extensive witness of Scripture[14] and Rahner's axiom (the economic reveals the immanent) make a different case. Most basically, the relations among the persons are not "interchangeable." "The Father alone speaks, the Son responds in obedience; the Father, through the Son and with the Son, is the giver, the Holy Spirit is pure recipient."[15] Von Balthasar maintains that there is in the Son's relationship to his Father an asymmetry that he alternately describes as the Son's "surrender," "obedience," "indifference to divine will," and "receptivity." The mutuality and reciprocity among the processions are not absolutely uniform; there is something like an initiative and facilitation of the Father that eternally marks the dialogical life of God.

At the same time, the doctrine of the Trinity does require that we interpret the relationship in a way that (1) preserves the Son's loving *unity* and *equality* with the Father, and (2) is consonant with our basic sense of what a loving relationship is. And so, whatever "obedience" means when applied to the Son's relationship to the Father, it cannot include those negative qualities associated with some human experiences of obedience—for example, inequality, antagonism, power relations, and heteronomy.[16] But even "earthly" obedience need not include these negative characteristics. We have seen that for von Balthasar interpersonal love includes a moment of obedience. The individual's response to the appearing form is always one of loving obedience or obedient loving. Loving the other means welcoming his or her address. In so receiving this address, the individual allows his identity to be shaped in part by the relationship with this other. His actions are realigned with the desire to "let be" this other. Thus obeying the beloved other need not be equated *essentially* with a submissive response to outside intervention, though we recognize that all too often in human relationships that element dominates. Rather obeying the beloved can be a faithfulness to that which is already in some sense, though not entirely, internal to us because of our loving commitment.

Interpersonal love, for von Balthasar, is a union of freedoms. It is a *union*, not a monophonic exchange. The voice of the beloved remains distinct and different from our own. This difference requires that we suspend our own willing and self-assertion at times in order to receive the beloved's gift of self. Receiving the gift of a child's crayon drawing means that we refuse to replace it with our superior version. Receiving the gift of a spouse means letting the spouse have his or her way in a matter in which the beloved has some wisdom or passionate interest. Receiving the gift of friends can mean letting them help even when we could do it better by ourselves. It is misleading to describe this receptivity to the other simply as a mode of *our* own willing—that is, *we* will that the beloved's will be done.[17] It is rather a *suspended receptivity* (or, indifference) to the essentially unknown and unanticipated, spontaneity and mystery of the other. This suspended receptivity, and not the element of coerciveness, is what von Balthasar underscores in his use of the language of obedience. This receptivity, we will see, is perfected in the individual's surrender to divine glory and his obedience to the Father's will.

There is something analogous to this suspended receptivity within the Trinity in the Word's reception of all from the Father.[18]

> . . . in [the Father's] self-surrender, [the Father] *is* the whole divine essence. Here we see both God's infinite power and his powerlessness; he cannot *be* God in any other way but in this "kenosis" within the Godhead itself. . . . It follows that the Son, for his part, cannot be and *possess* the absolute nature of God except in the mode of receptivity. . . . This receptivity simultaneously includes the Son's self-givenness (which is the absolute presupposition for all the different ways in which he is delivered up to the world) and his filial thanksgiving (Eucharist) for the gift of consubstantial divinity. . . . (*TD4* 325–26)

This personal and total surrender of the Father in generating the Son is the ur-kenosis of the triune life and its primal shape. The Son cannot be God in any way other than by following this pattern of self-giving. The kenoses of the Incarnation and of Good Friday and Holy Saturday and the regular pattern of earthly obedience are only new expressions of this triune way of being.[19] The Father's gift of himself to the Son has its own dimension of receptivity as it includes a perfect receptivity or openness to the Son's return of all to the Father and thus something like obedience.[20] The difficulty for many readers of von Balthasar is that he does not propose a completely mutual obedience among the processions. Instead he holds that a "hierarchy," an "irreversible order" remains in the processions of divine willing (*TD5* 88). Thus, when "the Father has a (primary) intention—perhaps with regard to the shape of the creation he has planned—he communicates this intention to the Son in begetting him" (*TD5* 88). But von Balthasar is careful to keep this ordering from becoming mechanical and unidirectional, as he must if he is to be faithful to the dynamic exchange of love he sees characterizing divine life. The Father "leaves it to the Son" to decide how to promote the Father's purposes.[21] The Father provides the governing idea of the divine will, but gives the Son latitude in fulfilling it. We will see below that von Balthasar uses the image of a play's production, with the Father as author and the Son as actor, to convey this polarity between the primal governance of the Father and the latitude of the Son.

This relationship between the Father and the Son marks the Christian's existence when he begins to participate in divine life. His actions will flow out of a grateful obedience to the Father's will, though they will also be touched by the space and latitude God allows those who have come to share in the life of his Son. We will return to this in chapter 3.

Mission: The Gift of the Father

The second characteristic that von Balthasar sees in the earthly Son's relationship to the heavenly Father is that the mission of Jesus as given to him by the Father is not extrinsic to his identity, but rather is his personal identity. Jesus is defined completely by his mission; he has no personal self lying outside of the task of the Father. The task of expressing God "through his entire being, through his life and death in and for the world, totally occupies his self-consciousness and fills it to the very brim" (*TD3* 172). Within the Godhead, the personhood of the Word is eternally received from the Father. In the Word's Incarnation, that personhood continues to be fully received from the Father, but now in the earthly modality of mission.[22]

For von Balthasar, the mission of Jesus acts as the heuristic lens for understanding what it means to be a "person." His mission is *person*-constituting; it transforms him into a unique individual with an identity out of which his actions and life choices flow and to which they give expression. Personhood then is not fashioned "from below," from the details we associate with a biographical sketch (i.e., son of a carpenter), but rather comes in the gift—we can even say "surrender"—of the Father in his bestowal of the mission. But we also see in the mission of Jesus that "given by God" does not mean "external to oneself."

> . . . when Jesus lays hold of his mission and fashions it, he is not obeying some alien power. The Holy Spirit who inspires him is not only the Spirit of the Father (with whom the Son is "one") but also his own Spirit. We cannot imagine his mission ever having a beginning: he has always laid hold of it already. (*TD3* 198)

We cannot get behind the mission to find in Jesus a neutral moment of personal freedom. To do so would abstract from the *procession* of the Second Person (i.e., from his identity as the one who is always constituted by the gift of the Father) and propose an isolated (tritheistic!) divine person who already bore his identity at his disposal and can now hover in indecision before the Father's task.

CHRISTOLOGICAL INCORPORATION

Von Balthasar's trinitarian theology makes several claims: (1) interpersonal language is appropriate for describing the relationships of the divine persons; (2) the Son's relationship with the Father is obediential; and (3) the Son's earthly mission is identity-constituting. These claims are important to von Balthasar's ethics because they shape his understanding of what it means for the Christian to be incorporated into the resurrected life of Christ and to live in accord with that new life.

Christ stands at the center of the drama of salvation, and he does so in such a way that he gathers and realigns all the other themes, images, and events of revelation. Christ is the one "who upholds the creation and is its justification." He is "the ultimate meaning of the whole creation and as the revelation of the Father inherent in it from the beginning."[23] But this also means that Christ cannot be interpreted apart from the events of salvation history—from creation, from God's decision to make humanity his covenant partner, from the silence of God after Israel's sinful departure from the covenant, and so on.[24] Von

Balthasar argues that these events converge toward the Paschal Mystery, which then becomes the heuristic key for all salvation history.

Here the unfathomable depths of God's commitment to his plan for creation shine through most brilliantly. God in Jesus Christ takes on the human condition *radically*, deciding out of divine freedom to give himself over in kenotic self-abandonment and to make the burden of finite freedom his own. In the descent into hell of Holy Saturday, Christ endures the full consequences of this condition, living in solidarity with sinful humanity and thus sharing their dreadful alienation from God. Scripture's depiction of God's wrath toward this sinful alienation is no "bloodless myth"[25] for von Balthasar. The wrath is demanded by God's covenantal righteousness (*GL7* 206). But the unsurpassable love among the triune persons envelops even this god-forsakenness. Through the perfect exchange of love between the Father and the Son in the events of Good Friday, Holy Saturday, and Easter Sunday, God makes the human narrative his own, drawing into the drama of his own internal life even the abyss of sin.

> But why should this [self-offering of Jesus] be efficacious for all the rest? There is no real help to be had here from a juridical doctrine of imputation (the merits of the pure one are credited to the sinners), nor from a doctrine of physical solidarity (by virtue of the Incarnation, Jesus represents the entirety of human nature before God). The only help is to be had from the New Testament's idea of the divine love that *out of love* takes upon itself the sins of the world; and this love must have a double character, as the love of God the Father, who allows God the Son to go into the absolute obedience of poverty and self-abandonment where he can be nothing else than the total object that receives the divine "wrath" and as the love of God the Son, who identifies himself out of love with us sinners (Heb 2.13), and thereby fulfils the will of the Father in free obedience (Heb 10.7). (*GL7* 207)

God bridges the chasm of human alienation not through an eternal decision lying solely within the Godhead, outside creaturely space and time, revealed though not accomplished in the Christ-event.[26] The absolute steps dramatically onto the stage of human existence and brings the drama of triune life to it, in order to lead the human drama, *from within*, to God's ordained conclusion.

This is the mission of Christ, "to sum up all things in himself" (Eph. 1:10), by leading broken existence into the fullness of trinitarian life. Salvation is not simply an assertion of God's continued love, now made visible to human eyes. "To sum up all things in Christ" means the more incredible gift of incorporating the human into divine life. This incorporation can only come about through the christological solution whereby in Christ, God embraces the finitude, poverty, even sinful contradiction of the human condition, inserting them into the triune exchange.

> If the impossible happens; if the absolute not only irradiates finitude but actually *becomes* finite, something unimaginable happens to existence: what is finite, as such, is drawn into what is ultimate and eternal; what is finite in its temporal extension, in each one of its moments and their interconnection, and not merely, for instance, in its final result. (*TD4* 132)

God's response to the gift of the Son is to preserve "existence in all its gravity," not just the "radiant moments," but to lift into the divine sphere the totality of human existence (*TD4* 134).[27]

The radicality of von Balthasar's anthropology emerges here. For he will root the subjectivity and agency of the Christian as deep within the trinitarian relations as the former's creaturely limits will allow. We are re-created, not just healed of our sinful brokenness, but raised to new, exalted status before God, or, better, *in* God. The insertion of the human creature into divine life is made possible only because in God there is already "other," triune other. God's relatedness to the finite creature compromises the integrity of neither party. In making the human person, one "so unfit for speech" (*TD2* 72), into a partner of God, God continues to be absolutely self-giving and personal love. At the same time, the human creature does not leave behind its humanity for a pseudo-divinity. Rather, the human person is lifted up—with his finitude and sinfulness—into the triune divine life *as human* at the point of interchange where the divine became human, that is, in the Second Person of the Trinity, Jesus Christ. Thus, there is no generic elevation of the person into divine life, nor an exalted encounter with a unipersonal God. God's work in Christ incorporates the Christian into the *particular* relatedness of the Son as he faces the Father. The central expression of Christian prayer, the Eucharist, embodies this new relationality; the Christian shares in the body of Christ while giving thanks and praise to the Father (*GL1* 575).[28]

At issue in the above is the idea of the *admirabile commercium*, the "wondrous exchange."[29] The teaching appears in early Christian literature, summarized in statements like that of Athanasius—"Just as the Word became [human] by taking flesh, [we] are divinized by being taken into the flesh of the Word."[30] For von Balthasar, the logic of the

Incarnation demands that the divine kenosis find a parallel in the ascent of human nature into God.[31] Otherwise, *either* Christ does not share in our nature *or* he has ceased to be the eternal Word of the Father. The claim that the Incarnate Word truly shared our human nature (including its temporal drama) without ceasing to be the God of dramatic, triune life, is the lynchpin of von Balthasar's soteriology, for it allows him to argue that God effects human reconciliation by lifting up the human drama—including its guilt and alienation—into the triune life where the ever greater exchange of absolute love between the Father and the Son overcomes even human sin.[32]

While the *commercium* is important for understanding his soteriology, it is the human side of that exchange, our being lifted up, that is crucial for von Balthasar's ethics. The Christian is incorporated into the life of Christ and thus is formed into his praxis. We can lift out of von Balthasar's thought two arguments for his strong participationist reading of the Christian's relationship with Christ. In the first, he offers a biblical justification based on the Pauline ἐν Χριστῷ (*en Christōi*).[33] In the second, he appeals to the doctrine of the Holy Spirit and its role in "liquefying" Christ.

Ἐν Χριστῷ

References to Paul's phrase "in Christ" appear throughout von Balthasar's writings.[34] And his reading of Paul on this point, unlike much of his scriptural interpretation, finds support in contemporary biblical scholarship. The phrase "in Christ" or its equivalent ("in the Lord," "in him") occurs 165 times in Paul's letters.[35] The incorporationist theme indicated by the formula (and related formulae—"with Christ," "through Christ," "into Christ," "body of Christ") touches on an important part of Paul's theology.[36] Because the theme is central to the oft-noted connection between the indicative and imperative, that is, between our being in Christ and the demand that we conform our lives to reflect that reality, it is likewise fundamental to his ethics. In developing his ideas along the lines suggested by the formula "in Christ," von Balthasar is not grabbing onto ideas that are marginal to Paul, and, correlatively, to the New Testament in general. Indeed, the theme is important enough that we may say something stronger: it is not only valid as a possible point of reference, but rather it positively merits the attention of ethicists interested in the connection between

Christian doctrine and ethics. Three aspects of Paul's incorporationist formulae are similarly part of von Balthasar's theological anthropology.

First, the formula "in Christ" itself refers to "a close union of Christ and the Christian." The union is a vital one (a "symbiosis") as it involves a "dynamic influence of Christ on the Christian."[37] Paul underscores the intensity of this influence through his use of reciprocal language: "yet I live, no longer I, but Christ lives in me" (Gal. 2:20); "Do you not realize that Christ is in you?" (2 Cor. 13:5). Von Balthasar similarly stresses the element of unity (Christ is linked "organically with all who are to be redeemed" [*TD3* 243]). And for Paul and von Balthasar, the Eucharist is central in making this unity with Christ real, visible, and empowering (1 Cor. 10–11; *TD3* 243).

Second, the Christian's incorporation into Christ leads him to become an image (εἰκών) of the risen Lord. Thus, Romans 8 begins with Paul's assertion that "there is no condemnation for those who are in Christ Jesus," and then goes on to indicate the fullness of God's plan for them: Christ: "to be conformed to the image of [God's] Son" (Rom. 8:29).[38] One key dimension of this christomorphic image is ethical conformity to the person of Christ. Paul will thus challenge his congregation to "imitate him," not of course because of any native virtue, but rather because he is "of Christ" (1 Cor. 11:1). As the Scripture scholar Morna Hooker puts it:

> [T]he behaviour which is required of those who are in Christ and who wish to be like him conforms to the attitude which *he* showed in becoming like us: he was obedient; he emptied himself; he humbled himself; he became poor; he identified himself with the sinful and with outcasts. And so, in describing his own ministry, Paul claims that he, too, has accepted all manner of humiliation and suffering for the sake of others; he, too, has accepted poverty and yet made others rich.[39]

The same ethical themes which for Paul define the image of Christ (obedience, poverty, self-giving love) likewise mark the Christ-form for von Balthasar. And as the individual Christian's life begins to image Christ, it will also embody these ethical characteristics.

But for von Balthasar, becoming an "image" of Christ is more than praxis or ethical conformity. A third element important for von Balthasar's ethics complements the above two: our being "in Christ" leads to our participating in his mission.[40] The "Second Adam opens up an area of Christian mission in which the latter [the human creature], *en Christōi*, can be given a share in his salvific work and suffering for the world" (*TD3* 241).[41] In von Balthasar's reading, Paul's frequent use of the "*syn-*" prefix underscores the Christian's capacity to co-labor in the mission of Christ: "For Paul, [his being seized by God] means that he must respond to Christ's personal love by surrendering to him in faith and by devoting himself to his apostolic mission. Thus *en* [i.e., 'in Christ'] becomes *syn* ['with Christ'], a participation in Christ's dying and rising and in his work (*synergoi*)" (*TD3* 247). Paul's claims climax with the assertion that in him (i.e., in *Paul*), God was pleased "to reveal his Son," in order that he might proclaim him to the Gentiles.[42] This, making Christ visible, is now the task of all who share in the one body of Christ.

The Spirit

Von Balthasar's position, however, does not stand or fall on the basis of an interpretation of Paul. What also compels us, I believe, to accept the stronger version of the participationist theme (i.e., participation as an active laboring with Christ), and what we do not find carefully worked out in Paul, is a doctrine of the Holy Spirit. Here von Balthasar can offer a helpful response to the concern among contemporary theologians that the Holy Spirit has been ignored and relegated to a "mop up" role, tidying up those loose ends that remain after christological reflections have come to an end.[43] Not at all a "pneumatological bauble" (to use Kilian McDonnell's felicitous phrase), the Spirit in von Balthasar's thought is the cohesive force of the drama of salvation and the "agent" who brings it to its fulfillment.

We have already noted that von Balthasar sees the salvific process culminating in the incorporation of human existence into the triune life of God, "into the sphere of glory between the Father and Son." The Spirit does not drive us into this new home; rather the Spirit opens our eyes to see the beauty, the *glory*, of the Christ-form and thus engenders in us a willingness, "called *faith*," where we "allow love to have its way" (*GL7* 401). This love is not an erotic, Neoplatonic movement. Since the God of von Balthasar is an interpersonal "handing-over" (*GL7* 400), so will be the union with God effected by the Spirit and thus our participation in that life. To be "in the Spirit," then, means to make this active and dramatic law of love the law of our active existence. Only through allowing the rhythm of the Spirit to become our rhythm do we enter into the kind of participation in divine life that God has made possible for us. We cannot storm heaven, but are received only through the surrender of faith.

Life in the Spirit is a participation not just in divine life but in the triune life of God. We might say that the Incarnation introduces human nature into the Godhead, and, in turn, God brings the Christian into the triune life "in Christ." The incorporation into Christ is accomplished through the Spirit. In the Spirit we too face the eternal Father in praise and adoration.

> [T]he dialogue [of prayer] is not between our spirit and the *Pneuma*, but between our spirit, borne by the *Pneuma*, and the Father, a dialogue in which the *Pneuma* cannot be other than the *Pneuma* of the Son, in whom we have come to share in sonship . . . [and are] drawn into the event of the eternal generation of the Son." (*GL7* 405)

Von Balthasar upholds the principle of "appropriation": God's actions *ad extra* are shared by the persons of the Trinity, though we can associate a particular action primarily with one or other of the divine persons. But the principle does not commit us to holding that God approaches us in undifferentiated unity. The grace of the Spirit is not "impersonal." Rather, the Spirit leads us into "a participation in the vitality of the interchange of life between the three persons."[44]

As the one in whom our love is borne, the Spirit can seem hidden in the background, a faceless God who is more "Sustainer" than personal Other.[45] Yet, while the Christian experience of God as personal Other, "Thou," should, in the traditional appropriation schema at least, center on the Father, the Spirit can, *must*, be understood as "personal." Just as in the cases of the Father and the Son, so too the person of the Spirit has a share in the freedom of the Godhead, only now that freedom is imaged in terms of an abundant, overflowing love which binds together the I and Thou into a "We." Von Balthasar, picking up on John 3:8, describes the Spirit as one who "blows where he wills."[46] As free, the Spirit is the prompter of new ways in which the love and the goodness of God can dynamically, interactively appear in the human realm.[47] The Spirit bestows the freedom, spontaneity, and creativity of divine love by gracing Christians—and even non-Christians[48]—with the gifts and apostolic tasks that will, in turn, "personalize" them and allow their unique share in the one mission of Christ. The Spirit transforms the believer, not so much into a disciple who follows the example and witness of Jesus Christ from the distance of time and finitude. Rather, the Spirit "liquefies" Christ, imparting to his historical existence a universal reach and granting the believer access to it through a simultaneity of mission (*TD3* 38–39).

The Spirit is the bond of the free and personal exchange of love first and foremost between the Father and Son. But the Spirit also effects this creative and free bond between God and human person. In the presence of the Spirit, the human response is given divine breadth. Even the limitations and sinfulness of the human person do not prevent the sort of participation in the mission of Christ that von Balthasar sees possible in the life of the Christian. The Spirit bridges and resolves the disparities between the divine and the human. The Spirit

> becomes part of [the Christian] and enfolds his discrepancies (perfecting, preserving them) in the loving differences within God himself. What vastness there is here, what great seriousness of love God reveals when he lets the tragic and apocalyptic differences between God and the world, God and hell, be fully expressed within his own all-embracing differences.[49]

The Spirit is the guarantor that the good and loving elements in the Christian's actions, always touched by human perversity, will be made a cohesive part of God's work of salvation.

THE DRAMATIC FORM

We can now bring the above into more explicit engagement with the ideas set out in our first chapter. Von Balthasar's aesthetics proposes a way of truly perceiving the world which involves more than a disengaged observation of facts. The world shows itself to us, in organic wholes, forms, which can be called beautiful because of their native capacity to claim our response. Our openness to the appearing form becomes a dialogical openness in the case of the human other. We receive, that is, "let be," the appearance of the other's self-expression and, forming ourselves as responding agents, also express ourselves. Furthermore, we can speak of the loving exchange itself as a whole, or form (i.e., the "we" of interpersonal love). It is a form that embraces the freedoms of both parties; the beauty of this form reflects the aesthetic rightness of the mutual exchange of gift given and gratefully received. This epiphany of goodness, we can suggest, is a theophany in earthly form of the triune life.

But, of course, the model of gift/gratitude does not reflect the full complexity of human relationships. To love as finite creatures in a finite world is an affair of choosing some goods over others, and sometimes rejecting gifts. Further, the hidden and not so hidden sinful egoisms imposed on the fragile interplay of human freedoms make discord inescapable. The human situation is one of conflict and tension, and yet it is also the place where God's revelation occurs. If God's glory, divine beauty, is truly to appear in our realm, it must do so without becoming distorted by these conflicts and tensions and by the sin and brokenness that underlie them.

On first glance, the challenge seems hardly insurmountable. Could not, for example, the life of a generous, self-giving individual who rejects the temptation toward hatred reveal the loving nature of God? Not according to von Balthasar. Besides showing God's loving nature, the form of revelation must be marked by two qualities. First, the form of revelation must manifest *divine* love. This means for von Balthasar that it must preserve the incomprehensible majesty of the divine nature, and it must show the triune nature of God's love. Second, the form must effect God's covenantal intent to include the individual human existence in God's triune life. Thus, it must make the brokenness and sinfulness of human existence and the particularities of the concrete human individual part of its form. God's revelation in Christ accomplishes each of these, as we will see. The question is how to view this revelation in a way that all these elements come to light. Von Balthasar argues that seeing revelation in terms of a dramatic form, or, more specifically, as tragedy, illuminates well the features central to God's work in Christ. And thus he refers to tragedy as "the great, valid cypher of the Christ event" (*GL4* 101).[50]

Von Balthasar's understanding of the dramatic form is a development of his interpretation of the complementarity between myth and philosophy (see *GL4* 43–313). According to von Balthasar, the Greeks made a real advance in their historical turn away from myth to a type of reflection (philosophy) that looked within or beyond particulars to uncover universal truths. But he does not view the intellectual development from myth to philosophy simply as the progress from a less to a more adequate construal of reality. The two approaches are complementary, and only a synthesis of both, which von Balthasar believes Christianity achieves, can provide an adequate portrayal of the human condition.

In von Balthasar's view, philosophy, by its very nature, suffers two deficiencies. First, it levels particulars to universals, and thus it makes the particular, creative freedom of the individual human person into a universal quality of human existence. Such a move undermines what von Balthasar calls the "positivity" of the finite—a positivity that is grounded in its relationship with the infinite. Because human dignity lies ultimately in the free and particular relationship which God establishes with the individual, it can only find expression in a form that includes the free interchange which this relationship involves.[51] The dramatic form, and not a universal system, is capable of this. Philosophy's second limitation lies in its inability to include the particular address of the absolute to the unique individual. Philosophy cannot incorporate such an address, von Balthasar believes, because doing so within a "system" necessarily undermines God's freedom and sovereignty.

Myth, on the other hand, seeks to explain the particular through a revelation from above. It is "fundamentally dialogical: glory streamed forth from the personally divine on to mankind who dared to interpret his temporal existence in this light" (*GL4* 155). Myth and philosophy are different historical ways of reflecting on and portraying the world. Fundamental to myth, however, is the belief that the nature of any particular human existence can be discovered only in the revelation of the divine to that individual, and thus describing this relation between the divine and the individual (and displaying it in story form) is myth's most important task. Unlike philosophy, myth does not offer a comprehensive perspective, one able to reflect on all human life. The gods cannot respond in a personal and coherent way to the multitude of conflicting wishes of a fractured human race, and thus cannot offer a universal perspective on human life. This is myth's deficiency. Greek thought moves toward the philosophical but not before exploring the mythical to its limits in the tragedies.

"The art of the Greeks," von Balthasar tells us, "culminates in the tragedians and then collapses" (*GL4* 101). The gods become remote and less personal in the tragedies, and thus impersonal fate more strongly marks human existence. The gods, however, are revealed in the darkness of their absence, that is, in what the reader senses should be there, but is not (e.g., the injustice of the good suffering is itself an indicator of justice).[52] The sufferings of the story's characters are neither denied nor shunned; they rather become the path to the gods and the mode in which the revelation of the "deep truth" of human existence now occurs (*GL4* 103). This is the glory of the tragic, that even amid the night of loss, there is no doubt that "it is God's night" (*GL4*

129). This is what von Balthasar believes philosophy cannot allow: glory to be seen where it appears most absent, "god in his opposite," i.e., in finitude and suffering (*GL4* 103). And it is why for him Greek tragedy, not its philosophy, is the "cipher" for God's work in Christ. What shines through and illuminates the tragedy of Christ's suffering and abandonment on the cross is both God's wrathful judgment on human sinfulness and an ever greater love that embraces even human brokenness and sin.

Myth does not survive the advent of Greek philosophy with its drive toward universalizing the features of human existence. Still, von Balthasar believes that the kind of fruitful reflection on concrete human existence that characterizes mythology over and against philosophy—that is, a presentation of the human in all its particularity and dramatic tensions in reference to an absolute judgment—survives in literature and dramatic productions. These, like myths before them, offer their audience an interpretation of concrete human existence as it appears within the often tragic interplay of human freedoms and uncontrollable natural forces. In drama, human action is interpreted in light of some overarching meaning that bestows a final and authoritative judgment on the agent's free historical choices of limited values and goods.[53] The capacity of the dramatic form to interpret concrete existence makes it a particularly appropriate tool of a theological aesthetics. The dramatic story of Christ—what von Balthasar calls the "theo-drama"—is the horizon in which the Christian interprets his concrete story. Like the beautiful form, the theo-drama awakens a particular response on the part of the person by inviting him to interpret his life in terms of the absolute horizon of covenantal love.[54]

The locus of the Christian narrative is the encounter of divine and human freedoms. The possibility that this engagement may be obscured when presented in terms of universal and abstract doctrines—where the event character of freedom, of word and counter-word, is subsumed into what is held to be universally true—strengthens von Balthasar's resolution to employ the category of dramatic form.[55] Presenting the Christ-event in terms of its dramatic form is not to abandon our "aesthetic" lens, but rather to move from an "iconic" aesthetics to a "dramatic" one. This will, I think, become clear in the course of the next section. As we will see, von Balthasar uses the theo-dramatic form to illuminate the Christian life in a couple of different ways. However, more than anything else, his reflection on the Christ-event along dramatic lines underscores one key theological fact: God has brought into the drama of triune life the drama of fallen human existence, so that "our play 'plays' in his play."[56] The whole *acting* human person and his historical drama have now been brought into the eternal interchange between the Father and the Son.

The Dramatic Christ-Form

The drama of Christ's life reveals God's glory. In it, we see *triune love* expressing itself. That is, in the *ad extra* expression of God's love (i.e., God's love for humanity) in the economy of salvation, we witness its immanent ground, the interpersonal love of the triune persons. Christ does not just reveal God's response to the human condition, but rather reveals *who* God is—not just love for humanity, but triune love in itself. And thus, the "Trinity, and not Christology," is the ultimate horizon of the revelation of God "in his dramatic relationship with the world" (*TD5* 56).

The Christian does not just "see" this trinitarian life immediately in the life of Jesus. Here von Balthasar's appeal to the dramatic form guides us in two ways. First, the dramatic form focuses our attention on the aesthetic whole. The Christ-event can only be interpreted in light of the history (Old Testament) of God's dealings with humanity. Second, the dramatic form illuminates the dramatic tensions that occur in the salvific narrative between human and divine freedoms. God "suffers more than anyone else at the ruination of his chosen [covenantal] form" and "does not draw back from revealing to the lascivious whore Jerusalem his form of suffering—the face of a lover who is not only humiliated, but who assents to this humiliation and even humiliates himself" (*GL1* 656). In the biblical drama, the Christian finds a God who rejects his covenant partner, who must reject her as "is his right as the holy God," and yet cannot reject her, but must "run after her, undeserving as she is, and bring her home with humiliating pledges and promises" (*GL1* 656).

Von Balthasar believes that this drama as played out in the Old and New Testaments witnesses to the dramatic triune life. Within the unity of divine willing and love, "something akin to a drama is played out between the sovereignty of [God's] judgment and the humiliation whereby he allows himself to be judged," and "these two voices in God are both united and kept distinct by a third, ineffable voice" (*GL1* 657). Not that God is in any way divided in himself. Rather, the Old Testament already offers hints of the drama of triune life that in the

New Testament becomes explicit, and it is in this context that we must interpret the Christ-event. In Christ we behold the capstone of this "most glorious drama" of the broken, covenantal history where divine love hands itself over, out of love, to the judgment demanded by divine holiness on human sinfulness. We see in this life a God who allows the distance between Father and Son to become the distance of sinful alienation in order that it be overcome through the ever greater unity of divine love. It is not, of course, that God *is* the economic drama, but rather in that drama we get a peek of who God essentially is: dramatic triune life.

Von Balthasar explores the dramatic form as interpretive lens of the Christ-event in two "triads" associated with the production of a play: (1) author, director, and actor, and (2) presentation, horizon, and audience. These "triads" of dramatic roles are used as metaphors to illuminate, first, the economic Trinity and, second, the manner in which God accomplishes his reconciliation with humanity without compromising divine transcendence or human freedom.[57] These two metaphors will also serve as helpful points of reference in understanding von Balthasar's approach to the moral life.

The first triad consists of the three principal roles that are part of staging a drama: the author, actor, and director. Von Balthasar believes it to be "a perfect metaphor for the economic Trinity in the theo-drama" (*TD3* 532). God the Father is the author who shapes the drama and makes sure that it has its intended effect on the audience. He relies on the "freedom and spontaneity" of the actors and director (*TD1* 279). The author must "cherish their autonomy," while standing "above them" (*TD1* 280). Christ is *the* actor who makes real the author's dramatic idea. But there is nothing "mechanical about this making-present; it is a creative act for which the [author] explicitly and necessarily leaves room in his work" (*TD1* 284). Finally, the Spirit is the director who takes the text of the play and interprets it "in a living and spiritual manner" (*TD1* 299). He does this by prompting, inspiring, and organizing the actors as they bring their talents and energies to their respective roles.

I believe we can find in this first triad an alternate approach to the problem of unity-in-trinity. I sought in the first two sections of this chapter to sketch von Balthasar's trinitarian theology and the pattern of relationship he sees in the response of Jesus to the Father. His stress on the vibrant freedom of the divine persons threatens divine unity. However, the drama enacted by the triune persons is one, and thus we can speak of an ontology of unity that is dramatic. That is, the drama itself manifests the divine unity even while indicating the distinctiveness of the persons. Furthermore, the noetic priority of the economic Trinity means that this dramatic ontology must have some precedence over other ontologies of unity (e.g., the Greek idea of the Father as the font of the one Godhead). We cannot peel away the events of salvation history to get to the (one) God who is revealed in them. Content and form are inseparable. God is loving action, and the narrative whole that is seen in the divine action *in itself* reveals that God. Again, it is not that God *is* the drama; that would wed God to worldly events. But within the complex plots and subplots of the economy of salvation we can discern a unity of vision, purpose, and intent, an aesthetic whole in and through which the Godhead is revealed.[58] The divine persons, in ways appropriate to the "manner of subsisting" of each (to borrow Rahner's term)[59] enact and make real this one divine will and vision in dramatic form. Hence God the author brings the drama "into being as a unity" (*TD1* 268); God the actor conceives and executes his role "on the basis of a single, unified vision" (*TD1* 284); and God the director comes up "with a unified vision embracing both the drama (with the author's entire creative contribution) and the art of the actors (with their very different creative abilities)" (*TD1* 298). While these "roles" of the persons are metaphorical images to help us imagine the unity within the dramatic triune exchange, they are, nonetheless, not entirely artificial. That is, they do reflect the way in which this triune life has revealed itself *ad extra*.

Christ is the tragic figure who now does what Greek tragedy could never do: tie the contingent to the absolute in a universal way that stamps every existent with its pattern. He is the one finite figure who acts out the *one* plan of the Absolute, who (as Father) is author of all and (as Spirit) universal gift and with whom he, the Christ, is one.[60] Thus Christ overcomes the divide between the philosophic and the tragic, between the universal and the contingent. He is the concrete universal. But to see this fully, we have to turn to the way in which Christ opens for the finite, historical creature a stage in which his finitude is granted eternal (absolute) meaning. The dynamics of the above remain in place. Whatever form of divine command ethics appears in von Balthasar, it must be interpreted in light of a God who "authors" our play and gives us our (christological) roles but who also makes room for our contribution as we are prompted by the Spirit.[61] Von Balthasar refers to the second triad as that of "dramatic realization":

presentation (dramas are performed *for* someone or group), audience (dramas are observed by individuals not just passively, but with some expectation), and horizon (dramas offer some larger horizon that unites the characters in the plot and, potentially, their audiences). Von Balthasar uses this to show how the drama of human existence is drawn (actively, through the intentional choices of the agent) into that of the economic Trinity without losing its relative autonomy.

For von Balthasar, there is a human need to which the drama responds and which secures its emergence in history. For "as long as theatre has existed," people "have sought insight into the nature and meaning of existence, things that cannot simply be read off from its immanent course but radiate from a background that explodes the beautiful and gripping play on the stage—which suddenly becomes inwardly relevant to the spectator" (*TD1* 314). Dramas bring their audience satisfaction by revealing truths about human existence.[62] They offer "patterns of possibility" which "turn up in human lives with such a persistence that they must be regarded as *our* possibilities."[63] The distinction between the spectator and the story blurs because the drama is also about the truths of the spectator, and thus it includes him or her. The drama responds to one's need to see oneself within "something that transcends and gives meaning to the limited horizon of everyday life" (*TD1* 308), and one experiences pleasure when the enacted story presents one with such an interpretive horizon.

The dramatic presentation introduces that element of the divine address which von Balthasar argues is missing from philosophy. God's dealing with the world provides, in dramatic form, the ultimate horizon for judging values and goods, and ultimately ourselves as moral agents. As is the case for human plays, this Christ-drama does not supersede our individual dramas. Such a play would have no interest for us or appeal that made it worth observing. Rather this divine play invites us to see our play in its light. It offers a vision, one that is attractive to behold, that can heighten and dignify the broken dreams, fragmented goals, and failures of our finite existence by showing them to be not manifestations of a "pitiless destiny" but creaturely realities embraced in the divine drama by "grace and forgiveness" (*TD3* 535).[64] The Son's death is redemptive precisely in that "it manifests the ultimate horizon of meaning, which is God's all embracing trinitarian love" (*TD5* 331).[65] Through Christ and in him, the Christian is given a "stage" on which to act and a story to give that acting a coherent form.[66] The Christian stands in grateful awe before the narrative of love that gives meaning even to the sinful rejection of God.[67] The faith that it awakens leads him out of his spectator seat in the ardent hope that this narrative can be his own, that his identity can be one with it. I referred to this use of the dramatic form in the chapter's introduction as "trinitarian." We will see in chapters 4 and 5 its importance for von Balthasar's ethics.

DIVINE COMMAND ETHICS—INITIAL CONSIDERATIONS

Chapters 1 and 2 have sought to provide a framework for von Balthasar's ethics. The first chapter examined the (theological) aesthetic horizon of human action, and this chapter has explored its trinitarian and dramatic horizon. Von Balthasar interprets the drama of creaturely existence in light of the theo-drama of the salvific narrative. This drama already includes within itself accounts of divine and human encounters which unfold interpersonally and narratively. All that remains is that the story be extended, that new roles and tasks within it be assigned, and that the new and various displays of human freedom be "directed" into the one meaning of the story (thus the Spirit and the church). However, the ultimate ground for our inclusion in the salvific drama lies in the "space" within the trinitarian life itself. The voices and responses of human creatures can be included in God's life because that life is already a communion of voices absolutely united in the Spirit. Of course, the human voice in itself is meager and wretched, radically unfit to share in the divine discourse. The Spirit takes this insignificant whisper of a word and gives it divine depth and breadth. The Spirit is the cohesive force of the theo-dramatic form, working our words into the one drama. It does this by incorporating the Christian into the point of divine–human interchange, that is, the person of Jesus Christ. We will explore this more in the next chapter.

Noetically this inclusion into the drama can come about because of a certain latitude of meaning that characterizes our actions. Our actions are not self-interpreting, but rather depend on a more comprehensive context for evaluating them. The theo-dramatic form provides such a context or horizon. In the illuminating light of the economy of salvation and its interpretive center, the Christ-event, the person interprets his life as "trinitarian": the person now lives in response to the will of the Father in the prompting of the Spirit. Everything that makes up earthly existence is now noetically and ontologically tied to the in-breaking of the vertical, that is, the address of God in Christ Jesus.

We can pause at this point to make some preliminary observations about how this approach aligns with an ethics of divine command. Divine command ethics holds that the goodness of at least some acts depends in a nontrivial way on God's will.[68] For von Balthasar, God's personal address to the individual makes a claim on the individual and is important to that one's identity. The centrality of this divine address gives von Balthasar's thought an orientation to divine command ethics. Yet there are important differences that distinguish his ethics from the type of ethics typically associated with many instances of divine command theory. Von Balthasar's distinctive brand of divine command ethics can be best seen by contrasting it to the ethics of Karl Barth, whom Christian ethicists generally see as the most able defender of divine command theory.

For von Balthasar and Barth, the new relationship that Christ effects between God and the human person is not at all peripheral to daily existence, but rather is an essential part of our manner of being in the world. We exist within the "sound" of God's Word (*TD2* 73). Furthermore, both underscore the personal quality of this new relationship. God's address is preeminently personal, both in that our individuality and unique personhood are addressed and in that the God who addresses us does so as "Thou." Like any relationship, this divine–human relationship implies interchange, address, and response. And if our covenantal relationship with God is constitutive of our identity as a human person, as von Balthasar and Barth hold, then it follows that the address given us by God and our response to it affect us to our core; they establish us as persons.[69] Human action before the divine address, then, cannot be understood as something that consists "only in carrying out something that God wishes." Such action would be an expression peripheral to ourselves and undeterminative of our identity. "Action means not only to choose and realize this or that, but to choose and realize oneself in this or that."[70]

Divine command ethics has a natural consonance with this type of theological anthropology. First, divine command ethics understands moral action in terms of a response to God's personal call. It thus maintains a kind of transparency between call and response—that is, one responds directly to God's address—which can be obscured in ethical theories focusing primarily on weighing intramundane goods.[71] For von Balthasar, God's relationship to us is free and personal and thus "cannot be recast as some kind of impersonally valid natural law" (*TD2* 292).[72] Second, divine command ethics also maintains a particular ordering of the covenantal relationship. The relationship is not, of course, symmetrical. In the dialogical space that God's word establishes, his address to us is "infinitely more important" than ours to God, and we can respond as we should "only through a constant hearing of the word."[73] For Barth, such sovereignty is due both to the absolute asymmetry of the divine–human relationship and to human sinfulness. However, for von Balthasar the sovereignty of God's address is also due to the fact that the God–human encounter reflects the image of the Trinity and thus shares in the polar dynamics between the Father and Son as revealed in Christ.

In this ordering of the divine–human relationship, we have an example of how von Balthasar's thought is more, not less, christologically governed than is the case in Barth. That is, for von Balthasar, obedience is not only a creaturely submission to God but also a participation in Christ's receptivity to the Father's will. Another example of this christological governance is evident in the nature of God's command itself. Both von Balthasar and Barth affirm the concrete specificity of the divine command *and* its person-constituting dimension. Barth, however, accents the former, and von Balthasar the latter. Thus, even though von Balthasar will make comments that reflect a Barthian emphasis on the total concreteness of God's address,[74] he places greater stress on the identity-shaping, aesthetic wholeness of the command. He does so because it is, he maintains, what we see in Christ's relationship with the Father. Shaped by this same dialogical relationship, the address to the human existent, like the address of the Father to the Son, is autonomy-granting,[75] personalizing,[76] and individualizing.[77] These qualities converge in von Balthasar's concept of mission —the unique yet universal task given to each Christian by the Father wherein the Christian shares in the one mission of Christ.[78] God addresses humanity not only universally but personally, giving each of us a christological "name" that constitutes our identity and the norm of our conduct. Thus, in describing divine desires for the human agent, von Balthasar rarely uses Barth's favored term, "command," preferring instead terms such as "call," "will," and "address," which have less punctualistic and occasionalistic connotations.

What most separates von Balthasar's ethics from Barth's, however, is not their different takes on how Christ governs Christian action, but rather in how they interpret the trinitarian horizon of Christian existence. Barth's thought leans in a modalist direction, albeit of an orthodox type.[79] He begins with the God who confronts the human person as the one subject, the wholly transcendent and absolute Thou[80] in a tri-mode revelation of Father, Son, and Spirit. God "'economizes' himself into a triad."[81] For von Balthasar, divine life is dramatic in the analogous sense that it includes spontaneous exchange and creative love. And because the Godhead is already dramatic life, God can encompass our drama into the one divine drama. This is the meaning and fruit of the Christ-event. The drama of revelation is a new moment in the already existing drama among the processions.[82] Since Barth does not ascribe to the persons of the Trinity the kind of freedom and personal Otherness that we find in von Balthasar's thought, it is more difficult for him to find a place for a *human* otherness, which is autonomous and dramatic. For Barth, the "Catholic And," as he refers to it, threatens the singular priority of the Christ-event by situating it in a preexisting neutral reality, one indifferent to Christ. For von Balthasar, however, the "And" is part of the glory—the "masterpiece," as he calls it—of God's act of establishing a covenantal relationship. He lifts up a genuine dialogue partner, by creating a space where divine and human freedom can encounter one another, without the latter becoming a moment in the former.[83]

Von Balthasar sees in the dialogical receptivity of the human person a way of negotiating between the one divine goal and intention in creation (it is oriented *exclusively* to the covenant established by Christ), on the one hand, and the *relative autonomy* of human existence (it cannot be reduced to the covenantal relationship), on the other. We *receive* in God's call our identity, but we do so as creatures actively *open* to that call. With his defense of the Catholic "and," we can rightly expect that von Balthasar's ethics will make a more vigorous defense of human autonomy than is generally found in Barth, all the while endeavoring to maintain Barth's strong theological (divine command) governance. Without the presupposition of such an autonomy, there can be no "masterpiece." The contingent, free yes to God's address is the place where God's glory shines through in the earthly. Eliciting this free yes is the goal of the divine drama in Jesus Christ.

3

Divine Commands and
Human Fulfillment

———————◆◆◆◆———————

THE CHRISTIAN BELIEF IN A COVENANTAL GOD can pose particular problems for ethical theory. To speak of God as personal vis-à-vis creation is to make God not only an object of human knowing and willing but, potentially, an agent counterpoised to human agency. But how can the absolute and sovereign God "play" on our field without radically disrupting the rules of our game? Or, as von Balthasar asks, once God enters the stage, can anyone else perform?

We can preserve the integrity of the natural order by keeping God at a transcendental "distance." The influential Catholic moralist Josef Fuchs argues strongly for such a transcendental interpretation of God. He makes a distinction "between *creaturely causality* in this world and God's efficaciousness as the *transcendent* ground of all created reality."[1] Instead of a God who acts as Personal Other, we limit God's personal presence to the causal fringes of creation: God is the one "who" holds all things in existence, grounds its autonomous laws, and bears human freedom.[2] The "influence of natural law in past centuries," Fuchs goes on to suggest, "has reduced to a certain extent the relevance of talk about 'God's commandments/laws' and about 'God's intervening presence' in worldly events."[3] Because of the distinction that a transcendental approach to God makes, it can claim both that ethical laws are immanently grounded and rationally perceived *and* that they are established by God.

This model of God's governance of the ethical order supports a continuity between the objective moral order, the operation of practical reasoning, and the truly good. Practical reason judges the objective requirements for a flourishing world and decides on that basis what is the truly good response. Moral reasoning in such a framework determines what is the good act based on a consideration of immanent goods (e.g., the yearnings, hopes, and desires of the human person for fulfillment), and not on concerns discontinuous with these goods, which a command from God could represent. Because of this continuity between the ethical obligations of the human person and her own reasoned insight into the possibilities of human flourishing, God's creation has "space" for human agency, freedom, and autonomy.

However, some theologians, for example, Jacques Ellul and Karl Barth, disagree and argue that God's sovereign involvement in the world impels the Christian to distinguish sharply between the creaturely and the divine. They go so far as to characterize the kind of human control over ethics advocated in natural law approaches as instances of sinful human pride.[4] Like these thinkers, von Balthasar underscores that God's personal address will be (at times at least) discontinuous with the immanent operations of reason and moral discernment. It represents an ethical claim that is not grounded in the horizontal (creaturely) order or discovered by the immanent operation of human reason. It *transcends* these and thus can only be *received* through some form of obedience (e.g., submission, assent, consent). However, von Balthasar also argues that the introduction of this discontinuity between divine and human ethical viewpoints does not threaten human integrity but actually preserves and fulfills it. Thus, the discontinuity of the divine command need not undermine the Catholic desire to maintain a "space" for human autonomy and creative freedom.

In this chapter, we will examine how von Balthasar's thought preserves the integrity of human agency (i.e., autonomy and freedom) in the face of the discontinuity which God's call represents to the person. We will do so using the categories of obedience and human fulfillment. The two represent key (and seemingly opposing) emphases found, respectively, in Barth and Fuchs. These two foci have the additional merit of representing important themes in *Theo-Drama*. If von Balthasar is able to harmonize these themes, and I believe he does, then we will be able to incorporate the theoretical goods that each offers (e.g., the prioritization of divine sovereignty, on the one hand, and human autonomy and freedom, on the other) into a coherent ethical theory.

The first part of the chapter will show how von Balthasar sets the obedience of the human agent—an ethical response that can be given indiscriminate commendation by some Christian thinkers—clearly within the drama of salvation. The second part takes up von Balthasar's approach to human fulfillment. It focuses on issues of self-identity and meaningful existence. These require, von Balthasar argues, the address of an absolute "word" (e.g., call, command, decision, etc.). The third section discusses von Balthasar's attempt to draw together obedience and human fulfillment into the idea of mission. Mission is the task assigned by God to each Christian whereby the Christian participates in the continuing work of Christ. I hope to show through this idea of mission that not all versions of divine command ethics are contrary to the "very presuppositions of the entire perennial endeavor of Catholic moral theology."[5]

Our focus in this chapter will be on the concerns that von Balthasar's approach raises for some ethicists over the integrity of human agency. There is another concern that must also be addressed: the discontinuity posed by the divine address seems to preclude any consensus-building among different social and religious groups. One strength of Catholic natural law, in contrast to divine command ethics, is that because it attends predominately or even exclusively to a rational consideration of intramundane goods, it provides a basis for achieving agreement on important moral matters. We will address this concern in the next chapter.

CHRISTIAN OBEDIENCE

The theme of obedience is a good starting point for exploring the relation of von Balthasar's ethics to divine command theory. "Obedience" is for some the true mark of the Christian. It serves to underscore the discontinuity of the divine claim with human expectations. For others, however, "obedience" mislocates the ethical question. The heart of the moral response is not submission or obedience to God, but love of human and creaturely goods (a love that is *also* the individual's answer to God's call). Obedience is an important theme in von Balthasar's writings, and therefore we might be inclined to place him with the advocates of obedience. But we have also seen that von Balthasar develops his concept of obedience through a reflection on the beautiful form. As a result, his concept of obedience has little in common with simple submission to an external authority. Obedience is tied to a genuine reception of the other's address. For von Balthasar, what is obeyed is first actively received by the agent. But the principal influence shaping von Balthasar's theory of obedience is not his aesthetics but his understanding of the narrative of salvation. The meaning of Christian obedience is formed through the history of God's dealing with humanity where it becomes, like gratitude and trust, one aspect of the faith response to God's salvific work.

The Moral Life and Our Response to God

I want to suspend for a moment the question of how God's address might change the content of ethics and consider one element of this intraeconomic interpretation of obedience: simply that there *is* a divine reference to Christian action. As a philosophical theory, divine command ethics holds to some form of theological voluntarism, that is, that the good in some nontrivial way depends on the divine will. But in its *theological* versions, divine command ethics often involves both something more and something less than philosophical versions. Its theological forms include something more in that they clothe obedience in religious piety, reverent affections, and, ultimately, Christian faith. But theologies that support divine command ethics can also be something less. They do not necessarily commit themselves (as do philosophical versions) to the theoretical position that the ultimate ground of moral goodness lies in divine willing and not in the divine intellect. Instead, these theological versions embody something akin to a "spirituality" of divine command ethics in which the commanding presence of God plays a central role in the life of the Christian. The explicit vertical reference of the human response, that is, its intentional responsiveness to the divine, is an essential part of Christian action for these versions even if they rely primarily on a consideration of creaturely goods to determine the content of morality. This minimal, but I think nontrivial, sense of divine command ethics is consonant even with some forms of natural law. Christians follow natural law principles in discerning the right course of action, but they perform these actions with an affective attitude of obedience to God's sovereignty.

Because the vertical reference plays such an important role in von Balthasar's ethical thought, it reflects, at the very least, this spirituality of obedience. The Christian response is elicited by the appearance in earthly form of God's glory. In the first two chapters, I argued that von Balthasar interprets this glory as the appearance of divine beauty whose fullness is manifested in the complete surrender of Christ to the Father in solidarity with sinful humanity. Because it is divine (not earthly) beauty that shines forth, this divine manifestation also judges all immanent aesthetics. Correlatively, it places a demand on the perceivers that they suspend all previous valuations and realign their affect with this standard of beauty.[6] The form of the crucified love "is so majestic" that its perception "exacts" something from the beholder, an "attitude of adoration."[7] The perception of the glory of God does more, however, than transform one's affect; it *transfixes* it: the Christian lives and acts in the horizontal but with eyes of love turned upward. The moral good now includes a contemplative dimension, not only in discerning the good but also as an essential aspect of what it means to live that good. This essential verticality opens our lives to the *personal* God of Jesus Christ because it is in this moral response tied to God that we are receptive to being surprised, challenged, disturbed, undeservedly called, and unexpectedly favored by God's addressing word.

Von Balthasar's theory is at odds then with those approaches in Roman Catholic thought which introduce a split between the horizontal and the vertical. In such approaches, strictly intramundane (horizontal) considerations (and thus theologically neutral) determine the rightness of the act. Theological or vertical references (e.g., God, faith, the biblical narrative) are included as part of the motivation of this otherwise theologically neutral act. The Kantian tendency to focus on the discrete, "big" ethical acts and on the public dimensions of such acts (i.e., how they look to an outsider) makes plausible, and for good reason, the claim that the believer and the nonbeliever do essentially the same thing when they, for example, tell the truth in a particular circumstance. And thus, the argument continues, we can bracket the vertical reference of that act without distorting its integral meaning. Von Balthasar does not deny the genuine insight of such reflections. However, his starting point is different. Rather than beginning with a moral space already fixed by immanent and determinate moral laws, he begins with the economy of salvation as the context of the human ethical response. In this context, the legitimacy or usefulness of bracketing the vertical becomes less compelling. For at the very least, this context will highlight the possibility and appropriateness of a deep, existential gratitude which desires *out of its own autonomy* to respond with a spontaneous and creative gift to the one who has given so much. The reference to the divine claim within such a sense of gratitude is subjectively immediate and insistent and objectively constitutive for any adequate construal of the response which follows.

Obedience within the Economy of Salvation

Von Balthasar believes that obedience is an integral part of the Christian life not because it is the logically appropriate response to a God who is omnipotent and free,[8] but because it is the response required by God's revelation in Christ. It is the God of the economy who commands, not the God of the philosophers. And because the context in which Christian obedience takes place (i.e., the economy of salvation) develops historically, so also will the nature of Christian obedience itself. Von Balthasar interprets the organic tie between God's Word and human response "theo-dramatically," looking at the way it is shaped by the twists and turns of God's dealings with a sinful humanity. God allows humanity's response to influence how God addresses humanity and what God expects of it. God is not the one actor in the drama of salvation. Von Balthasar wants to preserve the ontological thickness of historical events before the eternal — the "positivity of the finite" as he calls it. Creation, God's decision to establish the covenant, and the sending of the Son are, of course, *events;* something *happens.* But so too, von Balthasar stresses, are Abraham's response of faith, Israel's infidelity to that covenant, and the work of the prophets. The biblical narrative *develops*, unfolding in dramatic form through the shifts in God's engagement with human freedom that follow upon the events of the economy of salvation. There is not just one "player" controlling the unfolding of the economy of salvation; God responds to the contributions of human freedom, even when sinful. Correspondingly, the fall and the breaking of the covenant are not just two instances of the same human proclivity to sin.[9] Rather, Israel's infidelity to the covenant is a qualitatively different sort of evil. In it we see the full depth of what *sin* is: the specific rejection of God's free, personal, and gracious offer of friendship to the human person. What was to be the earthly site of God's glory—a people awakened in freedom, responding to God's call with love and service and walking in the light of his righteousness—becomes the darkness of a free human "No" to God and his glory.

How God and humanity are to respond to each other must change and be radicalized if a covenant is to survive. What happens at this point in the history of the relationship between God and humanity is no automatic continuation of the covenant, a preprogrammed response, if you will, which takes over once an infraction occurs.

> God could indeed save sinful Israel; he has the power to do this. But does he will to do so? Sin—interpreted as conscious infidelity—must in its intensification necessarily reach the point where the limit of the bearable is attained, where the covenant, which was made with a view to mutual fidelity, must count as broken and therefore as dissolved. . . . Can the covenant, which must be dissolved, nevertheless continue to exist because of grace? . . . Would not [God's] entire glory wipe itself out, if he were to enter into a relationship with that which is opposed to himself? (*GL6* 222)

If the covenant is to continue, it requires an even greater outpouring of divine self-giving and abandonment than anything God has yet done. The New Testament recounts the dramatic lengths to which divine love has gone to establish a new covenant. But the beginning of that work and the context for interpreting it lie in the preparatory stage of the Old Testament.[10]

For ethics, one old covenant "preparation" is of particular importance: the obedience of the prophet. Von Balthasar does not suggest that the obligation to follow God's will arose only at a particular stage in the economy of salvation. But responding to God's will is no formally static act, and the witness of the prophets represents a defining moment in the dynamic unfolding of human response to God. Certain "notes" are present in the modality of obedience that appears in the prophets. Not only must there be a willingness to hear, but those who hear must subordinate themselves, making themselves humble servants (*GL6* 231), for the command may come to the prophet with "an almost incomprehensible harshness" (*GL6* 232). One element of that harshness is that the prophet will not completely understand his task or what God hopes to accomplish in it. He must seek only that level of understanding which is desired by God. The prophet's obedience is more blind and burdensome than what covenantal fidelity had generally required. It is forced to lift itself out of the mire of human faithlessness and walk not in the light but in a dark unknowing. And yet it is also the place where glory appears even more brilliantly, precisely because of the dramatic contrast with the night of human disobedience.

With the collapse of the old covenant through human infidelity, obedience becomes a "stairway" constructed by God for the establishment of a new covenant with humanity. *That* one *obeys* gains a certain praiseworthiness and prominence in the prophetic literature. To pick up on our earlier interpersonal language, if the covenant is to be the sphere in which divine and human freedoms are joined in a divinely established mutuality and joyful exchange, it can only continue if the two parties go beyond the casual ease of interpersonal exchange and bridge the alienation of sin by giving themselves over to one another. But should this happen (and it can only happen through the gift of God), obedience becomes not only the means for continuing the covenantal relationship even in its brokenness but also the act which reveals both the glory intended in the covenant and the catastrophe of its loss.

On von Balthasar's reading, the prophets are not only instruments for relaying God's word to an unfaithful people. More importantly, in the response of the prophets to God's call appears the immediate radiance of human freedom aligned with its absolute ground. In prophetic obedience humanity attempts to offer an adequate response to God's address, to become as radicalized as is God's response to humanity. Prophetic obedience is a concrete human response that is both the light of the covenant continuing in the midst of human sin and the imperfect anticipation of the christological solution to it. The prophets demonstrate that obedience leads not just to a certain form of righteousness before God or the attainment of some acceptable level of goodness. Rather the prophets' expectant stillness before God's address is the fertile soil out of which God will harvest great and abundant fruit for the covenant people. Their obedience has a "mission" orientation; we might even say anachronistically that it is an *apostolic* obedience. Thus the verticality of prophetic obedience flows into horizontal service.

While in their lives and words the prophets fulfilled the task given them, to make God's glory present at a particular point in salvation history in the form of word and address, they also prepared the way for the coming of Christ by providing imperfect anticipations of a christological obedience. The lives of the prophets expressed and intensified God's addressing word to the Israelite people, but they could not effect the full reception of that word. The word was heard, but it did not have the power to claim its hearers in the depths of their being, to open their eyes, and to enable them to embrace the truth it proclaimed. The call to obedience by the prophets does not effect Christian freedom because the response that it demands does not fully participate in the freedom of Christ. As the economy unfolds, from the former covenant to the new, the raw (i.e., blind and unknowing) obedience of the prophets modulates into an obedience that is also an expression of triune love.[11] Von Balthasar follows John's Gospel in locating the radiant center of Jesus' glorification in his sacrifice on the cross (and not in the Incarnation or the resurrection and ascension) because the cross is where the radicality of divine obedience and love is manifested. Only here, in the Word made visible as love, and not just "heard," does that Word claim the full and perfect response of its recipients, a response that is not only obedient but loving.[12]

But the mode of prophetic obedience is not simply annulled by Christ. The economy of salvation includes not only creation and redemption, but also the preparatory stage of that redemption, of which the prophetic witness is a part. And for von Balthasar, the person who shares in the story of salvation will share in all its stages.

> Theologically speaking, we only know man as he exists in history, participating simultaneously in various "*status*" which he goes through; the succession of these stages implies the dramatic dimension of human life. Something in man must be identical to his original state (*status naturae integrae*), something must be identical to his fall from it (*status naturae lapsae*); something in him must correspond to the historical phase of his preparation for redemption in Christ (*status naturae reparandae*), and, finally, something in him must correspond to the effect in him of this transformation wrought by Christ (*status naturae reparatae*). Thus any "static" definition must always take into account the whole drama that takes place between man and God. (*TD2* 12–13)

The Christ-event is the central act of the drama, its unifying center, and the point at which the economy becomes a coherent drama. However, the Christ-form is perceived only by attending to those acts prior and subsequent to the central act of Incarnation, death, and resurrection. Those acts are themselves part of the *form* of Christ—not in the sense of component elements but rather, in line with Irenaeus's idea of recapitulation, they are the beginning and promise to which Christ is the end and fulfillment.[13] We begin to understand the meaning of christological obedience in the preparatory stage of the old covenant. The lives of the prophets form epistemic fragments that are collected and unified by Christ. The discontinuity that we see in prophetic obedience between human desires and expectations and God's demands— for example, the absoluteness of God's, in contradistinction to human, measure proclaimed by Amos (*GL6* 238), the necessary disposition of all spheres in Hosea's life for use by God (*GL6* 239), the awe and submission that the divine majesty evoked in Isaiah (*GL6* 248), the (seemingly) total futility of Jeremiah's mission (*GL6* 259), the surrender of Ezekiel's very self to the mission he was given (*GL6* 268)—are gathered and perfected in Christ's obedience.

Other elements of christological obedience are present in the prophetic witness in addition to that of discontinuity. In obedience the prophet is called to a real "entering" into the historical matrix of his life and world, as the place where he both hears the call and lives out its task. Thus, Hosea's message is not extrinsic to his life situation, i.e., to his loving fidelity for unfaithful Gomer, but emerges from within it. The fact that God's call leads the prophet to root his vocation in the concrete—that is, in the features of his life and in the lives of those he is to serve—means that the prophet's response to God's word adds a noble bearing to the mundane features of that life. In addition, because the prophet's life in all its concrete particularities is bound up in service to the Glorious One of Israel, the concrete existence itself, and not just the words that the prophet speaks, bears God's glory. Finally, prophetic obedience leads to a task that is given by God for the sake of God's chosen people. This task works to achieve new forms of covenantal fruitfulness and to advance God's relationship with his people. This purposefulness is not lost even when the prophetic work is rejected, as in the case of Jeremiah.

The earthly obedience of Christ includes these elements of prophetic obedience. In the dramatic events surrounding Good Friday, however, Christ transforms these elements into a cohesive expression of divine love. In Jesus' complete solidarity with sinful humanity, his vision of the Father darkens and his obedience becomes blind and absolutely self-abandoning. But here the drama undergoes an unexpected reversal. The obedience of Christ becomes "the place where the glory [i.e., God] may give utterance to itself" (*GL7* 265) and reveal itself as "boundless self-giving love" (*GL7* 283). In Christ's fidelity to the Father's will, the human word stretches to heaven and begins an unbreakable dialogue of love between the Father and sinful humanity. And as the Christian comes to share in the story of triune love, not merely as a recipient of its gift but also as a real participant in the central role, so too will the Christian's life reflect the layered richness of salvation history, including the notes of the discontinuity of prophetic obedience as recapitulated in the obedient and loving surrender of the Son.

THE QUESTION OF FULFILLMENT

While von Balthasar does not equate obedience to God with a mere submission to divine omnipotence, some might still find von Balthasar's emphasis on obedience incompatible with human autonomy. One helpful way of determining the extent to which God's command threatens human agency is to examine obedience in relation to the idea of fulfillment, since obedience seems to undermine goods generally associated with human fulfillment (i.e., freedom, use of one's own reason, and autonomy). The Roman Catholic tradition has generally interpreted the moral life along teleological lines, reflecting a traditional Catholic conviction that ultimately the moral life cannot be at odds with human fulfillment and indeed must further it. Moral acts affect not only the world but the agent who performs them. They "order" the agent to her fulfillment. This conviction places a limit on the type of ethical demands that God can lay upon the person. "If we can see no connection between our human fulfillment and the obligations under which God places us," the Catholic moralist Gerard Hughes reasons, "then we would have no grounds for believing that our God was a moral God at all,"[14] and thus no grounds for believing him to be "worthy of worship."[15] Von Balthasar, we will see below, argues that God can be deemed "worthy of worship" without making human fulfillment the criterion of that worthiness. But, in addition to the importance the theme of fulfillment has in the Catholic tradition, there is a second reason for examining the theme: von Balthasar himself makes it an important part of his reflections in *Theo-Drama*, where he argues that the ethical task given in God's call is precisely where human fulfillment is realized.

Even though von Balthasar's ethics incorporates the discontinuity between divine and human standpoints associated with divine command ethics, his ethics is ultimately teleological. His understanding of the human telos reflects the contemporary emphasis on personalist dimensions: for example, the integral wholeness of human life, its historicity, interpersonal yearnings, uniqueness. For von Balthasar, the desire for human fulfillment is composed of two aspirations: the desire to overcome sheer and meaningless contingency and achieve a personal identity grounded in the absolute, and the desire to gain self-possession through interpersonal love. Since the fulfillment of both of these deep aspirations requires the agent to embrace what is other, some kind of discontinuity is inescapably part of human perfection. Ultimately for von Balthasar these longings find their telos in, and only in, the human person's participation in the Christ-form.

Meaningful Existence and the Absolute

For von Balthasar, human fulfillment, at least on a natural level, is achieved in a life form that draws together the contingencies of one's life into a free, adequate expression of one's most fundamental self to a personal other. The project of freedom is the project to bring to expression a personal identity that is truly and autonomously our own, one that we can embrace in our deepest act of freedom, and one that is unique and irreplaceable for all time. We endeavor to make our existence an absolute word that expresses an irrevocable "I." But cast in these terms of finite identities and the absolute, the idea of fulfillment leads to questions of meaning and freedom vis-à-vis the contingent reality that makes up our lives. Who am I? What is my identity? How do my finite choices establish that identity? What role do the finite contingencies "fated" to be part of my life have in making up my identity?

These are not questions Aquinas could have asked. The essentialist categories that structured his thought, however much balanced by his insights into the contingency and particularity of moral action, led him to focus on the one, universal goal of all human agents and not on the unique "I" that was in transition to that goal. Since the agent was but one member of a species of like agents, all sharing common faculties and the same absolute end,[16] concern about how the unique, irreplaceable, and incommunicable core of the subject-self was to be realized in the moral life was not made an object of reflection.

Both von Balthasar and Thomas, however, understand the moral life in terms of its proximate and ultimate purposefulness. For Thomas, our actions are purposeful in that we act for the sake of some desirable goal. Since human action is not simply self-contained, but rather fits in a larger schema of purposefulness, that act likewise can, and perhaps must, be interpreted according to an ultimate end which shows it to be not only purposeful but finally fulfilling for the agent herself. Von Balthasar, however, interprets this purposefulness narratively. For him, an individual's actions are given purpose by being united by and interpreted within a story that describes something "true" about the agent-self and is therefore constitutive of that agent-self.[17] Thus, the fullness of life is not achieved through a linear development of human capability, that is, through an "ascent" or progress in virtue. It is instead gained in what might be called a narrative completion: the fulfillment "completes" the entire drama of one's life (in a way that parallels Christ's completion of the Old Covenant), and thus clarifies the sense and purpose of the events of one's life. Von Balthasar's ethics is teleological in this sense, that we seek to fashion a completion of meaning (i.e., a narrative completion) out of the activities, accomplishments, and events of our lives. Our ethical existence will correspond to the life story which embodies this narrative fulfillment. In this narrative sense, von Balthasar's ethics can be described as teleological.

Narrative ethics interprets the contingencies and concrete events of existence in light of the complete story of one's life. "To tell a story," as Stanley Hauerwas suggests, "involves our attempt to make intelligible the muddle of things we have done in order to be a self."[18] The endurance of loneliness (because it was an inescapable part of a self-giving vocation), the wasted years spent in frivolous pursuits (that became the occasion for conversion), the act of disloyalty in refusing to honor a parent's desire or hope (because one felt called elsewhere), the cross of aging and diminishment that is simply borne (as a way of being faithful to the gift of life) are common ethical responses whose full and correct meaning requires a larger life context, what Thomas calls circumstances. Von Balthasar expands Thomas's insight and makes the horizon of interpretation not so much the circumstances of the act as the narrative life identity of the individual. We identify our "selves" not with the isolated acts and facticities of our lives but with the meaning they come to represent in being narratively *interpreted*.[19] We can judge past and prospective actions in light of how they further or weaken, enrich or impoverish, the self of one's narrative identity. And if this life story is itself genuinely meaningful and fulfilling, then we can say that, *prima facie*, those actions which assist in shaping that identity are themselves good. We will see that for von Balthasar, the narrative identity of the individual is formed around the unique christological mission given to her by God.

But this raises a problem. The potential chaos of our contingent choices and facticities can be given order and meaningfulness through a reality that transcends them, and this, we hope, our personal story does. But what is the ontological status of this story? In what way is this *assembled* story true—true, that is, not merely in terms of the parts that are assembled, but in the completed assembly itself and the interpretation which the story involves? But also, and more importantly, why is this story true *for me*? Why is *my* identity given in this assemblage of the concrete? The two issues at stake here, the ontological status of the story and its existential validity, cannot be resolved through any immanentist project—that is, through the sheer effort of the finite creature. Such immanentist projects fail, first, because the assembled story of my life can never attain permanent existential validity. There will always remain an unbridgeable gap between what can be called the "narrative I" and the "subject I," that is, between the identity constructed by one's narrative history and one's own most inward sense of self. None of the stories that can be fashioned out of the actions and counteractions, worldly blessings and curses that make up one's existence can be embraced by the "subject I" absolutely. I will always sense the suspension between my most privately possessed "self" and the self of my narrative construction. The fact that the story of one's life can never be completely embraced by the "subject I," in turn, casts some doubt on the ontological status of the story—that is, whether the story is true. However, for von Balthasar, immanentist projects also fail because the finite person desires and needs a judgment about her life which is not just relatively or tentatively true but is absolute.[20] The finite creature cannot, however, render such an absolute judgment on herself. Thus, while for Thomas the highest act (the one that represented the fulfillment of the person) was the knowing, willing, and loving the absolute, for von Balthasar, it is becoming a "self" in relation to the Absolute, to relate the *unique* "I" that is one's identity to the absolute.[21]

Von Balthasar considers two solutions, each using the idea of "role," but rejects them both. First, my identity can be formed out of the limited ethical role that is allotted to me by some more comprehensive reality (e.g., the Stoics' order of nature, civic society): to be a mother, or friend, or defender, and so on (*TD1* 495). While this role is finite, it shares in the dignity of the higher reality.[22] However, there is still no necessary convergence between my inward sense of self and this external story which has been given me in life, and thus the role presents no internal claim on individual freedom. There is an advance here, however, and it is one that von Balthasar will capitalize on when he turns to the Christian narrative. One's free identification with the grander scheme of things (e.g., a Stoic order, the cosmic cycle of life and death, the cause of human emancipation, one's family history) softens the unchosen givenness of one's lot. Nonetheless, one's role is not a full participation in this larger reality, but only a limited part of it. Thus the self who identifies with the larger reality can still be alienated from the constructed self occupying this concrete, finite role. The second approach embraces this alienation. The human person, stuck "in the fragility of the temporal," anchors her identity by looking upward to the divine (*TD1* 545). However, by taking her stand in eternity, she alienates herself from her life here below. She reaches the absolute only to lose the unique "I" of her historical existence (*TD1* 544).[23] Nonetheless, these two "dead ends" (role as limitation and role as alienation) are instructive in that they indicate where von Balthasar feels the solution must lie: taking a stand in eternity, engaged fully in the finite.

What cripples both of the approaches is that they attempt to unlock the identity of the self by placing it within a larger system impersonally and abstractly conceived. Such a system might be able to situate contingency and the absolute together in a way that preserves them both, but it cannot do so without obscuring the dimension of personal freedom (i.e., the agent's free choice of this identity). For von Balthasar, the achievement of personal freedom occurs when one is able to grasp one's deepest identity and express it to the other. It is a project that cannot be controlled by something beyond the domain of one's "I" (e.g., Stoic fate, social expectation) and still remain the project of freedom. But what cannot be controlled can be freely invited by the call of another. This is "God's masterpiece," to awaken through love a free response that embraces God's freedom and with it God's absolutely free "idea" for each individual. I suggested in chapter 1 that for von Balthasar, the two poles of freedom (self-possession and relationality) are realized in the dialogical encounter: the individual responds to the other and in doing so expresses and forms herself. We can then speak of two teleologies of human fulfillment: first, a narrative teleology where one's narrative identity is grounded in the absolute; and, second, a teleology of freedom, achieved in the interpersonal exchange. The two movements both require a suspension of one's own agential aims and pursuits in order to receive what is other. The first suspension arises when we consider whether to interpret our lives in light of the absolute; the second occurs when we pause to listen actively to the personal address of the other. Von Balthasar never himself isolates the two movements or works out a systematic relationship between them, though they are present throughout his writings.[24] At this point, however, we must amend our earlier statement to include both these teleological movements: human fulfillment consists not just in the "self in relation to the Absolute," but the *person* in relation to a personal Absolute.[25]

The Ignatian Movements of Love

Von Balthasar's resolution of the two movements begins with a concept of human love for God that draws together the Neoplatonic love of Augustine's thought and the descending kenotic love of Christ. Von Balthasar's thought complicates but does not eliminate the roles that self-realization and eros-love have had in the Catholic approach to the moral life. His theological aesthetics retrieves beauty as a heuristic lens for understanding divine revelation and the believer's response, and eros-love has a central role in this endeavor. But through his theological aesthetics, he also argues that our response to the beauty of Christ is not an unbroken continuation of self-love but a decentering of that self-concern and a recentering in the appearing other. It is a fundamental principle of von Balthasar's aesthetics that human fulfillment is not found in an ek-static, one-directional movement of love toward the beloved. Rather it is found in a bipolarity of receptivity and agency, as is reflected in freedom's dimensions of relationality and self-possession. This bipolarity, which is absent in the Neoplatonic view of human fulfillment, is found, von Balthasar believes, in the spirituality of Ignatius of Loyola.[26]

The effort to incorporate an Ignatian movement of love is explicit in von Balthasar's essay "Homo Creatus Est."[27] Here he explores a tension he finds in the Catholic tradition between the erotic Neoplatonism that marks the Augustinian-Thomistic legacy and the Ignatian (and, he suggests, more biblical) stress on our obligations to God. On several levels, von Balthasar criticizes unguarded versions of the former.[28] Ignatius's "First Principle and Foundation"[29] offers a counterpoint by fixing an appropriate ordering between the claim of God on the human person and the innate human aspiration to self-realization. The primary telos of the human person, according to its opening line, is to praise, reverence, and serve God. The concern with human fulfillment remains, but it is subordinated to our prior surrender to God: "[we are] created to . . . serve God, and *by this means to save [our] souls.*"[30] There are two movements here: the giving of self to God and the reception of self from God. For von Balthasar, these two movements reflect the bipolarity of interpersonal love.

However, this dual movement is not only a dimension of creaturely existence. It is also a participation in the dynamics of triune life. The Father gives himself over to the Son and receives from the Son his answering Word. The human spirit's movement toward its fulfillment is swept up into a participation in the kenotic movement within the Godhead. The Christian's prayerful movement "upward" (*de abajo*, to use Ignatius's phrase), toward God,[31] enters into the tripersonal surrender of the Godhead "downward" (*de arriba*). The creature's surrender to God becomes a participation in God's surrender to it, and, ultimately, in God's kenotic movement toward creation and its redemption. Here, we will see, the creature finds its fulfillment. The eros striving of the human spirit remains, but now it is integrated into the divine, self-giving movement of *agapē* (kenotic) love.[32] Furthermore, God's surrender to the creature is personal, and so will be the creature's surrender to God. We saw one example of this free, personal interplay between God and humanity in the section on prophetic obedience. Through the prophets, God responded in a new, creative, and free way to sinful humanity. Because God's involvement in the world is personal (i.e., voluntaristic and dramatic), the way God calls forth human participation in that drama will likewise be personal.[33]

The relevance of all this for our concern with discontinuity is that if an "Ignatian" view is adopted, as von Balthasar believes it should be, it affects how we perceive the relationship between the divine will and morality. The emphasis on the personhood of God introduces a kind of suspension between the goodness and lovableness of creation and God's personal choice about how we are to love that creation. There exists a personal "distance" between God and creation that can be likened to that which arises in the interpersonal encounter. The other is good and lovable, but that does not wholly determine one's response to her. Rather one's response will be creative, new, and free and not something that the other's goodness causes in a mechanical fashion. All the more so for God, whose infinitely creative ways of loving always exceed our own. God loves creation not just "appropriately," as fits creation's goodness, but personally, laboring for it and in it, sometimes in ordinary and anticipated ways, and sometimes in wondrous and astounding ways. God's love for creation is always free and not a formulaic response according to what is due. Correlatively, Christians' love for God leads them first to enter this same suspension (what Ignatius calls "indifference") between the immanent goodness of things and divine choice. Then they allow themselves to be attuned to divine choices and loves for creation. Thus, in the *Spiritual Exercises*, Ignatius has the retreatant make a choice about one's direction in life not only, or even primarily, according to what seems good or through a weighing of the various advantages of one direction over the other, but rather according to the particular choice of the divine person for that individual.[34] The ultimate ground of Christian love of the world is found, not as for Augustine in the ontological participation of created things in the one goodness of God, but in the personal willing of God—a personal willing that, of course, includes God's decision to create and his providential care of that creation. Christian love for the world contains an internal bipolarity: the movement of the creature *de abajo*, from below upward to the divine love and glory seen in the Christ-event, spontaneously issues forth into a movement *de arriba*, from above, where creation is embraced with the passion and intensity of divine love. Ethical judgments of the particular ways to love self, neighbor, and creation are complete and final only in light of this divine, personal willing.[35]

I have used different terms—for example, active receptivity, obedience, suspension of judgment—to describe that openness to the beloved which must be part of any loving relationship. The individual freely allows himself or herself to be affected, changed, and transformed by the wishes and addresses of the beloved. Since the individual cannot predict or anticipate all of the free expressions of the beloved, these addresses sometimes represent a kind of "break" (or "discontinuity") with what was anticipated. A similar suspension occurs in our relationship with God. For von Balthasar, Ignatian indifference[36] is not so much a permanent stance vis-à-vis creaturely things, but rather one moment in a dynamic posture toward them. Indifference moves back and forth, *from* an initial detachment in regard to earthly goods (in a flight from the world in order to make oneself available to divine movements), and *toward* a reengagement of those goods, now with desires and love attuned to those of God.[37]

> This co-operation [with God in the perfection of the kingdom] can no longer remain at the level of indifference in the sense of *merely* letting things happen; no, the particular will of God, which is to be actively grasped and carried out, must also be actively pursued. (*GL5* 104–5)[38]

Indifference to created goods is necessary because simply accepting God as one's supreme good does not yet give an answer to how finite goods are to be part of our lives; that answer is given only in one's entering into the dynamic, personal rhythms of God's love for creation and for oneself. At the same time, full, active engagement in the affairs of the world is necessary because God's love for his creation will lead the individual to likewise love creation and thus labor for its good. Finally, the active, free, and spontaneous living out of God's will includes the availability to love the *idea* of one's self as God does, and thus to love and actively pursue the person whom God wants one to be.[39] The person is always already seen and loved by God. One's love for God *de abajo* will always be met by God's loving gaze toward one. And in this gaze, the promise of myth—that is, of a personal, identity-constituting address of the Absolute—attains its realization.

OBEDIENCE AND FULFILLMENT

The First Level of Obedience: Creaturely

The initial discontinuity between God's desires for us and our views of the moral life does not lie *first* in the particular tasks or commands that might arise in our lives—the kind of prophetic obedience we saw above. It is true that, apart from a faith commitment, those addresses would seem at times like bizarre and excessive demands. Moreover, appearing to the world as a "holy fool" or simply a fool is always a genuine possibility for the Christian.[40] But the *primary* discontinuity in von Balthasar's approach lies in the transformation brought about by the Christ-form, that is, in the tragic and glorious love displayed on the cross and the faith response awakened by that appearing glory. Thus von Balthasar distinguishes between two levels of obedience:

> [F]irst, the subjection of our whole nature and person to the service of Christ inasmuch as we are made for him who is our divine head; second, the simultaneous inner adoption of the mind of Christ, whose divine inner freedom and personhood are identical with his obedience to the Father. *Under the first aspect, our obedience is that proper to the creature; under the second, it is divine.*[41]

We will return to this second level below. The first obedience, the basic, creaturely response of faith, is "demanded" by God from the one who perceives Christ-form not heteronomously but rather "aesthetically," as a free response of gratitude.[42]

> The form and the word within [the form] awaken and summon us; they awaken our *freedom* and bid us attend to the call that comes to us from the form. . . . The power of aesthetic expression is never an over-

whelming power but one that liberates. . . . [I]t grants freedom. It illuminates, in itself and in the man who encounters it . . . the realm of an infinite dialogue. (*TD2* 28)

Von Balthasar grounds the claim of the divine address neither simply in the sovereignty of the one making the claim nor in the self-generated dicta of human reason, but rather in the aesthetic claim of divine beauty. "We must recall," von Balthasar suggests, "that the triune love of God has power only in the form of surrender (and in the vulnerability and powerlessness that is part of the essence of that surrender)."[43] Because it is based not on a power relation or demand of logic, but rather on an appeal to freedom, the aesthetic claim is both softer in its engagement with human freedom yet more effective. Through his theological aesthetics, von Balthasar leads his divine command ethics out of the mire of heteronomy which threatens Barth's ethics, while being faithful to Barth's commitment to a strict theological governance of ethics. However, a similar claim about the aesthetic appeal of the Gospel can be found in Barth, though it is carefully circumscribed. Thus, the contrast here with von Balthasar should not be overstated. Indeed, a comparison between the two is instructive because it shows, I believe, the cogency and coherence of von Balthasar's theological aesthetics. While both Barth and von Balthasar maintain the appropriateness of describing God's work in Christ as "beautiful," only von Balthasar pursues the full implications of such a characterization for ethics.

Barth vigorously affirms the radical discontinuity between divine and human notions of the good.[44] However, Barth also rejects the idea that the divine claim has anything to do with the assertion of divine power.[45] More importantly, the ethical command is, as in von Balthasar, interpreted *within* the economy—for Barth within the doctrine of election and its component ideas of mercy, forgiveness, and covenantal desire. Barth will go so far as to say that God's command to the person will take the "form" of the good news and will, therefore, be a communication to the individual of God's merciful desire for fellowship.[46] Such a command cannot be considered *simply* irruptive or heteronomous.[47] Instead, Barth defends a *genuine* autonomy, that is, not just a *de jure* positing that God's command does indeed grant autonomy, but a real, subjectively experienced autonomy.[48] The *pro nobis* context of the command and the agential liberation that it effects lead to a Balthasarian conclusion, and Barth draws it: beauty is both a legitimate and a necessary description of God's glory.[49] The Christian's response to God is one of "awe, gratitude, wonder, submission and obedience," but also a "joy" that has as its object the beauty of God.[50] God's glory has the "peculiar power and characteristic of giving pleasure, awaking desire, and creating enjoyment."[51] In its beauty, it is a "persuasive and convincing form."[52] Barth, however, keeps this chord carefully subdued. Beauty is, he tells us, only an auxiliary idea[53] and cannot be included with the "main concepts of the doctrine of God."[54] This subordination of beauty frees Barth from the necessity of fashioning any systematic coherence out of what are on first glance discordant themes (e.g., delight, joy, persuasion, on the one hand, and obedience, submission, and judgment, on the other).

Von Balthasar, of course, makes the opposing claim, elevating beauty into a central theological category, and this difference with Barth, perhaps more than their well-known dispute about the analogy of being,[55] gives von Balthasar's ethics a markedly different form even while sharing in common features of divine command ethics. In pushing ahead to integrate the discontinuous and continuous themes in an aesthetics of the theological form, von Balthasar redeems divine command ethics for his Catholic audience. Perceiving the beauty of the human other always includes a moment of obedience or discontinuity, and this discontinuity is radicalized before the divine Other. Von Balthasar's theological aesthetics preserves the objective discontinuity of the divine and human judgments (divine glory is not earthly beauty) without postulating a disruption of human agency (i.e., mere heteronomous submission) in order to make this discontinuity tangible. His ethics offers an aesthetic version of what Paul Tillich describes as "theonomous" ethics.[56] Thus, on the one hand, he underscores the independence of God's commanding Word. God's Word is "pure objectivity," finding "a foothold neither in the hearer's desires nor in his fears" and thus demands only one answer: "assent and obedience." It does so not because God's word conforms to our expectations but rather because it "possesses the quality of glorious lordliness and proclaims a will which takes hold of man beyond all appeal." At the same time, the power of this Word does no "violence" to human willing, but rather "summons insistently" (*GL6* 58–59).[57] Exposure to a masterpiece can radically alter our aesthetic sensitivities. We could not construct its beauty on our own, but neither can we perceive without recognizing its invitation to transcend our previous standards of beauty. While there remains a discontinuity between the nature of divine and earthly aesthetic claims, the heightened claim of the divine object is matched by its power to draw forth a human response of love.[58] The first and most fundamental moment of human response to the divine is not a Herculean attempt to meet its claim but a single-hearted recognition of its glory and majesty. Creaturely obedience is one dimension of the decentering effected in the appearance of glory.[59] The movement of the human spirit before God's word is not, *pace* Hughes, due to the recognition that it is fulfilling but due to the recognition that it is glorious.

The Second Level of Obedience: Divine

It might seem that such a response lacks the kind of (secondary) creative and creating freedom traditional to the Thomistic tradition. However, von Balthasar maintains that it is the divine intent to bring forth such a freedom, that is, a human freedom that is distinct from God's own. The paradox that arises in the two affirmations, the sovereignty of God the Father and the freedom of the Christian, is illuminated, though not explained away, by the doctrine of the Trinity, where the complete receptivity of the Son to the Father's will is one with his personal freedom. Here mission is the key cipher. I have indicated the basic features of von Balthasar's concept of mission. It is grounded in the triune life of God and has its archetypal expression in the person of Christ. Christ reveals that the Second Person of the Trinity is not only Word, but Answering Word—the one who responds to the Father not in words that convey something in addition to himself but in the Word which expresses who he is. The task of Christians is likewise to shape their lives into a response in which the unique word that God has made them to be is given expression. In an analogous and obviously imperfect image, we can say that the mission of the individual is where one becomes a christological "person" of the Trinity. Shaped into the image of Christ, the Christian's life is introduced into the divine conversation.

> And whoever shares, *by his obedience to mission,* in [the] truth and freedom of God, *shares also in the choice,* the plans and the providence of God himself. He no longer meets God as one who lays before him petitions of his own designing; his petitions and desires are included in the decrees of God. . . . by God's elective will in Christ, the human word is included in the trinitarian dialogue between Father and Son in the Holy Spirit.[60]

There is a paradox here that Christianity has consistently affirmed: autonomy is achieved by an ever greater dependence on God. Von

Balthasar's contribution is to view this paradox in a trinitarian light and to see interpersonal relationships as an intramundane analogy to it. Adhering to God, living in dependence on his will, calls for an obedience to the earthly mission God has planned for us. The mission is the point in which God's triune life is opened to us and, as the participation in the person-constituting dynamic of the processions, the form in which we can autonomously invest completely all our personal energies and sense of identity.[61]

While von Balthasar's ethics can appropriately be characterized as one of "divine command" on account of its theological voluntarism vis-à-vis the created order and our need to submit to God's personal will, the characterization is by itself incomplete. Von Balthasar's idea of Christian obedience is informed not just by the image of the Son's surrender to the Father, but also by an interpretation of the Spirit as the one who fosters creative freedom within the unity of the Godhead. The one, absolute freedom of the Godhead has room for the "otherness" of human freedom because, as von Balthasar repeatedly stresses, God is already "Other" in the unity of the Spirit, and this divine otherness is the basis for every created otherness.[62] The gift of genuine autonomy is as much a pneumatological fruit as it is christological, because it is the Spirit's work that allows the otherness of finite freedom to be welcomed into the unity of the Godhead. The freedom that the mission gives to the creature is a real sharing in the sacred space of triune life.[63] While von Balthasar recognizes the particular challenge of bringing the Spirit's personhood into focus, referring to the Spirit as "a mysterious Someone of his own," he describes the Spirit not just as the unity between the Father and the Son, but as the one who expresses and seals this unity in "a personal manner."[64] By the latter I take him to mean that it is precisely the Spirit's qualities of personhood —that is, spontaneity, creativity, interplay—that complete the absolute, loving bond of the Trinity. Thus the personal qualities of freedom and creativity will likewise be part of the human person's bond of unity with God.

Since the space made available to the individual through Christ's mission is not "a mere fluid medium" but rather "a personal and personalizing area" (*TD3* 249), the Spirit's prompting will direct the person to embrace more than just general ethical norms or universal principles. She will be called to the unique, personal norm that is her particular way of freely and creatively participating in the divine interplay.

But for the Christian the norm [of his choice] cannot be provided by his own opinion, or by some general ethical consideration. For him, because what is involved is the following of the supreme example of the God-man, the norm itself must be divine; and because, again, what is involved is the practice of personal, imitative discipleship, the norm must be personal too. The only such norm is the Spirit . . .[65]

The Spirit is the intimate gift of God's presence to our inmost being and thus not so much the place where we meet God as personal Other, or "Thou," but where the wellspring of divine, personalizing freedom becomes our own.[66] Through the personalizing presence of the Spirit, we reach into absolute freedom and form ourselves into the "I" that God created each of us to be. Thus the Spirit is the gift to us of both "a concrete plan of the future, in accordance with our own mission and hence with our own personality, and the inner free spontaneity to carry out, recall and follow this plan" (*TD3* 52). Because the Spirit fosters our autonomy, as a freedom that is truly other than divine freedom within the mission given by the Father,[67] there is a sense in which the work of the Spirit is the mode whereby God allows the divine self to be "receptive" to human freedom. Thus, through the Spirit, the Father gives Christians "an acting area in which they can creatively exercise their freedom and imagination" (*TD2* 273). In our ethical lives, we do not "trace a path already marked out for us, as if we were immature children"; rather divine freedom "has 'prepared' a personal path for each one of us to follow freely, a path along which our freedom can realize itself" (*TD3* 52). Since there is ultimately only one single mission, that of the Son (*TD5* 392), the personal identity given to each person and the ethical path it entails will always be christomorphic. But within *this* realm as shaped and defined by the eternal Word (and not simply that realm of action available to the person through the use of intellect, will, and finite freedom), God gives the Christian a "voice" in the Godhead.

Is the Christian then freed from the burdensome, harsh obedience required of the prophets? The kind of obedience evidenced there, a type of obedience that I suggested continues to be required of the Christian, seems far sharper and more disruptive than the aesthetic response described in chapter 1 (in which "obedient hearing" is already integrated within "ecstatic seeing") and seems entirely absent from the trinitarian mission described above. Prophetic obedience requires only word and hearing, not understanding or vision. I believe the kind of "dark" obedience that God genuinely demands of the

Christian at times is part of what von Balthasar refers to as the second, divine level of obedience. The paradigm of this divine obedience is, of course, the Son's surrender on the cross. This obedience is characterized by von Balthasar not so much as a creaturely submission to the divine will, but as a receptivity within the eternal dialogue of love between the Father and the Son.

Nonetheless, both levels of responses, creaturely submission and triune surrender, are present and converge in Christ's self-sacrifice.[68] A twofold theological aesthetics, iconic and dramatic, gives von Balthasar a way of supporting these levels of obedience which the Christian response will involve. Every response presupposes the fundamental act of Christian existence, the act of faith, and von Balthasar never describes this act in terms of a blind obedience, but rather as a kenotic beholding of the divine beauty displayed in the story's central character.[69] The story of Christ draws the individual to enter its story (first level of obedience). Christ's narrative becomes her narrative. The Christian in faith moves *from* the immanent narratives available to her through her community, family, occupation, etc., and *to* the narrative that comes to be hers in faith. Because she identifies herself entirely with its central character, the desires and wishes of the Father become, in *divine* obedience (second level), her own. The story that will be authored for her in God's commands to her will always be the story of his Son. But in this story, there will also be moments of dark obedience, including the demands for acceptance of suffering and forbearance within it. The Christian will be called to enter "the hard and painful corners of finite existence: death, disease, betrayal in love, hunger"[70] and to forgo certain paths in order to serve God in others. But this kind of blind obedience is not a self-violating obedience. God's commands will never, existentially or ontologically, direct the Christian out of the story of the Son or away from the idea of unique personhood eternally guarded for each person. The Ignatian rhythm of indifference and engagement, of contemplation and action, that is part of this story forestalls any disruption by the divine command of the individual's most inward sense of self, since that self has in its deepest freedom identified itself with the personal freedom of God as displayed in Christ.

Von Balthasar's image of a personal, triune God pushes the limits of knowledge and language; some might even argue that he exceeds them. But if Jesus Christ is the revelation of the relationship between divine and human freedoms (the concrete analogy of being, as von Balthasar describes him), then the relationship of these freedoms must be characterized in personal and obediential terms, as argued in chapter 2. At the same time, the Spirit's presence to the individual indicates another dimension of the Christian's encounter with God: God's freedom not only engages human freedom dialogically and interpersonally but also comes to the individual as the one who bears her freedom. Human freedom and divine freedom do not simply operate on the same level. This is the element that Fuchs's emphasis on God's transcendental presence rightly underscores. The doctrine of the Trinity points us to both dimensions of God's presence to the human creature —transcendent and interpersonal. At the same time, as the revelation of the incomprehensibility of God, the doctrine of the Trinity is not merely a positive assertion about the divine, but rather the mystery to which Christian apophaticism must be faithful. Von Balthasar's ethics reflects an attempt to be faithful to this revelation by allowing it to shape his understanding of human action, all the while recognizing that all he has offered are inadequate images and models of the Christian's participation in this mystery.

Fulfillment

Von Balthasar wants to press his claim further: his trinitarian ethics not only does not violate human agency; it positively fosters human fulfillment. In this his ethics finds a secondary vindication. This fulfillment is eschatological, though von Balthasar emphasizes the "already" of the eschatological life in such a way as to introduce some unnecessary problems for his theory, as I will indicate below.

For von Balthasar, human fulfillment consists not in our human knowing and willing Absolute Being, but rather, as suggested above, in a personal relationship with the personal Absolute. God is the absolute "Thou" of the human "I," and the unique and irrevocable name by which God calls each person is the seal of that person's dignity. God's missioning name is not something additional to one's identity. It does not reflect any misunderstanding of who one is. It represents no alienation between the individual and God. In short, it is the perfect, irrevocable, and fulfilling address of the absolute Thou. The question of personal identity which the tension between the ambivalence and flux of finite existence and the longing for the absolute now provokes has its adequate answer: in the mission, one's personal name is written on the absolute.

This unique mission grants individuals their true autonomy. It does this by giving them a concrete form (i.e., their labor in the mission) to grasp as their own.[71] The Christian story not only gives one new motivations, though certainly gratitude plays an important part of moving one to respond to the call of Christ. More importantly, it fulfills the "narrative teleology" of human existence. It does this by allowing Christians to see the diverse particularities of their lives as part of the biblical drama: the occasions of their success and failure, their acts of minor heroism and those of unnoted mediocrity, their rebellion against God and their repentance. The story of Christ, the *Christians'* story, offers a horizon that illuminates the *who* that Christians are within these fragments of particularity and points them to an identity that they can embrace with all their energy.[72] In embracing the name the Father has given to the Christian in Christ (the movement *de arriba*, from above), the Christian is moved to do more than put on a costume and memorize a part. In following the currents of the divine will, Christians eagerly engage in the task at hand with all their love and intellect, their passion and creativity.

For von Balthasar, the missioning name that God gives to each of us also defines the form and shape of our ethical existence.

> All biblical ethics is based on the call of the personal God and man's believing response. God describes himself in his call to man as the One who is faithful, truthful, just, merciful (and other paraphrases of his Name), and it is on the basis of this Name that the name of the one who responds (i.e., his unique personality) is determined. [In the call, the person] is given his mission, which becomes a norm for his conduct henceforth.[73]

This mission, given its christological shape, will involve a eucharistic surrender of self-giving love. But it will not lead to a self-dissipating love. Von Balthasar generally ignores the danger of self-destructive forms of self-giving, and as a result can be incautious in his praise of relentless self-giving as the norm of Christian existence. While the Christian can look to the triune life for a paradigm of the simultaneity of perfect self-giving and perfect self-realization, the Christian will have only glimmers of that eschatological perfection within the horizontal relationships of her present existence, not sustained experiences of it. It is not enough to say that the Christian is called to be "for others"; rather the Christian is called to be a "*person* for others." The radical self-giving of the Christian must include not only positive acts of beneficence but also acts where the Christian "consents" to leaving good works undone in order to be faithful to the person willed into existence by God. Von Balthasar can be read as suggesting as much, but he rarely, if ever, makes the idea explicit.

For von Balthasar, human fulfillment is not simply a matter of the horizontal (e.g., human projects, social roles) or of the vertical (e.g., God's personal address). Von Balthasar's appeal to the dramatic form offers an aesthetic solution which does not force us to choose either the vertical or the horizontal. Our lives do have their relative meanings, seen in their multiple tasks, their varied, contextualized identities, their plots and subplots. However, these relative meanings lack any kind of truly permanent fixity or finality; some new insight or event in our lives can throw these meanings into question. The openness of the individual's life to multiple meanings, an openness that is the lot of finite temporal existence, is itself an availability to an absolute address. The ambiguous meanings that can be ascribed to one's discrete and finite acts become sharpened and clarified in light of the Christian story that is one's own: the Christian's acts become ones of kindness, moral failure, remorse, conversion, and surrender. The narrative horizon that the Christian story gives to one's life does not interpret away the relative meanings of one's life, but rather illuminates in them Christlike patterns of living and, in these patterns, the glory of divine love. It does so because the Christ-event has really become, through the Christians' incorporation into Christ, their story, not just epistemologically (i.e., the lens through which they interpret their lives), as it might seem in some works of narrative ethics, but ontologically, as the fruit of the Spirit's power to "liquefy" the Christ-form, to use von Balthasar's language, by stamping it onto the lives of his followers. Obviously that aesthetic pattern will not so much be evident in an isolated act, and it might not be evident at all to those who look at that life apart from faith. But there will be concrete patterns of surrender, acceptance, love, reconciliation, and so on, which, once acknowledged, allow one to see in the narrative of this person's life a Christlike form and a unity that can appropriately be termed interchangeably one's "identity" and one's "mission."

Nonetheless, von Balthasar places an excessive emphasis on the "already" of the individual's eschatological fulfillment. This excess is evident at two points. First, one's identity in von Balthasar's thought seems too closely wedded not only to the concrete, but to the *ethical* concrete, however interpreted through the Christian story. The concrete stories of our lives are *not* the whole of our identities. They are tainted in that the story of human existence is always also the story of individuals fleeing from the name God wants to give them. Moreover, in light of the stories of some, for example, those with tragically shattered existences or who face de-humanizing disabilities, it seems clear that the brokenness of the world has prevented some persons from ever being able to embrace the names that God wants to give them, names that God instead preserves and guards for them in heaven. Again, von Balthasar's reliance on the dramatic form helps him at least address the problem. The story allows us complex judgments of the events of our lives. Some are subplots and thus not at the core of our identities; others are more central. And even more important is the fact that the story is not complete. The eschatological fullness is not yet ours, though we have begun to share in it. In the stories of many Christians, that fullness is present much more as promise and hope than as present reality. The note of this "not yet" needs to sound more resoundingly in von Balthasar's thought if he is to succeed in his project to incorporate all of the stories of Christian existence, the full ones and the shattered ones, into the one story of Christ.

Second, he presupposes without clarifying an idea of the *unity* of the mission, one that is, however, hard to see in the various identities of one's present historical existence (e.g., spouse, parent, carpenter, teacher, politician, friend, etc.). Von Balthasar refers to the lives of the saints, such as St. Paul or Thérèse of Lisieux, as examples of this unity of life aesthetically formed in the mission. But these examples mislead more than clarify. The concept of a person-constituting mission cannot, generally at least, be defined in terms of a single task, purpose, or goal of substantive material content (i.e., something more than the formal task of being Christ's disciple), though it might seem the case in the lives of some saints (e.g., Paul's "mission" to proclaim the gospel to the Gentiles). A tasklike unity is simply not the reality of the daily and pluriform witness to Christ characteristic of most Christians' lives. The term "mission" (*Sendung*) does properly indicate the trinitarian basis of one's ethical existence and the fact that, like Christ, the Christian is sent "from above." But the term must be allowed some semantic flexibility if it is to indicate the aesthetic whole that appears within the task-varied narrative of most Christians. Again, a greater note of eschatological reserve could help von Balthasar. For now, the Christian walks in the hope that God will finally bring her to her intended personhood within the scattered directions her life does in fact take.

Von Balthasar's claim, however, can be made more moderate: within the many tasks to which Christians are called in their lives, they begin to find themselves shaped with a particular character, an ethical personality that is manifested in their particular story. The concept of "mission" would then refer to the characteristic way that God calls each Christian to live a christomorphic life. The lives of the saints teach us one thing: growth in Christ is not growth into ethical sameness. Just as the saints and great literary figures reflect certain characteristic qualities, habitual ways of responding to situations, and even predictable patterns of acting, so also as the Christian grows into unique personhood, the Christian's life will come to have a particular ethical shape. The tasks that form this ethical character arise sometimes from the proximate demands of neighbor and world, sometimes from a more direct inspiration from God. Perhaps one of the tasks will serve as a heuristic lens for all of the Christian's other works (e.g., missionary work). Ultimately, however, all the divinely missioned tasks give expression to the unique idea of personhood (i.e., the Christian's character) that God has willed for each person in loving her into existence, and thus are grounded in, and thereby unified by, the one love of God. This is not a direction von Balthasar pursues, though it is consonant with his thought.

CONCLUSION

For von Balthasar, the persuasive power of the Christ-form is such that it can integrate the splintering fragments of human existence into a single coherent form. We have examined how two of these "fragments," obedience and the human longing for fulfillment, can be harmonized in the light of the divine economy.

Von Balthasar maintains that obedience is the appropriate response of the creature to God, and he does so with the same zeal one finds in Barth. However, this response of obedience is also carefully interpreted. Creaturely obedience is a response not to the display of infinite power but to the powerlessness and kenosis of triune love. The glory that appears in Christ deepens and radicalizes the receptivity of persons so that they can genuinely and autonomously receive the "word" that God speaks to them in Christ. But even this creaturely response is "recapitulated" in Christ into a new form. The active receptivity that always marks the creaturely mode of perceiving the other becomes, in the trinitarian horizon of Christian existence, a share in the radical surrender of the Father to the Son. The obedience of the prophets, whose radical servitude to the divine call sought to close the growing wound in the covenant opened by human infidelity, imperfectly anticipated the radicality of Christ's reconciling obedience to the Father and the cruciform path along which the Christian is to follow.

Yet, with Augustine and Thomas, and the mainstream Catholic moral tradition, von Balthasar maintains that this surrender is not just an appropriate response to God, but already in the present begins to tap into the deep human desires for fullness of life; it is *intrinsically* fulfilling in an eschatological sense (i.e., already *and* not yet), not just the prerequisite for a fulfillment to be bestowed at some future time. Human persons yearn to write the absolute name of their existence on the fleeting realities of their lives. But one-sided projects to achieve the absolute cannot succeed. Persons can find their names only if they are first spoken to them by the absolute. Von Balthasar situates the dynamics of divine address and human response explicitly within the trinitarian horizon of Christian narrative. The name that God gives the individual is a missioning name; the individual is sent to further the divine plans and hopes for creation by participating in the mission of Christ. This mission is not an additional task to one's identity; it *is* one's name and identity as viewed from a different vantage, that of the Father lovingly beholding creation through his Son.

The "Catholic" horizontal and the "Barthian" vertical intersect in the mission. The mission gives the individual a voice in the eternal dialogue with feet planted firmly on the earth. Yet the image of dialogue is imperfect, for what we come to share in is not simply an interpersonal exchange. Rather the Father is the Absolute Person whose address to us establishes our identity. Our lives are not just words to the Father, but always *answering* words. The address of the Father to the individual is ultimately one and is identical with the christological identity of the person, but in general it is given to the individual in multitudinous ways within the events and goods of one's existence and across one's narrative history. These particular addresses will involve greater or lesser degrees of knowing or blindness, of ease or heaviness, but they will always lead one to one's own eucharistic act.

4

Creation and Covenant

———————◆►◄◆———————

W̶E SAW IN THE LAST CHAPTER that von Balthasar modifies
Augustine's understanding of love for God by introducing
an Ignatian element: our friendship with God (the upward,
Augustinian movement of love) leads to our loving the world and the
things within it, not merely according to their own claims, but in the
personal way that God loves them (the downward movement). We
must, correspondingly, suspend our valuing of the world so that God's
desires can shape our love for it. But this same suspension (or indifference) would on first glance put a severe limit on our use of creaturely
goods as guides to divine willing. Creaturely claims do not completely
coincide with divine desires. The loss of a horizontal mediation of
God's will undermines two positions traditionally associated with Catholic ethics: that the Christian moral life is intelligible and that it is so
even to non-Christians. The two levels of obedience discussed in the
previous chapter point to the same conclusions. On the first level, the
radical, transforming effect of the Christ-event entails an equally radical (and new) praxis. The story itself commands the Christian, and as
a result of the particularity of this "command," the Christian's love for
the neighbor will appear "strange, offensive and scarcely decipherable
for the world."[1] But even for those within the Christian community, it
is not simply *understanding* the moral situation that reveals love's
demands but obediently *hearing* God's call to follow particular paths
(the second level of obedience). At both levels, the claims of the created order are insufficient for ethical guidance. Thus, von Balthasar's

theory limits the kind of moral universalism otherwise possible when
the exclusive object of ethical reflection is the same created order
shared by all persons across time and culture.

Nonetheless, I want to argue that von Balthasar's thought preserves
a relative autonomy of the horizontal order and with it a noetic component (i.e., understanding, reason) of the moral life. The horizontal
order is "thick" enough to mediate the Christian moral life, that is, the
divine claim and human response, and to gain for that life a basic intelligibility. Thus, God's commands will not appear as alien intruders
within our moral horizon. Moreover, because of this "thickness," von
Balthasar's ethics, though refreshingly new in its approach (and, at
times, frustratingly idiosyncratic in its terminology), has a decidedly
Catholic orientation and succeeds in reuniting Catholic ethics with its
spiritual tradition (especially, but not only, that of Ignatius of Loyola).
At the same time, the noetic dimension of the Christian's life for von
Balthasar is not such that it allows a clear and conclusive method for
determining the rightness or wrongness of action. We might call the
type of rationality it does allow an aesthetic "rationality": a genuine
perception of the world in light of the Gospel leads to general guide-
lines about the range of actions fitting to the situation at hand. A theologically informed and reasoned consideration of the matter at hand
assists, but does not simply determine, judgments about the right
thing to do. These general guides will be evident to those within the
Christian community but can also, albeit in a limited (though not
entirely ad hoc) fashion, be accessible to those outside it.

This chapter examines how for von Balthasar the good is mediated
in the created order and what noetic element this mediation allows.
Von Balthasar's thought permits a greater role for practical reason than
might be expected, though less than Catholic ethicists of a universalist
stripe would want. In response to the concern that von Balthasar's
ethics is insufficiently "universal" and too Christian-particular to be
authentically Catholic, I make a brief case in the first section that
Catholic ethics can and should include a note of Christian particularism. This particularism is balanced by von Balthasar's commitment to
the covenant, which requires the relative solidity and autonomy of creation and the full agency of the human subject within it. By way of
helping to understand the prospects for general moral intelligibility
within von Balthasar's particularist framework and the limitations to
moral universalism that follow from it, I conclude with a discussion of
the key ethical act in von Balthasar's thought: neighbor love within the

I/Thou encounter. In the final chapter, I will try to integrate the horizontal emphasis of this chapter with the strong vertical dimension defended in chapter 3.

CHRISTIAN PARTICULARISM

While Catholic ethics is not monolithic, it is distinguished by certain shared presuppositions and recurrent themes.[2] Principal among these is the conviction that the moral life is objective and rational. Reasoned reflection on experience, attentive observation of the world, and a critical appropriation of the commonly shared moral wisdom lead to objective insights into how one's personal and social life should be ordered. The confidence in the possibility of a universal moral order transcending culture and historical context is grounded in the belief that God has endowed creation "with its own stability, truth and excellence, its own order and laws" and the human mind with the capacity to comprehend that order.[3] I will refer to this Catholic commitment to a universal and objective moral order that is rationally discernible by all as its "universalism" strain. In contrast, divine command ethics is committed to a particularist view: at least some of the ethical claims which confront the Christian will not be shared by all persons but will, rather, be particular to the Christian. Furthermore, because it distinguishes between the merely apparent moral claims of the natural order and the true good of God's will, divine command ethics endangers what the Catholic tradition has viewed as the relative autonomy of the created order. The question then is whether the form of particularist ethics proposed by von Balthasar and the emphasis he places on the divine will are consonant with a "Catholic" affirmation of universalism and of the integrity of creation.

Von Balthasar's ethical particularism develops out of his conviction that in Jesus Christ God addresses humanity personally and concretely. At the same time, von Balthasar maintains that God's address does not violate the order of creation, and thus he strikes a balance between particularism and the Catholic tradition's deep commitment to ethical universalism. We will return to this below. But we can note here that von Balthasar is not alone in including a particularist dimension in his ethics. A number of philosophical trends have raised doubts about the traditional view of moral universalism: for example, the awareness of how much historical context conditions practical and theoretical thought; the existentialist emphasis on the particularity and unique-ness of all persons; and the recent stress on narrative and tradition. Many Catholic ethicists have been influenced by one or more of these trends and as a result espouse versions of natural law that are more qualified than those characteristic of the pre-Vatican II era. These the-ories hold to a kind of universalism that can accommodate historical and personal particularization. Catholic ethicists sympathetic to what has come to be known as proportionalism (e.g., Richard McCormick, Charles Curran, Lisa Sowle Cahill, Bernard Häring) generally argue for such contextualization of ethical norms.[4] Not all Catholic ethicists agree, of course. Germain Grisez and John Finnis argue for universal moral absolutes based on the requirement that the moral agent must always preserve basic human goods. And in his *Veritatis Splendor*, John Paul II has strongly criticized the rejection of moral absolutism by many proportionalists.

My point here, however, is not to take up the contentious issue of moral absolutes. Rather I want merely to suggest that there is already a kind of particularization of ethics that many Catholic scholars have espoused. However, unlike much of contemporary Catholic ethics, von Balthasar's particularist strain arises not so much from philosoph-ical influences as from his theological commitment. The revelation of Jesus Christ is distinct and divine. Through it, God addresses human-ity in a way that provokes and enables a new response on the part of the human person. For von Balthasar, we cannot, therefore, continue with "natural ethics" as if Jesus Christ were not "the norm of every-thing."[5] He is thus committed to a "faith ethics" approach in which theology and Christian faith determinately shape ethics.[6] I believe that there are good theological reasons why such an approach is valid from a contemporary Catholic point of view. Specifically, I want to argue that sound Christian ethics needs an adequate theological anthropol-ogy and that such an anthropology will require some element of Chris-tian particularism.

While there is no one contemporary theological anthropology, there is broad consensus that the approach to grace and nature that domi-nated nineteenth- and early-twentieth-century Catholic theology was flawed. A number of new approaches—proposed by some of the key theologians and philosophers of the early twentieth century: Henri Bouillard, Maurice Blondel, Yves Congar, Teilhard de Chardin, Henri de Lubac—tried to correct these flaws. However, moral theology often failed to fully incorporate these new insights. While I cannot argue this exhaustively here, I can trace out a trajectory in the development of Catholic views on nature and grace which will indicate this selective appropriation. The trajectory begins with the work of Henri de Lubac and culminates in the thought of Karl Rahner.[7] The insights associated with this trajectory were incorporated into the teachings of Vatican II.[8]

Henri de Lubac argued that Cardinal Cajetan (1469–1534) misinterpreted Thomas Aquinas's approach to the nature/grace distinction (that is, the distinction between what is proper to human existence in its "natural" state and what derives from its participation in the order of grace). Cajetan believed that human nature was sufficient in itself and thus was not naturally ordered toward God. Grace gave not only the capacity for knowing and loving God, but the very desire for God itself. Cajetan, wrongly according to de Lubac, attributed this position to Thomas.[9] Other influential commentators on Thomas followed his view (including Domingo Bañez and Francisco Suarez[10]). As a result, the Catholic tradition which followed Cajetan sharply distinguished in the human person a twofold end—one natural and the other supernatural.[11] Apart from grace, there is neither the capacity nor the desire for the supernatural end. To claim otherwise would, in a Thomistic-Aristotelian perspective, require that God bestow divine grace on the human person, since God, as the author of life, implanted the desire for the supernatural end in the first place.

> There is no example of a natural appetite that is not accompanied by the active means to fulfill it. Hunger tends to food, the eye calls for light, but they also possess . . . an organism of means which enables them to take hold of these things. But we do not see that [human nature] has at its disposal natural energies and instruments that would be capable of taking hold of God.[12]

Furthermore, since every nature must have an end, and since the "natural" end of the human creature cannot be supernatural life with God (however much it is the eternal, divine intent to bring it about), one must suppose the concept of a "natural beatitude"—some this-worldly end toward which one's moral life would have been directed had the order of grace not been established. Because both orders now exist, those theologians who followed Cajetan's lead espoused a two-layered anthropology, the supernatural laid on top of the natural so that they interpenetrated "as little as possible."[13]

The result, what de Lubac called the "bitterest fruit," was a marginalization of God's grace and Christian faith. "While wishing to protect the supernatural from any contamination, people had in fact exiled it altogether . . . leaving the field free to be taken over by secularism."[14] The earlier anthropology posed particular problems for ethics. The teleological approach favored by Catholic ethics could not allow the existence of *two* unintegrated ends. The manuals of the nineteenth and early twentieth century resolved the problem by including the natural order within the supernatural order and making the former subordinate to the latter.[15] However, the hierarchy of the dual ends was more conceptual than practical since the two ends contributed in different modes to the determination of the moral act. The natural end provided the justification and methodology for the generation of material norms, while the supernatural end provided a formal specification of the act, giving the act its proper metaphysical (though not necessarily intentional or motivational) orientation toward God. The manualist Henry Davis represented a common view of pre–Vatican II moral theologians when he argued that there were two conditions for an act to order the person to eternal life: the act must be morally good (that is, in keeping with right reason), and the act must be done *under the influence* of grace.[16] Grace changes nothing in regard to the material nature of the act. It only determines whether the act is *also* sanctified or not. As the dimensions of faith and Christian discipleship were carefully quarantined in the formal specification of the act, a neat and tidy moral rationalism came to dominate the material determination of the act. This rationalism took the radical and eschatological sting out of biblical injunctions, provoking one complaint that Catholic morality had "systematized into a science the pulsing vitality of concrete Christian life."[17]

Vatican II taught that moral theology should "draw more fully on the teaching of holy Scripture and should throw light on the exalted vocation of the faithful in Christ."[18] However, the incorporation of the renewal in the theology of nature and grace into the field of ethics has had the odd result of effectively countering those exhortations. This unfortunate state of affairs is due in part, I believe, to the fact that the theological anthropology that ethicists often assume in their ethical theories reflects only a truncated form of de Lubac's theory of grace. De Lubac maintained, first, that the human person is fundamentally (naturally) oriented toward life with God and, second, that the loving encounter with God made available in Jesus Christ is the fulfillment of that basic orientation. But the theory of grace which guides the ethical thought of some scholars stresses, almost exclusively, the first of these, that is, the immanent dimension of grace. God works in and through the fundamental dynamisms of the human agent, that is, in and through his knowing, loving, and desiring of the world. While de Lubac's approach does support a gentle harmonization of grace and nature so that grace reorients and strengthens basic human drives for the divine, he also underscored the newness and transforming nature of God's revelation in Christ. "Revelation . . . has changed everything."[19] This objective quality of God's work—that is, the fact that grace is tied to an objective, transformative event and is not just an internal operation of the Spirit—plays only a minor role in much of Catholic ethical thought. The thought of Karl Rahner, who was influenced by de Lubac's approach, has often served as the proximate guide for this merely subjective, immanent understanding of grace among many Catholic ethicists. But I believe his thought is misapplied by these same ethicists. A more faithful reading of Rahner's entire theory will indicate, I believe, a theological grounding for a particularist view of Christian ethics.

Rahner's anthropology retains the concept of a hypothetical "pure nature." The concept serves to indicate the theoretical possibility of integral human existence apart from the offer of grace. However, the reality of a "pure nature" has never been actualized, since God's self-communication has accompanied all human existence from the beginning. Rahner's concept of a "supernatural existential" is meant to underscore that this gift of God's presence forms a "constant dimension of human existence, always present, yet not part of human nature as such, affecting the whole of our being and directing us toward unsurpassable nearness to the triune God."[20] Like de Lubac, Rahner does not view grace as an extrinsic addition to human life but instead sees it as permeating in and though the entire range of human consciousness (i.e., its willing, desiring, reasoning, judging, etc.). Since God invites all into a new relationship, grace is not the unmerited gift of salvation to the few but the ubiquitous presence of God in the world.

And this immanent dimension of grace is the aspect that most Christian ethicists appropriate. Grace acts as a constant, universal backdrop of all moral activity. As part of every moral situation and human act, grace is no longer a discriminating factor in moral reflections. The previous object of natural law reflections, "natural human existence," can now be substituted with "graced human existence." Grace does establish a new human reality. But, since this new existence obtains universally, we can presume nonparticularity and universal accessibility to moral truths. Rahner's concept of the "anonymous Christian" is read as supporting such a conclusion. The mistaken perception is that Rahner defends a purely "internal" understanding of grace; the transformative effect of grace occurs primarily, even exclusively, in its presence to and activity in human subjectivity. The encounter of graced existence with the personal God revealed in Jesus Christ effects only a thematization of what has always been the case, perhaps adding additional motivation but no new qualitative change in the person and thus no new moral demands. Since the effect of God's transforming presence has already been accomplished in the universal gift of grace, revelation can only strengthen and clarify human reasoning. Thus, Richard McCormick, interpreting Rahner, writes that "Christian ethics is the objectification in Jesus Christ of what every man experiences of himself in his subjectivity."[21] Gerard Hughes likewise implies that the transformative power of grace lies primarily in the internal gift of grace when he argues against any necessary dependence of ethics on revelation because all persons "have grace offered to them, whether or not they ever have the opportunity to respond to revelation as such."[22] Charles Curran explicitly commends the substitutionary tactic of replacing human nature with graced human nature for natural law reflections:

> I deny that on the level of material content (actions, virtues, attitudes, and dispositions) there is anything distinctively Christian because non-Christians can and do share the same material content of morality even to the point of such attitudes as self-sacrificing love. Unlike some others, I base this, not on a common human nature abstractly considered, but rather on the fact that in the present existential order all are called to share in the fullness of God's love.[23]

There are good reasons for the view that Christian ethics is only the fullness of human ethics. One need look no further than the doctrines of creation and the Incarnation for justification. However, the problem that arises when grace is interpreted simply as an internal divine work is that all those elements particular to the gospel that might be interpreted as radical calls for a costly discipleship are excluded from the start. The transformation of the human person which grace effects is not directly tied to an encounter with the person of Christ and his saving story. We can thus bracket this encounter and allow secular notions of the human ideal to interpret the nature of that transformation. There are, however, different meanings that can be given to the claim that Christian ethics is truly human ethics. As David Hollenbach states, there is a "significant difference between the statement that the Christian story 'discloses' the meaning of the normatively human and the statement that this story 'confirms' insight into this meaning."[24] I believe that an argument can be made from Rahner's theology of grace that the Christ-event does indeed effect a theological particularization of ethics. It is an implication that Rahner himself draws.

A full defense of this (more "Balthasarian") interpretation of Rahner's theology of grace is not possible here, but we can note briefly the following. One critic of Rahner has stated that his thought naturalizes the supernatural and reduces grace to the *a priori* of created existence.[25] While this criticism may apply to some Rahnerians, it is misplaced as directed toward Rahner himself. The gift of the supernatural existential is not Rahner's only word on grace. Like de Lubac, Rahner ties the fullness of grace to the objective encounter with the particular revelation of Christ. Humanity's conditioning by grace attains its full radicality only in a thematic response, and thus there is a difference between grace and grace experienced as (or recognized as) grace.[26] This distinction corresponds in the ethical realm to a distinction between a graced response to the demands of "the good" and a thematic response to God's call. Rahner states that without God as the "accepted partner" in neighborly love, "interpersonal communication in love among men cannot reach its own radical depths and its final and definitive validity."[27] The encounter with God is such that it transforms worldly ethics and refuses the hegemony of natural law.

> And the ultimate meaning of this revelation [in Jesus Christ] is a calling of man out of this world into the life of God, who leads his personal life . . . as the tri-personal God, in inaccessible light. God is thereby bringing himself immediately face to face with man with a demand and a call which flings man out of the course pre-established by nature . . . [T]here arises the most immediate possibility that [God] might issue commands to mankind which are not at the same time the voice of nature, are not *lex naturae*. And if God calls man in this command of his revealing word to a supernatural, supramundane life, . . . [then the world] is condemned to a provisional status, a thing of second rank, *subject to a criterion which is no longer intrinsic or proper to it.*[28]

The engagement with the divine, personal Other introduces a new dimension to the moral horizon of the human agent (and not just an "internal quality" to his agency) that cannot be flattened to the immanent nature of things. There can be a type of moral reasoning within such an engagement, as I will argue below, but it will not make itself indifferent to this personal encounter in order to undertake a non-particularistic discernment of the good.

In short, the new approaches to nature and grace found in the writings of de Lubac and Rahner did not advocate a merely internal understanding of grace's activity. While *philosophical* arguments against an absolute moral universalism have been readily appropriated by many Catholic ethicists,[29] the *theological* arguments for a particularism in ethics, which this new approach to grace provides, have met a fair amount of resistance in the Catholic community. This might be attributable to a variety of factors: ecumenical sensitivities, tensions over the role of the magisterium, and a desire to maintain at least some latitudinal accessibility of moral judgments (i.e., access across various groups within one historical period versus a longitudinal, transhistorical access). But theological, or, specifically Christian, particularism need not be sectarian or lead to judgments opaque to human reason, as von Balthasar's approach demonstrates. Von Balthasar's commitment to a "thick" created order ensures that his ethics has room for broad, extramural intelligibility.[30] Because it does so without sacrificing its particularist vision, his ethics offers us one approach to relating faith and ethics that is both "catholic" and distinctively Christian.

THE PRESUPPOSITIONS OF THE COVENANT

Von Balthasar does not provide us with any clear indication of what role he believes moral reasoning should have in the Christian life. At times, he associates it with rationalization and the human effort to circumvent the demands of the gospel. But the encounter of divine and human freedoms, which is central to von Balthasar's theology, presupposes human agency and with it both a human freedom distinct from divine freedom and a capacity for reasoned moral choice. The suspension that we developed in the last chapter between our judgments about the goods of the world and God's cannot be made absolute lest it undermine the conditions of concrete, historical human agency by emptying the goods and values that make up its horizon of action of any moral meaning. A world void of its natural goodness could not be available to be made into a word of God (or the Word of God) and thus would impair our ability to hear and respond to that word. And without word and response, there can be no covenant. Unfortunately, while recognizing that Christian moral discernment does rely on earthly goods in making its judgments, von Balthasar offers little in the way of guidance as to how exactly those goods are to be evaluated. As a consequence, we are left with the task of demonstrating von Balthasar's tacit support for what in most Catholic circles is conventional moral wisdom—that is, that ethical discernment includes a thoughtful consideration of the nature of things—by gleaning the substance of that noetic dimension from different ancillary discussions.

The theological doctrine of creation has traditionally offered one argument for the intelligibility of moral choices. The Catholic tradition is not alone in making an appeal to it, of course, but gives it a particular twist by understanding the human creature's capacity for rational moral discernment as the means by which the creature pursues its ultimate end of knowing and loving the Absolute. More than just a providential gift, the rational pursuit of the good is the way in which the creature participates in the dynamics of God's love and knowledge. Similarly, von Balthasar argues that the Christian life, under the aspect of one's personal "mission," is the way in which the person participates in the dynamics of divine and triune life. The question before us now is to what degree the formal aspect of that participation (i.e., obedience to the divine will) takes material shape in concrete actions whose goodness is humanly discernible. If the material order is not to be inconsequential for hearing and responding to God's missioning call, how exactly is it to be evaluated?

A starting point for understanding von Balthasar's position can be constructed out of his critical interpretation of Karl Barth.[31] Here we see von Balthasar's characteristic concern to protect the full radicality of what God has accomplished in Jesus Christ. Barth describes creation as the "external basis of the covenant" and the covenant as the "interior basis" of creation.[32] Von Balthasar finds this description completely acceptable as a way of relating the two orders, but believes that Barth himself does not always do full justice to creation. Although there has always been only one human reality, i.e., the graced existence of the person called and destined to be one with Christ, it remains important to preserve a conceptual distinction between the orders of creation and grace. This is necessary not so much in order to protect the gratuity of grace by postulating a "pure nature," sufficient and meaningful apart from grace, but to exclude any hint of what von Balthasar calls "theopanism," where creation is emptied of any ontological reality and instead all that is real in the covenantal encounter is attributed exclusively to the domain of grace. The distinction of the orders underscores that grace works in and through an order that has its own integral, albeit relative meaning, even while leading that order to its perfection.[33]

Since humanity has always existed within the call of the Word and the presence of the Spirit in the one economy of God, the "nature" that grace presupposes cannot be uncovered by bracketing the historical "addition" of Christian revelation. However, without attempting to describe some clearly delimited "nature" with which to contrast "grace," von Balthasar believes we can peer *through the present economy*, within the epistemological brackets of the Christ-event, and offer some general observations about human existence apart from the full light of Christ. Thus instead of starting from "principles drawn from the revelation in creation to arrive at the revelation in the Word as the crown and summit," von Balthasar proceeds "in the reverse direction, from the revelation in the Word to that in creation," "by determining what the word of revelation itself presupposes and implies."[34] Again, the goal here is not a counterfactual investigation of "pure nature" but rather an examination within the economy of that "nature" which is already on the way to the advent of the covenant. If grace preserves the human, as the coexistence of Christ's divinity and humanity indicates, then we have methodological permission to reflect on and make tentative observations of the creaturely aspect of the individual as he exists within the one order of the economy. Von Balthasar approvingly finds hints of this approach in Barth,[35] and uses it for framing his one sustained reflection on ethics.[36] Three claims about the created order are of particular significance for ethics.

First, there is a center of creaturely activity and agency distinct from God that remains creaturely even when this finite existence is drawn into a relationship with the absolute. Creation is a "divinely willed counterpart to God,"[37] a "center of activity outside of God."[38] In the covenantal relationship, creation's "otherness" is not effaced but ennobled; the otherness separating creature and Creator is elevated into the otherness of the I/Thou. The glory of God's accomplishment in Christ lies in part in that God has effected a relationship that is polyphonic; the human partner, as creature, gives forth a word of response to God that is more than a weak echo. The glory of the Trinity, of divine community in absolute unity of love, cannot appear in the creaturely realm if the human person were something akin to a "Mrs. John Smith," that is, someone whose identity is given absolutely by his relationship to another.[39] Instead that glory appears because of the very elements that would seem to offend divine sovereignty were not God already triune other: "distance for the sake of nearness, autonomy for the sake of exchange and love, irreducible otherness for the sake of genuine union."[40]

Consequently, human freedom should not be bifurcated into two levels: an active and spontaneous creaturely freedom vis-à-vis the neutral (non-divine) things of the world, on the one hand, and a passive agency vis-à-vis God, on the other. Von Balthasar criticizes Barth's refusal to allow the creature *qua* creature to influence God: creation "as such, that is, as nature, does possess its own relative freedom within its own proper sphere both before and after the fall. But influence on God is something, as Barth saw it, that we can only consider inside the order of grace."[41] Barth's distinction cannot be maintained if the creature, precisely as creature, has been included in the covenantal relationship. Instead, the "causality of the creature achieves its true character and its fullest maturity in the order of grace."[42] The two freedoms, divine and human, do not simply encounter one another on the same plane, but neither does the human effort, or causality, reduce to the divine. At the very least, something like a Thomistic concept of secondary causality is unavoidable. But more importantly, we can say that creaturely freedom is not merely God's gift reflected back to God, but is itself a creaturely contribution to the glory of divine life, however much always borne and enabled by grace.

Furthermore, since the human agent acts as *one* existent within a graced, concrete, and historical context, we cannot separate human agency vis-à-vis the call of God from its agency vis-à-vis the claims of creation. Human responses to God and to the horizontal order are now linked in the economy of Christ. We noted in the last chapter that in one's "mission" the human creature is allowed a share in the divine interchange. In keeping with his critique of Barth, von Balthasar must root the mission in all the dimensions of the person's creaturely existence. It cannot supervene upon the person's temporal existence. Von Balthasar makes this point by repeatedly stressing that the mission does not trace a narrow path for the person simply to follow in blind obedience. Rather, it opens up our creaturely capacities—for example, our reason, creativity, freedom, natural gifts, and so on—for their participation in the mission of Christ. Human judgment about what is most loving or most fitting to the task at hand is a necessary part of our creaturely agency and our responsibility within the mission of Christ.

Second, the person has been "created and equipped as a creature

of nature to encounter and find God in all things."[43] Von Balthasar
favorably cites a passage from Barth: "God does not usually meet [the
individual] immediately but mediately in His works, deeds and ordinances."[44] There is a true revelation of the personal God in our surrounding world, however much the revelation comes about for the
Christian *only* in and through its being illuminated by the particular
light of the Christian narrative. As *one* creature, graced body and spirit,
the person does not encounter God's address as something hovering
over creation, as if this revelation within creation was given to human
reason *super*-naturally, and not also given precisely within the dynamism
of creation and the events of human history.[45] In the first chapter, we
saw the objective ground for this possibility: creation contains its own
openness, indefiniteness, and mystery, which God can use to express
God's unique Word. Here von Balthasar emphasizes the subjective side
to this, that creaturely eyes and ears have in grace been made percep-
tive of God's glory and address within creation. Thus von Balthasar
states that God's commands come only through the "veil of creation"
and the "medium of created things."[46] He faults Barth for insisting that
the concreteness of God's command is given solely from God's side and
not also from "the specific historicity of the individual."[47] Even the
nonbeliever is not excluded from this address within creation: insofar as
every person "looks out upon a cosmos that is noetically and ontically
saturated with moments of the supernatural, he will *also* be, at the very
least—without knowing it—a crypto-theologian."[48]

Third, the preservation of creation within the order of grace means
that there exist "spheres of meaning" that are neither isolated from nor
abolished by the order of grace.

> Though [creation's] autonomy is merely relative, it is nonetheless real.
> Yes, it may well be true that meaning ultimately comes from Christ, that
> we can say nothing conclusive about the (provisional) meaning of cre-
> ation until we have considered Christ. . . . But it remains no less true
> that this very relationship requires us to preserve scrupulously all rela-
> tive meanings as proper to themselves and to avoid any appearance of
> *deducing* them from their ultimate meaning.[49]

Von Balthasar offers as examples of these relative meanings, the
"sphere of culture" and "interpersonal relationships of I/Thou and
man-woman."[50] We cannot with any absolute confidence categorize
the ethical horizon in which the Christian acts in terms of what
belongs to the order of creation and what to the order of grace. But
we can have some confidence and hope, though perhaps less than

found in some natural law approaches, that the particularist view of the Christian can often find common cause with the outlooks of those guided and shaped by other narratives. This is due to the availability and predisposition of the spheres of meaning within the created order to the narrative of the economy. The economy of salvation has always been creation's interior meaning, to repeat Barth's helpful phrase, and thus its presence to the created order will be gentle, even if sinful hearts find it bitter. God's word thus makes itself "intelligible" to us using these spheres of meaning. Not even the natural human yearning for wholeness—that is, humanity's "'pre-understanding' of what God's 'redemption' might be"—is simply overturned but rather refashioned and transcended in God's revelation (*TD5* 53).

FOR THE GREATER GLORY OF GOD

These three conclusions about the created order—there is agency distinct from God's; God's call is perceived within creation; and creaturely spheres of meaning are preserved in the encounter of grace—together indicate that a certain kind of intelligibility will be characteristic of the Christian moral life. Because of this horizontal thickness, the intelligibility of the Christian moral life obtains not only for the believer but also, albeit in a limited manner, for the nonbeliever as well. But this is not to deny that the Christ-event has radically changed the nature of ethics for the Christian. We might describe the radicality as a heightening, perfecting, or completing of creation, but such terms are overused in Catholic circles to the point of losing any clear meaning. Most Catholic ethicists want to stake a claim to such terms. The question is, What is the nature of this heightening or perfecting? It would be helpful to examine first how the Christ-event "transforms" ethics for von Balthasar in order to gauge the kind of intra- and extramural intelligibility that we can expect to find in his ethics.

Von Balthasar offers no extended or systematic development of the sort of comparison we are looking for here between "natural" and Christian ethics (and the corresponding mode of moral reasoning appropriate to each). However, his understanding of the noetic element in the Christian moral life reflects what we might call an "Ignatian" template. That is, it follows the general Ignatian pattern[51] of contemplation and action, where the right course of action is discovered through a consideration of worldly goods viewed in light of the divine will. The faithful follower uses his reason and understanding to evaluate the goods and values before him in order to discern how he might best serve God in them.[52] This judgment occurs within a contemplative "beholding" of the situation in which the agent looks to the situation's dramatic horizon, that is, to the triune God who labors for humanity's reconciliation in this situation, on the one hand, and to his possible role in that labor (i.e., he imaginatively pictures himself in the "scene" of this situation), on the other. A proximate norm for his action is how he (with his particular talents, gifts, story, etc.) can work in this Christian drama for "the help of souls," and, laboring with Christ, achieve their full reconciliation with God and advancement in the spiritual life.[53] This evangelical guide is grounded in what is for Ignatius the deeper and ultimate norm for all Christian work: the greater glory of God.[54] And for both von Balthasar and Ignatius, the praise given by the human person is the privileged place within the created order where God's glory breaks into the world. It is a glory that is anticipated in the resolute obedience of the prophets, but now appears in the Christian's acceptance of the Father's will.[55] The task of the Christian is the doxological work of letting that glory shine ever more brightly by actively disposing himself to God's call in his life and working to bring about a similar disposition in others. There is a careful interplay in Ignatius (and von Balthasar) between the earthly and divine dimensions of ethics. The Christian works (actively, through reason and personal initiative) for earthly goods and values. But he does so in consideration of what transcends and relativizes these goods even while appearing within them, the ever greater glory of God. The goods and values of human existence are the necessary notes for our song of praise, but it is God who is songwriter and choirmaster of that hymn.

There are two dimensions in the above, both of which are present in von Balthasar's ethics (though not in any systematic fashion): the beholding of all creaturely goods in the light of the theo-drama and the contemplative consideration of one's own response as an element internal to this "beholding." In regard to the first, the Christ-form acts for von Balthasar so as to give the *general* and *fluid* meaningfulness of the world a *particular, christological* shape. While not overriding the world's spheres of meaning (e.g., of family relationships, professional demands, the civic order), the drama of the economy does lend them a distinctive form by illuminating in them a specific meaning vis-à-vis the economy of salvation. This is, as I suggested above, the interpretation that von Balthasar wants to give Barth's formula (creation is the exterior ground of the covenant; the covenant is the interior ground of creation): the Christ-event does not simply insert itself into the horizontal order and substitute itself for various meanings formerly found there (that would be to trump creation); nor does it just confirm the goodness of what is already there (that would be to eclipse the giftedness of the covenant). Rather, among the various meanings any human reality can sustain, it gently places in relief and completes the christological meaning it was always intended to bear in the one plan of God.

The transformation of our daily drama then is a "sharpening" and "clarifying," bringing the light of God's revelation to help us see what is "there" in creation. God uses the stammering words of creation to speak the *one* eternal Word and brings the world's drama beyond its inherent ambiguity to the singleness of meaning in Christ (*TD1* 20).[56] As the light of the gospel falls on the different parts and dimensions of creation, however, it illuminates them in different ways. Von Balthasar on occasion appeals to the image of creation as concentric rings encircling a center point at which Christ stands and from which the light of his truth radiates. The Christian "sees all worldly considerations as grouping themselves concentrically around this center, which in its peculiar quality of a *mysterium* radiates its light over all existing things."[57] But since "everything is not equidistant" from the center in Christ, there will be some spheres in which the Christ-event "totally eclipses" their general laws, "practically replacing them," but also other spheres "whose relative autonomy persists practically untouched."[58] The degree of transformation of creation, and of Christian ethics, is not uniform but will vary according to how the particular dimension under consideration bears upon the Christ-event. This diversity of transformation is von Balthasar's way of acknowledging the element of truth of moral universalism (e.g., that of the golden rule) without denying the ethical particularism found in the Scriptures (e.g., the hard sayings of Jesus, which demand a radical, eschatological witness). The Gospel narrative is the ultimate horizon of meaning for all the events of the world. But as its interpreting light is cast on these worldly narratives, the resulting shifts in the meaning of some will be more dramatic than those of others. Thus, we might say that the laws of physics, the usefulness of particular drugs for curing illness, the aesthetic quality of some ancient sculptures, and even the wisdom of some cultural proverbs remain largely unchanged when the illuminating light of Christ touches them. Similarly, there are ethical aspects for which

Christ's light does not do much more than brighten the goodness that is already there: the goodness of eating nutritional food when hungry, of not inflicting purposeless pain on others, and of educational opportunities. However, the meaning transformation of ethical realities closer to creation's christological center—for example, suffering and death, reconciliation and the response to evil—is more radical.[59] And the most important of these, we will see below, is interpersonal love.

For von Balthasar, even with the clarifying light of the gospel, the moral agent is continually confronted with an array of possible moral goods whose conflicting claims cannot be harmonized through an appeal to any immanent set of criteria or principles. While it is true that within the new Christ-informed interpretation of our moral horizon, different moral choices will become more or less appropriate, and thus we can expect to find some refining of moral possibilities (e.g., the hope with which we respond to the seemingly incorrigible neighbor), the Christian will still, nonetheless, often face a plurality of conflicting moral choices. God intervenes, however, to lead the Christian to a *subjective* unity; God fashions the concrete goods of the individual's life into a meaningful, personal whole, "like letters that form a sentence."[60] This brings us to the second dimension. In addition to beholding creaturely goods in the light of the gospel (first dimension), we also consider these goods in light of who God is calling us to be (second dimension). The fragmented goods and values of the world which occur within the field of Christian activity are reformed into a unity in the personal call given to the Christian. This unity is first established in Jesus, in the singleness of the mission given to him by the Father.

> As man, [Jesus] must continually measure the partial values that present themselves against the totality of the mission, of his Father's will; when he does this, the direction he is to take . . . becomes luminous. He sees the totality of his Father's will, and hence of his mission, shining forth from this partial value. (*TD3* 200)

As the Christian shares in the mission of Christ, the Christian comes also to share in the unity it brings, one which we saw in the last chapter is also a *personalizing* unity. The mission—the particular way God has called each of us to be an image of his Son—acts as a "grid" to guide us in the choices that we must make among the almost endless forms of earthly goodness available for Christian embodiment. It is the "magnet that gives the natural orders their Christian polarization" and "gives meaning and discrimination to [our choices] of secular ways and means."[61] Von Balthasar maintains that this commanding and person-alizing call is a principle of Christian praxis that was not fully recog-nized until Ignatius of Loyola.[62] But the revelation of one's mission does not simply appear from on high. It is given to us through these same goods and values. In the discernment about ethical choices, there is, therefore, a circularity where we move from "seeing" the world's goods and values to "hearing" within them God's "idea" for us and then to "assembling" these goods in accord with God's call to us.

We can say then that for von Balthasar a natural intelligibility of the good can be found in the world's concrete goods and values and that they are legitimate, albeit tentative, objects of ethical discernment. They represent "signposts" that are not by themselves infallible spokes-persons for God's personal call, but are, nevertheless, genuine point-ers to the absolute good,[63] and must be given at least "a loving appreciation" (*TD4* 465).[64] Von Balthasar, of course, does not wed God's will for the individual tightly to the worldly goods; it cannot be done, at the very least because the voices of the natural world are many and, as we have noted, conflicting in their claims. Yet the fact that the world's moral claims are cacophonous does not mean they are not gen-uine and constant expressions of God's will. Like the pluralism inter-nal to Scripture, the pluralism, the *symphony*, of the natural world does not undermine its status as an expression of God. In the cries of the hungry, in the pain of loneliness, and in the joy of new life can always be found the call of God. Whether it is *also* a personal call for a par-ticular individual is not, however, determined apart from the personal, christological mission.

In following the path that God has willed for them, Christians intensify the diffused glory of Christ and make the christological trans-figuration of earthly goods present and real for their sisters and broth-ers within the Christian community and for those without. The glory that appears in one's own life then strengthens the light cast on the world by the Christian narrative and makes brighter the paths of Chris-tian discipleship. But Christians' first priority, the glory and praise of God, will relativize the earthly goods that are at stake in their actions (sometimes more than others).

> Once this [Ignatius's view] is accepted, human nature, even when it is elevated by grace, cannot act as the guide for man in his praise, rever-ence and service of God; ultimately such guidance can only come from God and revelation of his will.[65]

In the apparently fruitless endeavor to proclaim the gospel in hostile arenas, in the humble and seemingly insignificant work of an educator working in a marginal situation, and in the tireless and unpromising efforts of a social worker to bring change to a neighborhood that is complacent in its despair are found not the exaltation of the world's goods but that radiance of faithful stewards following the path God has given them. These tasks will "make sense" to the outsider, but only to a point; other avenues of effort will seem more "reasonable." For von Balthasar, however, they are not at all wasted efforts, but the work of a daring and hope-filled love whose glory is revealed even in its tragic failure.

NEIGHBOR LOVE WITHIN THE I/THOU ENCOUNTER

We do not find in von Balthasar's thought a loss of horizontal meaning, but rather a sharpening and clarifying of it, and thus the continued possibility of a mediation of the divine (ethical) claim in the claims of the horizontal order. As an example of the creaturely "thickness" within christological particularism, we turn to the interpersonal encounter. It is an ethical event that is at the center of Christ's work and thus is radically and "dramatically" (in von Balthasar's use of "drama") transformed.[66] Because the interpersonal encounter among human persons is refashioned in Christ's light, it represents a boundary test case for the claim that creation preserves its relative autonomy within von Balthasar's Christian particularism.

We can identify six aspects that von Balthasar understands as characterizing Christian love for the other. While we have already encountered some of the elements of what follows, bringing all the parts together here allows us to construct a full description of the ethical act that lies at the center of von Balthasar's moral theory. These aspects, perhaps to the disappointment of some, do not immediately translate into material norms, but they do offer a normative model of neighbor love that, while general, is nonetheless instructive. The aspects serve to define a moral space in which the Christian must act. They are thus similar to what Karl Barth calls "formed references": they form a christological reading of a common ethical situation in which believers act (i.e., the interpersonal encounter) and thus can guide believers in knowing God's will and assist them in making specific ethical decisions.[67]

First, *in the new order ushered in by Christ, the neighbor is the mediator of God's call.* In the neighbor, the Christian "encounters his Redeemer with all his bodily senses" (*GL1* 423).[68] The neighbor as Christ corresponds to a key element of von Balthasar's soteriology: Christ saves humankind by entering into complete *solidarity* with it. This solidarity is in itself already a commitment to breaking down sinful patterns of isolation and of solitary exclusions of others.[69] But, more importantly, in his perfect solidarity with sinful humanity, Christ represents all humanity before the Father and in the Paschal Mystery's drama of love takes on the burden that its sinfulness entails.[70] Because of the natural solidarity among persons, Jesus Christ, through the "liquefying" work of the Holy Spirit, can represent the alienation of each and every person to the Father. Now when "the Father in judgment looks at the Son with the eyes of justice, he sees nothing that would call for judgment" (*TD5* 283).[71] From the "world's point of view, the man Jesus became an icon of the Trinity." "From God's point of view, however, he is the icon of the world, representing all human nature's conscious subjects on the basis of the real substitution he undertakes on their behalf" (*TD3* 341).

Here we can recall the Ignatian movement introduced in the last chapter: the human creature looks upward to heaven and finds the Father revealed in the person of Christ. In Christ, the creature returns to look downward, *de arriba*, to love the world as the Father does. But to do this, to love the world as the Father does, the creature must see in the world what the Father sees: the One who suffered and died for that world.[72]

> This changes everything, for from now on, one's fellow man—whether friend or foe—is the brother for whom Christ died . . . each individual who can be addressed humanly as "Thou" is raised to the status of a "Thou" for God, because God's true "Thou," his "chosen" and "beloved" "only Son" has borne the guilt of this human "Thou" and has died for him, and therefore can identify himself with every individual at the last judgment. (*GL7* 439)

The light which the Christian narrative brings to earthly goods transforms the way that the Christian views the world, and consequently, the way he acts within it.[73] He now sees the one who suffered for him in the cries of the poor and the despair of those broken in spirit. The new vision intensifies the claims related to neighbor need and prioritizes those needs over other responsibilities. It is not that other duties (e.g., professional responsibilities) are "irrelevant for the kingdom," but "with the poor and the abandoned," God's heart can only "beat in solidarity."[74] Furthermore, because in the divine economy Christ has entered into complete solidarity with the neighbor, von Balthasar can assert that "whoever endeavors to struggle against injustice and to bring about justice in the world works in a quite direct way with the God of revelation and of love and grace, whether he knows it or not."[75]

Second, *Christian love of the neighbor is also a loving response to the personal call of God which appears in the neighbor.* This vertical dimension of Christian neighbor love is implicit in the first aspect above, but it merits emphasis because of the importance von Balthasar gives it. He does not make an explicit vertical reference to God a necessary condition of every act of Christian love. But as part of the rhythm of faithful discipleship, the Christian should regularly view in the act of neighbor love a worshipful offering to God. The vertical dimension is "what distinguishes Christian love from every sort of humanitarianism."[76] Christian love is a participation in the triune love of God, and thus in their christological mission Christians are expropriated and sent (missioned) by the Father to bring their love to the neighbor. And in directing this love to the neighbor, Christian agents lift their response prayerfully back to God in christological praise of the Father.

The particular vertical dimension that von Balthasar attributes to neighbor love also distinguishes his idea from a similar idea found in Rahner. For both, the two great commandments, love of God and love of neighbor, come together in the act of Christian love. For Rahner, "the primary basic act" of the human person is "an act of the love of his neighbor and *in this* the original love of God is realized."[77] Von Balthasar likewise connects the two, going so far as to describe "idolatry" and "oppression" as "interchangeable terms" (*GL6* 316). But his synthesis of the two commandments differs from that of Rahner, he claims, because "the 'religious act as such' is primary."[78] It is not clear what sort of primacy is being advocated here (logical, metaphysical, phenomenological, experiential?). Rahner *does* state that "the reflected religious act *as such* is and remains secondary" in comparison to the unthematic, graced response to God within the act of neighbor love.[79] Von Balthasar, however, maintains that the synthesis of the two commandments is given only within the economy of salvation and cannot be assumed as something that has simply always and everywhere been the case.[80] Christ has given "endless value to the human 'Thou,'" and thus makes it possible for Christians to love God in loving their neighbor (*GL7* 441). But this love for God in the neighbor occurs as Christians come to see in the neighbor the God whom they have met in Jesus Christ. Thus "the reflective religious act" cannot be secondary because it is this act that effects subjectively what God has accomplished objectively in Christ: the unity of love of God and neighbor.[81]

Third, *Christian love is grateful answer to what has been given—not just a new moral act, but answer.* I have been "addressed by a free, loving Thou, I am both given an answer and called to give one in return. The gift implies a task. . . . [W]hat I have been given is to be transformed and freely given back" (*TD3* 458). This is true on a natural level. The complete "why-lessness" of every creaturely form transforms its appearance into a moment of natural grace: something whose Origin and Giver lie hidden has come to expression before me. When the creaturely form is that of a free, loving Thou, the sense of gift multiplies. This other, whose presence and agency lie beyond my own will, compounds his mystery by surrendering himself to me and by intentionally allowing his freedom to be tied to mine. Whatever response I will make, should it be appropriate (or aesthetically fitting), it will be enabled and guided by the gift I have received and my grateful recognition of it. This "natural" bond between gift and response is the trace of creation's divine author. The persons of the Trinity proceed through gift given and gift received. The rhythm of Christian love—from receptivity to activity, from contemplation to action, from gift to response—reflects not creaturely limitation but divine perfection.[82]

When we consider Jesus Christ, we see that God is not just personal Other, but the one whose gift of forgiving love to us is absolute. Our answer to this love will be motivated, enabled, and shaped by its gift. Most ethicists stress the first. Our answer will be *motivated* by a desire to return the goodness that has been given us; we will give the answer with greater ease and enthusiasm because of the gratitude we feel. Von Balthasar's thought, however, suggests two additional points of connection. First, the gift also *enables* our response. All addressing words within interpersonal encounters share in this power. But the word of forgiveness spoken to us in Jesus Christ is spoken precisely where there was no relationship, where the bonds of encounter had been broken. God's absolute word restores and seals this bond and names the human person as eternally related to God and covenant partner. Second, the gift *shapes* our response. The absolute word of forgiveness has been addressed to us; we should not choose a new topic of conversation. We have been named forgiven and beloved people, and that name is the identity out of which comes our answer to God's address. We must learn "what it means to be *forgiven*," and respond from within that reality, not as some past accomplishment, but as an ongoing dimension of our daily existence.[83]

God's gift of forgiving love is fully received by the person when the person "hears" and "obeys" the Christ revealed in the Christian narrative. The story itself claims one's gratitude. But that story includes the stories of all persons. Their words have been brought into the triune conversation through Christ's solidarity with them and enclosed into the one Word of God. The neighbor's word now comes to us as a gift of God since everything "in the created order, with the exception of sin, is enabled, through Christ, to be an expression of God."[84] God intends his encounter with the individual to be personal, and thus his call is no abstract, general word. It appears in its most expressive and personal form in the neighbor, whose graced, finite words to us can pierce through the world's sin and be made addresses of God. These temporal and limited words of pain and joy, of praise and judgment, of understanding and direction become God's particular word to the believer because, in Christ, God has decided to make these words part of the eternal triune conversation. They are always heard and understood within the one Word of forgiveness and mercy spoken in Christ and addressed to me and to the other, but, so heard, they are genuinely graced addresses to which the Christian is called to respond. The neighbor then is not only the recipient of Christian love but also the means in which God calls forth the Christian's response.

Fourth, *Christian love is moved by christological hope for the neighbor.* God establishes this hope by integrating our "horizontal time" into God's own "vertical time" (*TD5* 29–30). The gifts of divine love form bookends for the story of every human life (and of humanity itself): it *begins* with the outpouring gift of divine goodness and *ends* with the cruciform gift of endless mercy. The new meaning of human history is revealed in the entire divine economy, but especially in the Christ of the Triduum. The no of humanity has been answered and enveloped by the costly self-giving yes of Christ. His love dissolves the objective burden of sin, but it hopes to do more—to win back sinful human hearts by his ever greater love. This radical and daring hope of triune love which inspires God's work in Christ is the meaning that God has given horizontal history. The meaning is not an already assured victory effected from on high, at least not in the present, existential reality of human existence, but the *eschatological hope* that absolute love will draw forth a yes to God from every human person.[85] The strength and depth of this hope are revealed in its love for the most alienated. The "more remote" and "inaccessible" a neighbor is, the "clearer and stronger" does the light of "divine love that suffers for him" shine.[86] Christian praxis toward the neighbor thus hopes and believes that the gift of love will never prove irredeemably tragic. And the Christian acts out of this hope, because he knows that his own inadequate love has been made to share in God's own.[87]

The *theological* hope of the Christian is ultimately directed toward the reconciliation of all persons with God. But while this hope goes "beyond this world," it does not "pass it by" (*TD5* 176). Von Balthasar cites approvingly Jürgen Moltmann's observation that there is an "other face" to our reconciliation with God that "has always been short-changed" in Christian history: "the realization of an eschatological hope for justice, the humanization of man, the socialization of humanity, peace for all creation."[88] Theological virtues take root in earthly soil. The experience of the goodness and wonder of the horizontal order can dispose the individual to a faith, hope, and love toward the One who created that order, and move him to participate in the risky, daring drama of Christian love. And thus

> the Christian in the world is meant to awaken hope, particularly among the most hopeless; and this in turn means that he must create such humane conditions as will actually allow the poor and oppressed to have hope. . . . It cannot simply hope that others will attain eternal salvation; it must enable them to cherish this hope by creating conditions apt to promote it. (*TD5* 176)

For von Balthasar, the work for justice is a "natural" moral endeavor (i.e., a universally intelligible good) which is taken up in the Christian sphere and "recapitulated" as one part of the Christian mission (what for Ignatius was the salvation of souls) to reconcile the world to God.

Fifth, *Christian love of neighbor is a eucharistic love.* Christian love is radical self-giving for the other. I turn away from my own needs and desires, preferring those of the other because "Christ has preferred me to himself."[89] Von Balthasar cannot (and does not, I will suggest below) absolutize self-giving to the *human* thou; only God commands such complete surrender. Yet the radicality of the act is such that not only does the need for "balanced settlement cease" (*GL7* 140), but the Christian also acquires a share in the *pro nobis* of Christ (*TD4* 406). From a "natural" standpoint, Christian love will appear as supererogatory, as an inversion of justice, and an unmerited burden.[90] However, suffering love, especially *unjust* suffering love, shows itself within the Christian narrative as a share in the cross of Christ. Its lavishness and excess (we can even say its essential hyperbolic nature) extends to shouldering the wrongs of others through our gift of forgiveness and the bearing of evil's consequences.[91] In this sharing, it is transformed into the grateful surrender of the one who, in Christ, lives the mission of the Father and whose measure of love has as its referent not the *quid pro quo* of interpersonal fair play, but rather the Suffering Servant who laid down his life for him.

Moreover, suffering love universalizes the Christ-event, like the Eucharist itself. Borne by God's Spirit, the radical suffering love of the Christian makes Christ's own love visible in the broken bonds of human fellowship and his call to love audible to ears made deaf by sinful self-isolation. Christian love participates in the liturgical movement of the church's worship. Responding to God's Word, the gifts of the Christian are lifted up, so that they can be shared by the Father as eucharistic food for the neighbor. Von Balthasar is fond of citing a homily by Origen on this point: "And thus every man is capable of becoming a pure food for his neighbor according to his worthiness and the purity of his intention. . . . For these are mysteries of the Lord: every man has a certain food in himself."[92]

Sixth, *Christian love seeks communion with the other.* The goal or *telos* of Christian love is not one-sided affirmation of the neighbor. Rather it intends communion, and thus works to create conditions that foster a unity-in-difference with the other. The theological importance of genuine communion follows from much of what was said above. If our neighbor is the privileged place where the Christian encounters God, and if Christian love is a participation in God's covenantal love for the other, then more than any other creaturely event mutual love embodies the fruit of the economy in the horizontal realm.[93]

Furthermore, in no other place does the glory of the crucified and risen Christ shine more brightly in the Christian's life than in the eucharistic love that restores the bonds of fellowship with the alienated brother or sister. Christian love follows Christ and seeks communion with the one seemingly furthest from one: the sinner.[94] Reconciliation is more than one in an array of praiseworthy endeavors.[95] It is the goal that shapes the Christian's response to evil and to the fallenness of the world. The reconciliation among persons is formed first ecclesially, where God's saving work is gratefully recalled and celebrated in the Eucharist and made present for one another. Apart from this saving narrative, genuine I/Thou interpersonal communion will be, von Balthasar believes, tenuous and fragile. The vertical dimension naturally present in the Thou, that is, his sacred dignity, is more easily ignored —and the other more quickly made to serve one's own interest—if that verticality is not deepened and strengthened by a recognition of Christ's solidarity with this neighbor (*GL7* 441).[96]

The communion teleology of Christian love gives an additional contour to what we have described in the other five aspects above by placing neighbor love within two sets of "side constraints." These constraints are not limits placed on love but normative guides.[97] Von Balthasar never explicitly introduces these concerns, but I believe they represent a natural and necessary development of key ideas in his thought.

First, there are agent-relative constraints. Communion cannot occur if one party allows himself to dissolve into the identity of the other— whether the other is God or neighbor. Our everyday experience of love offers one confirmation of this: the devoted sycophant can make our lives easier, but he cannot offer us love's real reward—the gift of a "Thou" who is free and other, and yet turned to us. Difference, separation, and space between two individuals are required if a genuine image of the Trinity is to appear in the earthly domain. And thus there is a legitimate kind of self-regard that is essential for relationship with another.

We have already seen a second justification for believing self-regard a legitimate and necessary response of the Christian: our personal mission is given to us by God and to that we must be faithful over any particular claim of the other. The "I/Thou" relationship with God is primary and seals our identity. Loving *de arriba* means loving created things as God loves them, which includes loving the idea God has in mind for each of us in willing us into existence. God will call us to individual tasks and ways of serving his Son's mission. And within these life tasks, God calls into existence a unique individual that each person should cherish and nurture as one's own way of being before God. It is true that God does not give a rubber stamp to worldly self-regard in the form of desires to further talents and gifts and to pursue virtuous inclinations and vocational preferences. Nonetheless, these same inclinations and vocational preferences often serve as the means in which God draws us to our full personhood before him and thus must be respected and perhaps embraced. Neighbor needs, therefore, do not always trump worldly self-regard. The name by which God addresses each of us *alone* requires absolute obedience; we cannot attribute such an absolute claim to any horizontal mediation of that call. One could wish that von Balthasar had devoted more attention to exploring what kind of self-love is normative for the Christian. In those places where he refers to the theme, he generally associates it (not without reason, of course) with compromise and sinful self-regard.[98] But I believe that in his concept of the "mission," we find a foundation for normative self-love and a place to begin a theological reflection on it.

Second, there are neighbor-relative constraints. Following its triune archetype, interpersonal love is a dialogical relationship where the other is invited to "be" by creating conditions that allow him actively to express his self-identity in relationship with the other.[99] Christian love strives to empower the neighbor to achieve the idea that God has in store for him. In his "service of souls," the Christian cherishes what the person can be before God and offers assistance to make that identity a reality. The difficulty, of course, is that none of us knows exactly *who* another is to be before God—hence the "side constraints" on what Christian love can aspire to accomplish for the neighbor. The neighbor's relationship with God is one only he can choose to accept, and only he can make the final discernment about what personal path God has given him to follow. Nonetheless, since *all* are invited into covenantal life with God and since that relationship is mediated in the present created order, we can rightly expect that the kinds of particular supports and loves for the concrete neighbor demanded of the Christian will not be nominalistic. While reconciliation of the neighbor with God is the ultimate goal of Christian love, in this present age we participate in fellowship with God through our fellowship with one another, as we saw above. The work for divine reconciliation must for the Christian lead to the work of horizontal reconciliation. And the latter will include the endeavor to establish the basic conditions for agency, autonomy, and relationality (e.g., adequate food, shelter, and water; medical assistance; educational opportunities; etc.) out of which the neighbor can respond in freedom to the offer of fellowship.[100]

The above six aspects of neighbor love are clearly grounded in a particular narrative, that of salvation history. The six aspects both describe and prescribe the appropriate response to this story, with the descriptive element more dominant in the first three, the prescriptive more so in the last three. No academic investigation of morality independent of the story of this love will generate the same understanding of interpersonal love or of its normative claims. At the same time, the goods internal to this account of neighbor love are also earthly goods, and not merely constructed out of the particularities of the narrative. The christologically refashioned goods of this account, just like the Incarnation itself, assume the goods of the created order (e.g., the goods of relationality, of fulfilling love in the other, of the mysterious depths and irreplaceable uniqueness of the person). And thus even self-sacrificial love, daring and risky hope for the other, and costly reconciliation with the deeply alienated are not goods opaque either to the believer or the nonbeliever but responses appropriate to "reasoning hearts" in light of the natural and, for the Christian, supernatural depths of the human Thou.

CONCLUSION

For von Balthasar, the primary ethical task of the Christian is to respond in obedience and love to the expressed will of the Father. But the Father's desires for the companions of his Son are given within the voices of the world: its values and goods, its stories, the opportunities it offers for the bonds of fellowship—all seen now in the light of Christ. Christians will lift these goods to God in prayer to discover what particular path God is calling each of them to follow. These earthly goods engage the mind and heart and mediate God's covenantal relationship with humanity. The order of grace does not overturn the order of creation. Rather, creation is the "thick" presupposition that makes the next, wondrous act possible: God's covenantal relationship with what is "other." God's Word in Christ does not relativize the claims of the created order, but rather amplifies them and charges them with the dignity of a personal address.

It does not seem that von Balthasar's approach offers even the theoretical prospect that the ethical visions of faithful disciples and sincere non-Christians will converge completely and harmoniously. However, his theory does offer the hope that there will be more than "ad hoc" agreements on ethical matters, that there will be numerous convergences in regard to the nature of objective obligations and material norms, and that engaging in fruitful dialogue is possible in areas of disagreement. The kind of christological transformation of the order of nature that is effected by grace, while more substantive than often held to be the case in Catholic thought, does not obscure the natural beauty, goodness, and, von Balthasar will add, glory of creation.

It might seem that the more radical transformations of earthly goods, like those associated with some forms of neighbor love, will be opaque to the moral discernment of those outside the Christian community. But for several reasons, von Balthasar's thought permits one to hope for some convergences even in these issues. First, those who participate in the mission of Christ share in the power of the Christ-form to effect a response. Thus, the eucharistic life of the Christian can present the nonbeliever with a concrete ethical choice whose attractiveness elicits its imitation.

> [There are] situations in the created world that, however, emerge clearly only when the light of supernatural grace falls on them, initially of course for the one who believes and entrusts himself to the guidance of this light and, then, in some way also to the wider circles of humanity, when the situations and truths that have become the object of awareness are presented, tried out and made credible by believers.[101]

Second, the historical, objective presentation of the Christian message in the lives of its saints has already introduced Christian values into the general moral consciousness of the world. While von Balthasar might complain that the church has been "continually robbed and pilfered by secular humanism,"[102] such secular borrowing can spread (imperfect) refractions of Christian love beyond the domain of the specifically Christian and support the possibility of extramural conversation.

However, the deeper justification for the broad intelligibility of the moral life is that God respects the "otherness" of creation in order to bring that "otherness" into divine fellowship. God "has lowered and subjected himself" to our "human nature in order to become a partner and player *befitting man*,"[103] stooping down to the human level in order to engage us from within the same earthly horizon ("otherness") in which we act.[104] Von Balthasar's theological aesthetics argues as much: divine glory appears in the world in a way that the human creature can behold and answer it (*GL7* 399). And we can extend his theological aesthetic reflections to worldly values. Unless interpersonal friendship, just treatment of the poor, and sacrificial love in the "natural" sphere already held some moral purchase with us and were already radiant, evocative, and alluring, they could not be transformed and made part of the unique and divine Word of Christ.[105] And because the divine summons of the human to become partner of God begins already in the "natural" revelation of creation, even the non-Christian has a glimmer of the covenantal offer.[106]

5

Contemplation and Action

———◆►◄◆———

THE LAST TWO CHAPTERS examined different dimensions of
von Balthasar's ethics. In chapter 3, I focused on the vertical
dimension in his ethics: Christians receive from God a personalizing mission that is their share in the work of Christ. In the last
chapter, I tried to show how the values and goods of the world provide a proximate guide for Christian discernment. The two dimensions
are integrated in Christian neighbor-love: we love the neighbor now
seen as the one for whom the Father sent the Son.

In this chapter I want to show how this integration can be made
part of a Christian ethical theory. I will do this by revisiting and developing von Balthasar's idea of Christian perception. It is not the core
idea of his ethics ("mission" occupies that place), but I believe it can
play an important role in transforming the general theology of *The
Glory of the Lord* and *Theo-Drama* into a coherent ethical theory. I have
described von Balthasar's ethical theory as one of divine command for
a number of reasons. With God's revelation comes the commanding
claim of God on the human person. God's will is not completely mediated by intramundane goods. And God's will for the person is not
always available to rational scrutiny. However, von Balthasar's theological aesthetics reconfigures divine command ethics, providing it
with characteristically Catholic emphases (e.g., grace building upon
nature) without undermining divine command theory's stress on
divine sovereignty and the covenantal encounter. The Christian perceives God's glory as it is manifested in the economy of salvation. In
this aesthetic encounter, God invites the Christian to enter that story.

123

I referred to this aesthetic encounter as "trinitarian" because it involves perceiving oneself within a drama, a "form" that is also an interplay of personal freedoms. It is not simply a matter of either one's own personal story or God's story (and, thus, either subject or object), but, as I hope to show further below, a fluid, trinitarian interchange of both. I propose to "ethicize" this aesthetic encounter between the creature and the triune glory of the Christ-event. That is, this encounter takes place in our concrete lives, in time and through choices about intramundane goods. While the foundation of the encounter is laid in the domain of the church and Scripture, once laid, it establishes not only the possibility but the appropriateness of further encounters of faith in other arenas. Von Balthasar's thought provides only occasional hints about how this ethicization of the encounter can be executed. However, a complete, fully developed aesthetic ethics can be found in the thought of Iris Murdoch. I will use her ideas to assist in the project. The perceived images and forms of Christ within the horizon of our daily activities shape and attune our ethical character, much like Murdoch's Platonic good. We contemplate Christ within the concrete world and are moved to action in our response to him.

AN AESTHETIC ETHICS:
IRIS MURDOCH AND THE VISION OF THE GOOD

I suggested in chapter 1 that von Balthasar's aesthetic categories serve to generate concepts and images that help us see the truly real. Iris Murdoch argues more explicitly for a more metaphorical reading of the world, especially as it relates to our moral horizon.[1] For Murdoch, the reigning idioms (e.g., scientific/analytic categories) lead to a veiling of the world by precluding certain forms of "perceiving" that world.[2] Murdoch proposes an alternate portrait of the moral life in which vision of the beautiful and the good, and not rational choice, forms the key image. The morally good life is one of seeing the world rightly and without self-delusion, and not first a matter of choosing to do the right act. While the latter is important, the former is prior and more fundamental and leads to the latter. I want to suggest that von Balthasar's ethics aligns well with this alternate account of ethics and not with the standard version of ethics as rational choice.

For Murdoch, the process of coming to know the world is like that of creating good art; we fashion a picture which, through faithful attending to the world, comes to be an ever more adequate portrayal. The world we perceive through such attending is already and inescapably textured with evaluations. It is not just that values "pervade and *colour*" our perception of the world,[3] but also we cannot get around such valuations and still "know" the world.[4] Murdoch points to our use of secondary moral concepts (e.g., courage, humility, justice) to argue the point. In portraying a particularly brave act, we cannot simply do away with the (secondary) concept of "courage" and suffice with a factual description. We do not see the same world without bringing to bear such sedimented—not hardened—moral concepts.[5] In their light we see the world.[6] Thus, unless morality is "put in the picture from the start," that is, in allowing values to color our *Gestalt* of the world, the nature of morality will be misinterpreted, for denied its own integral domain it will be made to justify itself in alien tongues.[7]

For Murdoch, the moral agent is transformed through her "encounter" with the Good. The Good, transcendent and radiant, occupies a place similar to that of von Balthasar's aesthetic splendor. Both illuminate the world, giving it moral texture, depth, and attractiveness.[8] The perception of the beautiful and of the good have a formal similarity for Murdoch.

> Goodness and beauty are not to be contrasted, but are largely part of the same structure . . . . Virtue is *au fond* the same in the artist as in the good man in that it is a selfless attention to nature: something which is easy to name but very hard to achieve.[9]

We "are magnetically attracted" to the Good. The object of a considered action offers to the beholder a kind of agential empowering. "*Looking* (concentrating, attending, attentive discipline) is a source of divine (purified) energy."[10] Both von Balthasar and Murdoch offer contemporary versions of the classical Greek notion of *kalokagathia* (the integration of the beautiful and the good, *kalon* and *agathon*): what is truly good ultimately manifests a harmony of form that can be described as attractive to behold and valuable to embody.

Yet for Murdoch, only rarely, if ever, does the human agent experience this integration of the good and the beautiful. Her novels are filled with characters who are enthralled by comforting illusions and consequently morally paralyzed. Like Plato, Murdoch distinguishes the genuinely beautiful from its limited and defective incarnations, which form the object of so much (immoral) human pursuit. But vision, truly seeing the world before us, not only evokes an ethical response in the agent; it also encourages conversion. "Moral change" comes about from an "*attention* to the world" that involves a process of "unselfing."[11] This conversion involves not so much achieving some new standard of moral behavior as a development in the moral character of person. The person becomes one who sees the world well. Murdoch's aesthetics, therefore, has two implications for understanding human agency. First, it establishes a link between seeing and doing, and, second, it locates the process of moral growth not in the development of one's ethical performance but in the difficult task of developing a virtuous perception where one sees the world as it truly is.

Murdoch interprets the fruit of this conversion differently than Plato. In contrast to Plato's view, the escape from the cave for Murdoch does not lead to the more universal, but rather deeper into the finitude, contingency, and frailty of the world. The chain that imprisons us in the cave is not our fixation on finite things, but our fixation on our own ego and the consoling illusions it grants us—thus Murdoch's Freudian gloss on Plato's myth of the cave.

> It remains Plato's (surely correct) view that the bad (or mediocre) man is in a state of illusion, of which egoism is the most general name, though particular cases would of course suggest more detailed descriptions. Obsession, prejudice, envy, anxiety, ignorance, greed, neurosis, and so on and so on *veil* reality. The defeat of illusion requires moral effort. The instructed and morally purified mind sees reality clearly. . . . The original role of the Forms was not to lead us to some attenuated elsewhere but to show us the real world.[12]

Perceiving is an act of love whereby we come to the "extremely difficult realization that something other than oneself is real."[13] Like beauty, the raw particularity and givenness of the world reorient us away from our own being to a reverent gaze of the other. Below we will distinguish what von Balthasar and Murdoch each understand as the content of good "vision." We can note here, however, that for Murdoch a faithful attending to reality directs us not to the optimistic view reflected in Plato's philosopher king,[14] but to messy corners, to random, chaotic happenings, and ultimately to "the pointless necessity of the world."[15] The difficulty in truly seeing the world is that it is "not easy to do justice to this hardness and this randomness" of the finite things around us "without either smoothing them over with fantasy or exaggerating them into (cynical) absurdity."[16]

Murdoch's understanding of human agency is consonant with von Balthasar's, but, unlike von Balthasar, she develops it within an explicit ethical theory. We can distinguish two levels of moral agency in Murdoch. While both levels are implied in von Balthasar's thought,[17] making them more explicit can provide his thought with more ethical substance. The first is the correct or true "vision" of the world. This "vision" serves as a moral grid in which we spontaneously judge objects, acts, events, and so on as good or evil. We creatively fashion this grid like an art form; it grows out of the history of our experience of the world. We do not simply choose this "vision" or "moral grid"; the good shining forth in reality invites us to embrace it. The call of the good moves us not just toward isolated responses, but toward what von Balthasar refers to as an *attunement* whereby the entire person comes to be the type of person who "sees" a world in which these calls of the good can be "heard." Conversion is thus necessary not only as a (performative) prerequisite for doing the good, but also as a precondition for knowing the good act as good. And because the moral concepts which compose our vision are realities that hint at ideals not yet attained, and thus can be appropriated ever more profoundly by the subject, the process of conversion whereby we come to see them requires that we contemplate our world in an ongoing manner and continually struggle to attune ourselves to its call.[18]

The second level is the choice of a concrete course of action. The agent decides on particular actions out of the attunement that comes through true vision. However, these decisions are not punctual decisions, moral crossroads that must be decided anew at each turn. Rather, they tend to follow the grain of our moral vision of the world. Much of the difficult work of discernment has already been accomplished when we come to moments of moral choice.[19] Von Balthasar, like Murdoch, makes the first level of agency fundamental to the moral life: the agent must first see the world rightly. True perceiving is also a decision to be the kind of person who sees the world truly and feels the call to act in accord with that perception. We are moved to obey the beauty that we see. Murdoch will claim as much.[20] At the same time, the link between perception and action is not absolute for von Balthasar; nor can it be. We can draw back from the call once heard, defensively muffling it through self-deceptive strategies, before it drives us to the appropriate moral response.[21]

Von Balthasar's thought is amenable to a Murdochian development because, like Murdoch, it connects seeing and doing.

> Such a simplicity of the eye [i.e., the eyes of faith], allowing the decisive perception, presupposes the unity of the act of seeing and the act of liv-

ing. . . . This seeing . . . has its first effect on man a sinking down in adoration before the glory; but at the same time, it is the strongest impulse
for the subsequent thinking that converts what is seen into action. (*GL7*
14–15)

That this link is also "ethical"—that is, that it relates to human
response to earthly goods—is hinted in the fact that von Balthasar regularly links a contemplative view of the *world* (and not just Jesus Christ
or Scripture) with the action which follows.[22] The Christian is to be
"*in actione contemplativus.*"[23] Nonetheless, von Balthasar never ties
the idea of a "contemplative in action" to any formal ethical theory
(i.e., to a sustained reflection on how and why certain actions are right
or wrong). My belief is that von Balthasar's thought could be developed into a viable ethical theory by explicitly developing his notion of
attunement in the direction suggested by Murdoch's ethical theory. In
a way, I propose to "ethicize" the Christ encounter. Such an idea was
implied in earlier chapters. I suggested in chapter 4, for example, that
the attunement to the Christ-form helps us see the values of the world
in a new light: the neighbor before us is the face of Christ, and loving
self-sacrifice is now a participation in the mission of Christ. But my
emphasis in the argument that follows is not only on how the encounter with Christ has *already* affected the Christian, but also on how that
transformative encounter with Christ now takes place *before* the Christian, in the horizon of her daily existence, that is, in its thoughts and
actions, and in the objects of her attention and the people she meets.
Applying Murdoch's thought, however, represents a "development"
of von Balthasar because he does not explicitly gather the ideas that
support such a move into a sustained argument.

CHRISTIAN PERCEPTION

If we are to succeed in developing the idea of "attunement" along ethical lines, we must have a theory of perception which, like Murdoch's,
allows the moral agent to perceive (and thus be drawn to) the ultimate
moral object (the Good for Murdoch, the Christ-form for von Balthasar) in her or his day-to-day dealings in the finite world. Ethics involves
choices about the limited goods of our concrete existence. Thus, if we
accept the strong link between vision and ethics suggested in von
Balthasar's theological aesthetics, then the agent's encounter with the
Christ-form (as our ultimate moral object) must occur within this con-

crete, finite domain, or the vision of the Christ-form will be only indirectly related to the individual's concrete ethical existence.

I argued in chapter 1 that von Balthasar defends a general aesthetics (i.e., a "seeing" of splendor and beauty in the forms of the world) as propaedeutic to a theological aesthetics (i.e., the perception of God's glory in Christ). Von Balthasar explores the idea of a Christian perception throughout the first volume of his *Glory of the Lord* and gives it particular attention in his discussion of the "spiritual senses."[24] Von Balthasar's notion of "spiritual senses" is an important pillar for his theological project. The fruit of God's work in Christ is the new, covenantal relationship between God and the human person. The spiritual senses make it possible for this encounter to occur in the Christian's daily existence. Von Balthasar's strong emphasis on a realized eschatology means that this vibrant interchange already shapes human existence.

> [The] preparations are now over and . . . the main part of the drama can begin. The Spirit of the Father and the Son has been poured out over all the world, to the end that the Father's work of creation and the Son's work of reconciliation, both raised to the final trinitarian potency, can now show themselves to the world in their full form and impress themselves upon it with their full power. (*GL1* 408)

Von Balthasar's idea of Christian perception addresses how this display of God's triune "full form" before the human subject occurs. He excludes extremes: an empirical approach that begins and ends with our sensory immersion in the world and a mysticism "which can perceive God's presence directly" (*GL1* 366).[25] Because it is only through our senses that we perceive the world, the human person's encounter with God must "lie where the profane human senses, making possible the act of faith, become 'spiritual,' and where faith becomes 'sensory' in order to be human" (*GL1* 365).[26] Von Balthasar defends what Rahner calls the "mysticism of ordinary life," the human person's experience of the Spirit "in the *concrete* history of his life."[27]

Von Balthasar accepts that we cannot begin with the senses themselves or the subjective experiences of knowing, willing, and feeling and hope to discover within them some "spiritual" faculty. His argument takes as a working premise the view that the "spiritual senses" (i.e., seeing the divine in the earthly) can be successfully defended only within the framework of Christian presuppositions (*GL1* 367). The divine nature of God's revelation requires such an intramural move. The form of revelation establishes its own conditions for being seen.

The perception of faith's object cannot be subordinated to a worldly aesthetic scheme or governed by the particular mode of human perception. By free divine choice, not by some latent capacity in the world, the earthly now speaks the divine Word.[28] In addition, the need for an intramural appeal is also created by the (contingent) circumstances of the present intellectual climate. As I indicated in chapter 1, the loss of a sense for creation's beauty and glory in much of contemporary thought has weakened our ability to see the world's natural radiance. The task of defending creation's native radiance and the human capacity to perceive it falls primarily to the Christian.[29]

Christian experiences of the divine must be understood in light of that object which alone creates the possibility of such experiences: the glory of God as it appears in Christ.[30] Von Balthasar maintains that by making this object of faith "visible in itself," the "mystery" of the spiritual senses can be "demonstrated" and made "comprehensible." What we find in making faith's object "visible" is that this object itself testifies to the possibility both of God addressing the human person and, in turn, of her response. "God's Word, from the outset, wants to be fruitful in the fruitfulness of the believing person. *In the very form in which it addresses man*, the Word of God already wants to include the form of man's answer to God" (*GL1* 538; emphasis added). The full glory of the Christ-event appears only in being met by the total response of human freedom, that is, the grace-inspired surrender of faith. The human response is seen first in its archetypical form in Jesus' relationship with the Father and then in the disciples' experience of God in Jesus. The fact that the canonical writings include the establishment of the *church* and the experiences of post-Easter faith is significant for von Balthasar in that it shows that the response of faith is not just the desired *consequence* of God's work in Christ, but is itself part of the form of revelation. The human answer is not peripheral (like miracles or historical assertions) but central to the Christ-event.

If the interchange with God is to take place within the concrete interactions of the Christian's daily life, there must exist something like "spiritual senses"—a capacity to encounter God in and through our sensed experiences of the world. Furthermore, if grace does not violate or overturn nature, we would expect to find anticipations or preparations of such a spiritual sense already in the natural realm. This "natural" spiritual sense would, in turn, offer a kind of secondary confirmation to the existence of a genuine "sensing" of the divine. Von Balthasar finds such an anticipation of the spiritual senses in the person's encounter with the human other (*GL1* 380–81). The person who faces the other does so not just as a sensing entity but in her or his "concrete and individual wholeness" and as a corporeal-spiritual being (*GL1* 380). Even on a natural level, one's sensing of others is not just an apprehension of empirical facts of the other, but a "dis-covering" of the other and a "linguistic event" of "reciprocal expression."[31] This spiritual knowing of the human other through perception occurs in view of the relationship for which we were created. The complex ways in which our interpenetrating human capacities allow us to experience and interpret a world of spiritual others can be "opened" by the Spirit to unveil God's approach to us. The Spirit lifts up our natural, spiritual knowing of the human thou into a graced perceiving of the divine Thou. While we may "sense and think" many things, in the Spirit we are fundamentally "God-perceiving."[32]

The power of von Balthasar's argument lies in its doxological and intuitive appeal, not in its discursive rationality. It invites a positive judgment based on the argument's capacity to make the Christian form visible. That is, the argument lights up features of the Christ-event which, once seen, are recognized to be truly part of that event. This particular argument will appeal more strongly to those whose Christian experience is significantly informed by liturgical life and sacramental practice, since the Christian drama (or Christian form) for them is already viewed as a rhythm of divine visibility and human response.

The Subject and Object of Christian Perception

Recalling von Balthasar's understanding of how God "appears" in the economy of salvation can help at this point. Christian faith is not a "naked, visionless" response, the "pure opacity of the *credo quia absurdum*" (*GL1* 460), but a response to a perceived object. Because the hidden and unfathomable depth of God's being becomes visible to human perception, we can speak of the "form" of revelation. But the form, if it is to be *divine* revelation, cannot be circumscribed or controlled by the earthliness of its manifestation. In the descent of the Divine Word into human form, in Christ's earthly poverty, humility, and obedience, and in his powerless suffering and death, God is concealed. Yet in this concealment, divine plenitude "appears": a perfect love which empties itself and gives itself over in love to sinful human existence. This concealment is a kind of formlessness (the absurd tragedy of a man of God with the power of the Spirit who suffers an ignoble death) which enters into the content of the Christ-form.[33] What appears is not simply available to human glance. It can only be grasped, as a form, through faith and in the presence of the Holy Spirit. And it can only be seen when it is seen *as love*, that is, the inexplicable love of Father for sinful humanity expressed in his Son.[34]

Faith is the total human response—intellectual, volitional, and emotional—that is given to this form through the gift of the Holy Spirit. It is neither simply the volitional act whereby one surrenders to divine mercy, nor the intellectual act in which one consents to truths inaccessible to discursive reason, but rather a self-giving to something that is experienced and apprehended. At the same time, as the subjective correlative to the divine manifestation, faith takes its bearing from the Christ-form and follows its kenotic movement. It is a self-emptying. We behold the mystery that appears only through a "death of the senses," a readiness to deny a self-imposing perception in order to "let God be what he is in himself" (*GL1* 406–7). Faith thus is a "non-seeing seeing."[35]

Christian perception requires not only a transformed subjectivity but also an adequate object: God's revelation in Christ. Through his idea of a "theo-drama," von Balthasar argues that the entire drama of human existence has been included in the triune life of the Godhead. This means that the human person's entire arena, the agent herself and the present moral stage on which she acts, has in its integrity been included within God's dramatic life. The whole created order, therefore, is given not only a new subjectivity (in the human person) but also a new objectivity (in what is seen and heard). And the Spirit brings about both as it "liquefies" (to use von Balthasar's phrase) the work of Christ so that all creation, subject and object, is included in his form.[36] The biblical "possibility of seeing the divine reality through the medium of what is visible in the world" and "of hearing the voice and the eloquent silence of God in the often strident voice of worldly events" arises because God's Spirit uses creation, especially the human neighbor, to communicate God's presence.[37] When Christians look to the world and find the form of Christ, they do so not only because of the Spirit's presence in them but because of the Spirit's labor before them. The world receives a renewed iconic capacity not only to point (statically) to its Creator but also to reveal the economic presence of the Trinity.

The work of the Spirit in "liquefying" the Christ-event is, however,

an eschatological task; it is already accomplished in our midst and yet
the world yearns for its yet unknown fullness. Since Christ is the *center* of what God has done in the economy, and not the sole act, the
form of the Christ-event includes other events and stories which take
their meaning from the central act. The inclusion of "other events"
into the form of Christ, however, is strict when considering the events
of the economy; it is eschatological when viewing all else. That is, the
prophetic oracles, the rise and fall of the kingdom of Israel, the establishment of the church, and so on have already been located vis-à-vis
Christ and given their meaning there.[38] But our own histories and the
events of the contemporary world are part of the form of Christ pro-
leptically; they wait for their final, christomorphic meaning in the age
to come. And yet as the eschatological actor, the Christian is to live in
anticipation of this final meaning. She does so as one who through the
Spirit shares in the mission of Christ and looks to the world with
Christ-formed sensibilities. She labors as part of a community of faith
for whom not all has been made clear, but yet who are guided by a loving knowledge of what God has revealed in Christ and the ardent hope
that all creation is being made to share in that event.

We can pause at this point to note how von Balthasar's understanding of the divine–human encounter differs from that of narrative
ethics. In chapter 4 I suggested that for von Balthasar the light of the
biblical narrative transforms earthly goods and values. They take on a
new, Christ-centered meaning and the Christian responds to them
accordingly. Such a narrative reshaping of our moral horizon is key to
narrative ethics, and thus von Balthasar could be read as one of its pro-
ponents. However, von Balthasar's project includes three elements that
are not part of most versions of narrative ethics.

First, for von Balthasar the Christian narrative has the power to
draw the believer into a new life. The biblical narrative does not "social-
ize" the Christian into a new personal story, but draws the Christian
ek-statically into it. Narrative ethics can ignore the uniqueness of *this*
story and how it forms and transforms in a manner different from
other socializing narratives.[39] Second, for von Balthasar the expansion
of the biblical story to include our own world is brought about by the
Spirit. The biblical narrative does not "absorb the universe" by trans-
lating the world's language into the idiom of Scripture (i.e., through
"intratexuality," to use George Lindbeck's term).[40] Because of his emphasis on the ongoing labor of the Spirit, von Balthasar more readily maintains the possibility that the Christ-form can appear in surprising new

places and ways in the world. Scripture— its language, themes, images, and so on—does not constrict God's work, however much it guides our interpretation of that work. And thus von Balthasar expressly cautions against limiting the work of the Spirit to the surface of the biblical text: the "form of Scripture is loose and perspectivistic, so that we will not cling to it and take the garment to be the body itself" (*GL1* 541).

These two lead to the third. The *encounter* between God and the human person is not constructed by the biblical narrative, however much it is mediated by it. Von Balthasar allows an extranarrative solidity to both the one beholding the story and the God revealed in it. Neither the moral agent nor God is submerged in the story, as they can seem to be in narrative ethics. Thus, even while underscoring the narrative form of revelation and of the human response to it, the encounter overflows the text in a way that enables new, spontaneous, and interpersonal exchanges between God and the human person.

Mediators of Christ

If a Murdochian development of von Balthasar's theological aesthetics is to succeed, it must be the case that the Christian's moral horizon is also a horizon where the form of Christ "appears." Analogous to the way in which Murdoch's moral agent responds to the Good as it is manifested in the world, the Christian moral agent responds to the Christ-form as it appears before her. The attempt to "ethicize" the encounter with Christ presumes that ethical choices are also responses to this Christ-form. Von Balthasar's thought assists us here by suggesting five earthly domains which mediate the Christ-form. They are earthly locations that can be interpreted in accord with the economy because they are also locations where the Holy Spirit can and does labor to impress dimensions of the event character of the Christ-form onto worldly images. In all of them, the creaturely form is respected; the light of the economy cast on each form by the Spirit gives it a new meaning without destroying its old.

First, and most general, the Christ-form appears in the forms of creation. The sensory environment of the believer,

> in which he lives and with which he is apparently wholly familiar, is through and through determined by the central image and event of Christ, so that, by a thousand open and hidden paths, his wholly real

and corporeal sense-experiences bring him into contact with that central point. . . . He stands in the world which has been determined and established by the appearance of God and which is oriented to that appearance. The reality of creation as a whole has become a monstrance of God's real presence. (*GL1* 419–20)

While the forms of creation (e.g., living things, forms of human society, the cycle of birth, growth and death, etc.) are not primary icons of the Christ-event, they do witness in fluid ways not only to the Creator but also to the goodness and beauty which God labors to redeem. These forms include the dramas of human lives, individual and social, limited, broken, and often tragic, which are reinterpreted in the light of Christ's drama on the cross.

Second, and more determinately than the above, the form of Christ shines within the corporate, communal, and worship-filled reality of the church. It is the place where Scripture is first proclaimed[41] and where the covenantal reconciliation of Christ begins to be lived out in the "we" of the community. The Christian's experiences here spill out into the world. The church teaches its members to see the world, to understand its christological language, and to "taste" and "smell" ever more perfectly Christ's concrete existence (*GL1* 421). Third, the signs and gestures of the church's life are symbolic images that point to the events of the economy of salvation. God uses this sacramental life to introduce different dimensions of the Christ-form into the life of its members. The washing of baptism, for example, is the process whereby the form of the dying of Jesus Christ is impressed upon the believer (*GL1* 578). Each sacrament "clothes itself in a generally intelligible cosmic image (the elements) or human image (laying on of hands, the act of man forgiving man)" and is understood by the believer "both because of pointers given by the earthly image and because of Christ's unique symbolic power as God and man." The convergence of meaning, christological and earthly, in the symbolic form empowers the believer to perceive and respond to the sacramental act as an act of Jesus Christ addressed to the believer (*GL1* 579).[42]

In keeping with the importance that interpersonal encounters have in his thought, von Balthasar is emphatic in introducing the fourth domain. He asserts that there is "*one* image, however, which stands wholly by itself and which is like no other image instituted by the Son of Man. . . . [T]his is the image of the fellow-man we encounter" (*GL1* 423). Von Balthasar underscores the sensory nature of the encounter.

The Christian encounters Christ "with all his bodily senses, in just as concrete, unprecedented, and archetypal a manner as the Apostles when they 'found the Messiah' (Jn 1.41)" (*GL1* 423). "In his love for his neighbor, the Christian definitively receives his Christian senses, which, of course, are none 'other' than his bodily sense, but these senses in so far as they have been formed according to the form of Christ" (*GL1* 424).

Finally, the believer encounters the Lord in prayer. The experience here will be filled with sensory, conceptual, and biblical images, though these images might be present only to be "transcended and annulled" in order to point us to the ever greater mystery of God.

These five "regions" are not simply on par with one another. Only the church, together with Scripture, mediates the Christ-form in a full and immediate sense, established and guaranteed by God's Spirit.[43] The others are images taken up by the Spirit's free movements and made to refract some aspect of the Christ-form before believing eyes. None of these images are made to convey Christ by the "brute effort" of Christian contemplation, but rather all of them "allow God all his freedom" (*GL1* 419).[44] In the case of the church and Scripture, however, we have forms that more fully reveal Christ. Their images, signs, and gestures are already gathered together in such a way as to guarantee the perspicuity of their interrelated forms to the believer, and thus have a certain christological solidity, not a rigidity that shackles the Spirit but a firmness of form that reflects the incarnational density of their archetype.

But while the church and Scripture together are the privileged mediators of the Christ-form, we cannot ignore the striking importance that von Balthasar gives, here and consistently throughout his writings, to the neighbor as mediating Christ. I do not believe that von Balthasar ever works out an ordering between the two (i.e., between Scripture and the church, on the one hand, and the human person, on the other), but in my proposal to "ethicize" the divine–human encounter, I imply one. The church and Scripture must be given a temporal and normative priority in awakening the faith response of the Christian. But once awakened, faith is deepened and nurtured in the interplay that develops among our various experiences of the Christ-form as the Spirit labors in our midst. The experience of Christ in the neighbor is not just an *application* of what one has already encountered in the church, but a continuing development of that first and most basic encounter.

The Covenantal God Encountered

More than our moral imagination is at issue here, applying biblical images to interpret the world. If we follow von Balthasar in the view that not only the Christian, but all of creation has already begun to participate in the dynamics of trinitarian life, then the interchange between the Christian and the Father does not take place only "vertically," in the inner chamber of prayer (with the subsequent ethical act only a follow-up to that conversation). Rather it occurs "before" the Christian, in the Christian's engagement with the world. The world is a sacred text to be contemplated with a christological lens. And just as we saw above that the content of Scripture for von Balthasar lies before the Christian not as an idea to be grasped but as a Person to be encountered, so also must our Christ-formed contemplation of the world's text lead us to something more than a Christian "concept" of the object. Rather, we can hope, tentatively and in the Spirit, to find in the five regions described above an experience of the covenantal encounter.

We cannot hope to describe the variety of experiences of God that occur within the Christian community. They will, of course, be governed by the biblical experience of faith but will also share in its experiential wealth. However, three general qualities will be experienced in the God who appears before us, because they are also those of the biblical experience of God: God as *mystery*, *active presence*, and *absolute Thou*.

First, our experience of God will be informed by the recognition of the "ever greater-ness" of God and the radical incommensurability of divine being with earthly images and forms. "Mystery" here is not merely a "not-knowing," the negative limit to our comprehension, though an awareness of God's incomprehensibility is part of it. Mystery is already part of the disclosure of God. The term points us to a fullness, a "positive mystery,"[45] which we can try to indicate by various concepts (power, freedom, beauty, goodness) but never capture. The more the believer comes to "know" God, the more God will be seen as positive mystery. The response of the creature to God witnesses to this fullness. Von Balthasar finds Rudolph Otto's description of human wonder before the mystery of God ("*mysterium tremendum et fascinosum*")[46] generally acceptable, but prefers "adoration" inasmuch as the term refers us to the positivity that this mystery manifests—that is, the wrathful judgment enveloped within the overflowing of gift and love (*GL7* 268).[47]

The experience of God's glory does not occur only within the Christian context. All individuals, we saw in chapter 1, can be struck by the radiance of creation, not just its natural beauty but something more appropriately called its glory—that is, the splendor of its divine Creator. For the Christian, however, the experience of mystery is christologically shaped, which means that the Christian sees the mystery through the prism of the kenoses of the Incarnation and crucifixion. The experience of God throughout the Christian's earthly existence is tied to the mystery of the exalted one who humbly comes to meet us in a face, in bread and wine, in suffering. And the ethical response to these appearances will be doxological, adoring the Creator who approaches us in earthly garments.

Second, the Christian's experience will be of a God who is active within the objects and events of one's horizon.[48] The image of God in Ignatius's *Spiritual Exercises* is appropriate here: God labors for and in the individual, humanity, and all creation. Interpreting the "where" and the "what" of the divine activity is not a straightforward matter, however much it will be consonant with the salvific narrative. Obviously, we must exclude a simple fatalism, tying God's will directly to historical and natural events. Instead all Christians can and must discern carefully in order to see where God's Spirit is active.

> The gift of discernment of spirits, which is the appropriate organ of perception for the Spirit . . . [is not] primarily a gift bestowed solely on the chosen few (1 Cor 12.10). Rather, it is the faculty, given with the maturity of faith (Heb 5.14), which enables one to read the manifestations of the Spirit objectively, as they are in themselves. (*GL1* 201)[49]

This "organ" for the Spirit is rooted deeply in the common spirit of the church and thus can never fragment into naked charismatic insights. The Christian's experience of God will be guided by a sense of the community's mind and an active submission to its common work to "give form to the Christian reality in the world."[50] Once we perceive this laboring activity, we must answer it with our lives. We are then to follow H. Richard Niebuhr's exhortation to see God "acting in all action" upon us and to "respond to all actions . . . as to respond to his action."[51]

Third, the Christian will experience God as personal. On a general level, this idea presents no difficulty. In Scripture and in the world interpreted in light of Scripture, we encounter a God whose free work of creation and redemption is offered to the personal "I" of each person. The prophetic oracles, Jesus' words of forgiveness, and Paul's exhortations are addressed directly to each of us. However, von Balthasar argues that the address of the Father involves something more than a general call to discipleship; it leads to a particular, personalizing mission. But how can one experience and receive a particular call in and through a reality (creation and Christian revelation) which, as object of an ecclesial community's reflection, is not particular to any one individual?

Rahner and von Balthasar have to answer different versions of this question, and for the same genetic reason: a strong and intentional Ignatian influence on their moral thinking. Both agree that the "election" of the retreatant to choose according to God's choice at the center of Ignatius's *Spiritual Exercises* has direct implications for Christian ethics.[52] Each of them, however, approaches the problem in a way that reflects his characteristic emphasis. Rahner's transcendental subjectivity leads him to underscore the mystical element; von Balthasar's stress on the visible concreteness of faith's object means that the personal "call" is refracted in a constellation of worldly forms.[53]

The transcendental subjectivity assumed in Rahner's approach to the problem (he begins with an "object-less experience of God")[54] places his solution on a different path than von Balthasar's. But the dissimilarity between the two is not absolute. Both locate the answer to the question of God's personal will in God's dynamic, existential address to the believer. In a lesser-known article on prayer, Rahner observes that our personal dialogue with God can and should be seen not as an exchange where "God tells us 'something,'" but rather as the place wherein "we experience ourselves as those who are spoken by God, who in the concreteness of our existence have our origin in and are at the disposal of God's supreme freedom."[55] The transcendental experience of God is fundamental, but we will also experience certain concrete choices and ways of proceeding as consonant with the pull of this transcendence. Thus within this fundamental experience of God and of being addressed at the core of one's identity, Rahner goes on to say, particular objects of consideration can come to be "regarded as spoken to us by God in and together with that fundamental address of God to ourselves."[56] Similarly, for von Balthasar what is given in the encounter with the personal God of revelation and mediated to us in the Christ-form "spaces" before us is not a communication indifferent to our identity but a word about who we are. This does not solve the epistemological problem (i.e., how does one know the particular, personal will of God?), but it does tie God's personal will to something deep within many Christians' experience: the experience of coming to know ourselves as God knows us. God does not mythically intervene in the secondary causal structures of the created order to make the perceived world "say" something positivist and idiosyncratic to each of us, punctuating our horizon with occasionalistic commands. The experience of God in our moral horizon continues the eternal Godhead's unfathomable decision to create each of us—the mysterious "my-self" which is already experienced as known and loved by God.

As a call to *personhood* (and thus a call to become, through time, a particular existent), our experience of a personal God will not, typically, erupt within time and space, but rather will be informed by them, that is, by the sedimented self-awareness of our personal histories and self-constituting memories of the ways in which God has been active and personal in our lives. Moreover, since the particularities that make up our individual lives are part of the identity to which God's personal word calls us, the way we experience God because of these facticities, that is, encountering *this* neighbor, hearing *this* homily, facing *this* kind of limitation or disappointment, being present in *this* liturgy, being victimized by *this* act of injustice, can be used by the Spirit to give color to God's personal approach to us. Because of the rich christological depths of the horizon before us and the Spirit's dynamic interpretation of it, we do not risk Stoic fatalism to see natural providence "as being actually in the service of God's will."[57] The Spirit offers no flat reading of reality. Nor do the objects of our horizon beckon to us merely as confirmatory notes to what has already been given in the subjectivity of the person (as one might associate with Rahner's approach). Rather, the Spirit uses the events and objects of our horizon to guide us along our unique personal path by illuminating in them the words that God wishes to speak to us. The Spirit can do this not only because of the latitude (not indefinite but christologically circumscribed) of meaning of all creaturely forms, but also because of the inexhaustible richness of the Christ-form itself. Each person can refract only one christological possibility in the life situation that providence has bequeathed her.

> [We] can never know in advance how the eternal will manifest itself in temporal form, what aspects will predominate this time, what familiar aspects will be deepened, what new, unsuspected ones will be brought to light, what dimensions will be brilliantly lit, what others will be left in semidarkness. Every human life is unique, and so each person's gaze will illuminate the Lord's archetypal existence in a different way. . . .

> [T]he love of God . . . plays an utterly fresh, original and inimitable melody upon the instrument of Christ's life. The instrument has a limited number of keys, just as the words of holy scripture are limited. But there is an unlimited number of possible variations on the one theme, which is the self-sacrifice of divine love and our initiation into the depths of divine meaning.[58]

Since the form of every Christian life is that of Christ, then it must be that the moral "individuality" of the Christian is not one of radical charismatic discontinuity. Rather it reflects an aesthetic distinctiveness within the uniqueness of the Christ-form. In its creaturely realities (i.e., its actions, history, personality, etc.) appear the free fashioning and expression of a *personal* life form that can be recognized as christological, that is, eucharistic and kenotic love.

From the Tragic to the Theo-Dramatic: A Balthasarian Development

The God who approaches in worldly forms does so in the drama of the economic narrative. Both von Balthasar and Murdoch use the dramatic form to draw together the horizon of contemplation (the chaotic, concrete world for Murdoch; creation, the church, sacramental forms, the neighbor, and prayer for von Balthasar) with its ultimate object (the "Good" for Murdoch; and the glory, activity, and personal address of God for von Balthasar). For both, the contemplated object is no pretty icon, but a reality that is marred by the chaos of contingency and sin (von Balthasar) or egoism (Murdoch). In drawing together the horizon of contemplation and its ultimate object, the dramatic form serves to bind together what would otherwise seem disparate elements: the dark undercurrents of reality (its sinfulness, its brokenness, its seeming purposeless) and the aesthetic (i.e., ek-static, erotic) response to beauty. Their respective uses of the dramatic form lead both to different versions of what I have referred to in chapter 2 as a "trinitarian" dramatic form: we are not only confronted with an objective dramatic form but "behold" the form in such a way that we see ourselves in it and are moved to act within it. The explicitly personal and trinitarian horizon of von Balthasar's theo-dramatic form supplements Murdoch here and makes his version of aesthetic ethics more successful, I believe, because it is better able to hold in tension the tragic dimension of ethics and its capacity to bring a type of fulfillment ("purified joy," to use Murdoch's phrase) to the moral agent.

For Murdoch, the moral task that confronts us is one of purifying ourselves of distorting and self-serving illusions and coming to live in obedience to the good as it appears before us in a true vision of the world. The world has a "pointless necessity" about it and is filled with "chance and its horrors,"[59] and yet something like what Plato calls the "Good" radiates in its midst (in, for example, the values that color its landscape) and comes to expression in the life of the (rare) saint. The dramatic form of tragedy—for example, the life of the noble person or saint whose suffering servitude to goodness leads not to reward but to further suffering and death—reveals this polarity of bleak contingency and radiant goodness. Peering at the world through the lens of the tragic form and acknowledging the truthfulness of its image can lead the individual to occupy a new narrative, one that no longer offers the solace of morality's utility. And yet there is a "purified" joy that draws us to this new, albeit tragic, narrative.[60] The "special unillusioned pleasure which is the liberating whiff of reality" allows us to "experience what Plato spoke of but wished to separate from art: the way in which to desire the beautiful is to desire the real and the good."[61] The "beautiful" is a dramatic story that is *also* our story. To paraphrase Murdoch, we are creatures who make stories of our lives and then come to resemble the story.[62] However, even the knowledge that we *have* a story can introduce illusion and false comfort in our "vision." The truth-seeker must hover between the tragic form which grants some understanding and insight into the human condition and the dissipation of that form for the sake of the truth which overflows it (i.e., the "truth" of the random chaos of mortal existence).[63]

But can the "beautiful," which the lover of wisdom seeks, be so ephemeral and still have the power to beckon to us, decenter us, and transform our self-centered desires? Murdoch corrects Plato's otherworldliness by situating the moral agent inescapably in the finite, contingent world. And yet a disembodiedness slips into her theory from another direction. One appealing part of Plato's ethics is that though his telos of human existence can seem strangely otherworldly, it centers on a worldly existence that we can imagine as fulfilling (at least for some), i.e., that of philosophical reflection. Plato's philosopher does not pursue this life in order to satisfy his (or her) own needs, but the life is, in fact, fulfilling. But while Plato's truth draws the moral agent beyond a focus on finite things, Murdoch's truth entrenches the moral agent all the more into the world. Like Plato's philosopher, Murdoch's saints live and act in truth. However, they do so without the philoso-

pher's (secondary) consolation of engaging in an intrinsically rewarding life.

Against Murdoch's explicit intention, the moral life she describes
seems disembodied. None of the agent's own desires and attractions
count morally. Murdoch makes no distinction between self-interest
and selfishness. Concerns about the self, on the one hand, and the
"purified joy" of the moral life are sharply opposed. A "kind of passion, a high Eros, or purified joy, which is the vision of the good . . .
comes about when . . . selfish desires, and the distress involved in their
frustration, are removed."[64] Murdoch praises purified desires, but
never gives them any earthly focus; they are desires for a "Good" that
seems strangely detached from the particular goods that energize the
moral actions of most individuals. Martha Nussbaum's criticism of
Plato on this point applies to Murdoch.

> One thing is very clear: that [Plato's] standpoint is nothing like that of
> the ordinary human being. . . . The *Republic* seriously underestimates
> the complexity of our appetitive nature when it ignores the aesthetic
> side of appetitive acts [e.g., eating] and the complex connections
> between such activity and other valuable ends.[65]

Of course, Murdoch could well respond that her saint is "nothing like
. . . the ordinary human being" because so few persons are saints. But
the problem here is not just that most do not achieve such a life of
purified desires; most do not feel morally bound to pursue such a life.
Her saints are angel-like in their lack of self-concern with basic personal needs. Murdoch could be right that such is the ideal of the moral
life, but I take it to be counterintuitive to what most hold to be the
case.

The Catholic tradition has resisted absolutizing self-forgetfulness,
and even condemned it at one point.[66] Though von Balthasar can be
excessive in his praise of radical self-giving, he consistently maintains
that the moral life is genuinely fulfilling. The eschatological horizon of
Christian life allows von Balthasar to retain Murdoch's insight into the
tragic dimension of the moral life while also introducing a note of
redemption to it. As is the case in Murdoch's thought, the individual's
drama is broken and tragic for von Balthasar. But because the horizon
of the individual's drama has been revealed as triune love, the tragedy
of her personal drama is redeemable. The particular dramas of our individual and social lives—from the pursuit of personal love to the contentious work of social reform—will always be marred with the
limitation, brokenness, and sin of human existence. And yet the hori-

zon of this same broken world has been encompassed by "the all-
embracing 'event' of the economic Trinity" (*TD3* 534–35). The trinitarian horizon of all-embracing love transforms the tragedy of mortal
existence into a redeeming drama. This redemptive promise offers a
more adequate foundation for Murdoch's "purified joy" than her
unalloyed vision.

I suggested in chapter 2 that the drama of the economy, precisely as
a unified drama and not as a mere sequence of events, reveals the
divine nature. In light of the discussion above, we can suggest that
God continues to be manifested in the world before us, not only in isolated events, but in the various dramas which occupy it. Thus we can
behold in our own contemporary struggle—for example, to overcome
suffering, hatred, alienation, oppression, and so on—the Spirit's expansion of the narrative of salvation. These dramas can do so because in
Christ the divine narrative has assumed the marred form of the human
drama and has made it a place of glory's appearance. All that is broken
—our individual sin, the hatreds of our world, the limitation and ultimate diminishment that life imposes upon us—receives its final, and
ultimately non-tragic, meaning in the light of this economic drama.
Murdoch observes that seeing "human misery" as beautiful "is what
we do when we enjoy great tragedy."[67] She maintains this, but, I
believe, von Balthasar's theo-dramatics offers a more persuasive account
of how this is so. The beauty that appears in the life and death of the
Christian "tragic hero" is not the memory of a now silenced spirit but
the eternal glory of triune love, and the praise for this fallen hero is not
the passing honor of a semidivine choir but the personal and absolute
love of the Eternal Father for his Son.

The full redemption of our tragic existence is eschatological, and
that means that for now the human actors in this trinitarian drama are
necessarily in fluid roles of givers and receivers of christological love
and forgiveness. Entering the Christian drama, beholding it, and
responding to it, does not lead directly to performative perfection, but
a painful recognition of our creaturely finitude and sinful limitation.
The Spirit, however, responds "to the manifold, fortuitous needs of
the moment and the changing potential of the troupe of actors" in
order to guide the performance and its "multifarious" and limited
human cast to what we can hope will be a truly christological drama
(*TD3* 533). The ultimate shape of our individual lives has been cast
and fixed: the "all-encompassing reality" is "grace and forgiveness"
(*TD3* 535). Grace and forgiveness: the salvific drama addresses us con-

tinually with both by offering us room on its stage for sinful failures *and* fruitful labor in the work of redemption.

This redemptive co-laboring, though, is an especially important consideration for the Christian, in von Balthasar's view. The drama "between God and God" takes place not only that we might receive forgiveness, but also so that our "com-passion can be transformed into the grace of co-atonement (Col 1:24)" (*TD3* 535). Von Balthasar is very serious about the Christian's participation in the work of redemption. The Spirit impresses the Christ-form onto the various dramas of the world, I want to suggest, by bringing forth among their human participants a christological response—that is, a willingness to forgo retribution, to renounce one's own desires, to give costly for the sake of another—to the brokenness and sinfulness that mark those earthly dramas. The Christian participates in the work of the Spirit in expanding the Christ-event by introducing into the many and varied worldly plays in which she participates the "act" of the christomorphic love. Occurring against the background of human pettiness and hatred, this act will shine with the light of the Cross, now impressed upon one more region of the world's drama. Von Balthasar's hope is a reserved one: not so much to rid the world of the drama of sin as to transform that drama into the glory of Christian "tragedy" by placing it under the sign of the cross.

In Christians' contemplation of the world's dramas, they see not only the economic presence of the Spirit, laboring to overcome human sinfulness, but the opening within that drama for a new role, their contribution to the play's success. In what we can call von Balthasar's "trinitarian dramatics," the pondering of the Christ-form is never for Christians just a beautiful sight to behold, but also a seeing of themselves in its dramatic form. The form in which von Balthasar's absolute "Good" approaches us is not a fixed icon nor (as for Murdoch) the uncertain promise of a fragile tragedy, but an *absolute* and *open* dramatic form, which both addresses us with a personal name and creates the space for our response.

CHRISTIAN ATTUNEMENT

"Doing good works *is* faith in its second potency," von Balthasar tells us in his discussion of Karl Barth's theology.[68] I began to show in our discussion of the "mission" (chapter 3) how deeply the Christian moral life is, for von Balthasar, rooted in the event of faith. The idea of Christian perception completes this tie between ethics and faith by extending the encounter that elicits the faith response into the realm of the daily and ordinary and thus into the horizon of human activity. In *The Glory of the Lord*, von Balthasar telescopes the encounter and its faith response into the moment of ecstatically perceiving the Christ-form. This event-encounter is at the basis of what I referred to in chapter 1 as von Balthasar's "iconic aesthetics." The telescoping is not inappropriate (it helps us understand, as von Balthasar intends, the object/subject dynamics that the event evokes), but it is not representative of most individuals' experience of faith. It does not describe the temporal process by which they come to faith; nor does it indicate the daily renewal that many Christians must undertake to preserve often fragile Christian commitments. However, von Balthasar's concept of the theo-drama, where our temporal, historical dramas are transformed by the light of the economic drama, points to a way of including the idea of a historically developing faith (i.e., a faith that does not arise in the moment). The Spirit in and through daily encounters (with neighbor, in the church's liturgies, in prayer) grants the Christian an ever deeper and more finely tuned vision of God's glory in Christ. And the Spirit does this by opening our perception to see Christ in the forms of the world. The faith encounter and its ecstatic response expand horizontally in and through concrete acts.

I suggested above in our discussion of Murdoch's idea of moral vision that the kind of moral life that one lives is governed by what the person "sees" or fails to see in the world. Von Balthasar is committed to this tie between vision and praxis in principle (in chapter 1 I tried to show the close bond between perception of the Christ-form and response), but does not pursue the full ethical implications of it for our daily existence. What the Spirit opens our eyes to see will draw forth certain moral inclinations and responses. For von Balthasar, the moral horizon is not given simply by the world before us but the historical drama of the world as it has been renewed in Christ. Thus, if we want to argue, as I want to "push" von Balthasar to do, that the proposed, close bond of vision and response governs the daily rhythm of our mundane encounters and ethical responses to them, then we must be able to speak meaningfully of our experience of faith's object within the forms of the world. But we are entitled to do so, we have seen, because of the pneumatic extension of the Christ-form into the forms of the world. Christian praxis, then, is a *contemplatio in actione*, a response to the form of Christ as manifested in the world.

The contemplation that leads to action is not a cerebral exercise or otherworldly mystical encounter. The subject of Christian perception is the same subject as that of faith's self-surrendering response: the *whole* person—spiritual and corporeal. Thus, the individual perceives God's self-communication not by means of one isolated human capacity, but through all the mutually interpenetrating modes (intellectual, volitional, sensory, and affective) in which the human creature engages the world.[69] "Constant contemplation of the whole Christ, through the Holy Spirit, transforms the beholder *as a whole*" (*GL1* 242; emphasis added). And it does so because Christian contemplation opens the entire existence of the believer to the irradiating beauty of the living God. God desires to enter into a relationship with what is other than God (creaturely human existence) and not an isolated dimension of grace. Thus the sensibility of Christ is given to Christians not only in the spiritual dimension of their existence but also in their "organic and corporeal nature." God gives this grace not "as a 'concession' to the multitude who cannot soar to purely spiritual experiences, but as the perfecting of the divine work of creation," which designed the human person "to be an indissoluble unity of body and soul and which desires to bring him to perfection as such" (*GL1* 247–48). The response that God desires of the person is not only a spiritual act, but one that reaches down to express all the dimensions of human existence.

We "see" (perceive, understand, feel) well by seeing as Christ does and by entering his sensibility. We could describe this as an ethics of character or virtue. The emphasis is not only on "doing" the good act, but "being" a particular type of person, one attuned to Christ. And like the life of virtue, Christian "attunement" will involve normative operations of the highest *and* the lowest capacities of the human creature.

> The whole man is permeated by this predisposition to submit to the power of the good, and this includes his senses, informed as they are by spirit. (Though the senses, abstracted from the human totality, cannot manage to perceive the good in itself, but treat particular goods as ends.) *The distinctive ethical task laid upon man is that of ethicizing (ethizesthai) his entire spiritual-bodily nature; success is called virtue.*[70]

Von Balthasar's concern in this passage is for the prospect of an extra-Christian ethics. But this trace of a virtue ethics is presumed in the anthropology of *The Glory of the Lord* and *Theo-Drama* (with its emphasis on the spiritual-corporeal wholeness of the person's faith response). Like Thomas, von Balthasar gives the attunement of the person its proper Christian orientation. Just as the virtue *caritas* gives formal unity and Christian particularity to the various virtues, the surrendering love of the Christian to the form of Christ provides unity and particularity to Christian "attunement."

While the need to *grow* toward Christian attunement and the process in which that growth occurs receive little attention in von Balthasar's writings (again, all is telescoped into the one "moment" of faith), growth and development in one's faith will be a normal part of the ethical task facing most Christians. Not only can the approach of *The Glory of the Lord* be read as consonant with such growth, the temporality and drama of human existence explored in *Theo-Drama* demands it. Attunement is a *process*, even a drama, not only because of sin (and the fact that conversion in general is difficult, never-ending, and often punctuated with periods of reversals), but because God respects the temporality of human existence. We change over time. To see God's call, we must first become the type of person able to see that call. The "sensorium" for the divine is not just a fact accomplished with grace's indwelling. Christological vision requires the often slow development both of recognizing "who" we are (sinners called to participate in the Christian drama) and of attuning ourselves existentially to the genuine goods and values that compose a true, God, savoring view of the world.

"Attunement" develops in the concrete acts of the Christians' lives as they struggle to see and respond to the Spirit's prompting before and within them. While for Thomas the person becomes virtuous primarily through the practice of virtue, von Balthasar places a greater emphasis on one's contemplative encounter with the good. We are pierced by the good that is perceived. Von Balthasar does not (or, at least, need not) deny Thomas's insight that we become virtuous by acting virtuously, but his emphasis lies in our first coming to recognize the good as good, and for him that means that we must first perceive what God has done for us in Christ Jesus. And because this "good" is now not just natural goods and values but the approach of God to us in human history, the training of the affect in this encounter is similar to that associated with good liturgy. The encounter takes place in a "fundamental imaginal framework" which "forms intentions in and through the affections that take God in Christ as their goal and ground."[71] The kind of encounter with Christ and attuning of our intentionality that appears within the community's celebration of Eucharist is the foremost instance of what can become part of the Christian's daily experience. The Spirit's work of impressing the form of Christ onto the forms of the world, a work that is both objective and subjective, means that we can and must allow the symbols and images of the narrative to sound the christological depths of the world of our experience—for example, how we understand a neighbor's hatred, hear God's word of judgment and mercy to us in prayer, experience ecclesial solidarity, and see where God labors in the arena of the world.

Attunement is a matter, to use an Ignatian phrase, of finding God in all things. The process of attuning ourselves to the form of Christ is one of entering the divine story by finding in our broken stories Christ's own story. This is the movement of Ignatius's *Spiritual Exercises*, the insertion of our lives into the drama of salvation—that is, the movement from a consideration of the "Principle and Foundation" ("we are created to praise, reverence, and serve God . . ."), to a reflection on our sin, on the work of Christ, and finally to the choice to follow Christ in his suffering and glory. An ongoing (we might even say vigilant) contemplation of this story and a "seeing" of our story in its light will lead us to become actors in it. The Pauline exhortation that we choose which Master we will serve—God or the world—becomes in von Balthasar's theo-drama the exhortation to choose which story we will enter—the delusional fantasy of a self-centered cosmos or the glorious drama of the cross.

Conclusion

In Praise of Glory

V ON BALTHASAR UNDERSTANDS the central act of the Christian, the response of faith, not primarily in terms of an intellectual or fiduciary response, but rather as the creature's doxological response to the glory of God in Jesus Christ. The glory that appears in Christ is sovereign. Not: "The sovereignty of the glory of Christ, once perceived, *should* be acknowledged by the creature." Rather the very perceiving of this glory leads the creature to feel and recognize its commanding claim and praiseworthiness, to suspend its own creaturely standards of beauty and goodness in the light of its "ever-greaterness," and to bend knee in adoration.

Von Balthasar underscores both the fact that in glory's appearance *something* is revealed (i.e., is manifested to human understanding and perception) and that God seeks to have that glory returned, glorified, in the freely given praise of the creature (and thus the need that God address the person in such a way that he can respond to God with autonomy). He also suggests that God's glory is configured in Christ "aesthetically," that is, visibly, noetically, attractively. Von Balthasar finds in "beauty" a useful earthly analogue for reflecting on the "visibility" of divine glory and its total engagement of the human agent. Like beauty, glory is enrapturing; it evokes the ek-static response of the agent. Thus, von Balthasar links (truly) perceiving the Christ-form and responding in faith. We do not look at the "beauty" of the Christ-event and hover in indecision over whether to allow it the honor it is due. Analogous to the experience of considering the beauty of a piece of art, we find our response pulled forth in the very seeing of the object.

150

In chapters 3 and 4, I tried to show how the two axes, the vertical (divine) and the horizontal (earthly), shape von Balthasar's ethics in different ways. Chapter 3 focused on the vertical dimension. There I distinguished two levels of obedience. The first is fundamental and determinative for the Christian life. It is the total self-surrender which appears in the ecstatic and transformative beholding of the Christ-form. Obedience here is the *creaturely* response to divine glory now revealed as absolute love. This event ushers us into the triune life, where we are made "theological persons" by sharing in the unique christological mission given to us by the Father. Another kind of obedience takes shape as we are allowed through the Spirit to participate in the divine interchange. We live the obedience of the christological mission, as a people turned to the world with an affect reshaped according to the Father's desires.

Obedience here is not a "dead echo," von Balthasar repeatedly maintains. We saw in chapter 2 how the triune God provides us with a christological space not only for our human creativity, spontaneity, and agency, but also for our personal, integral stories. In chapter 4, we explored the implications of the covenantal relationship for creation in general and for the human person in particular. Specifically, I argued that the horizontal must retain a certain solidity if human agency is to maintain any real meaningfulness before the divine address. I suggested how the transformation of creation effected by the advent of the Christ-event is such that a relative, natural meaning of earthly goods and values is preserved. A christological light is cast on these values without violating their immanent integrity. Thus, they do act as objects of moral reflection which can, in turn, point us along the moral path God wishes for us.

In the last chapter, I developed the idea of Christian perception, an idea which, I believe, draws together the themes of the previous two chapters. What at first sight threatens to split into two directions—the response of the human agent to God and to horizontal claims—is reconfigured around the one divine-human axis of the Incarnation. The bivalence (earthly and divine) of the Son's earthly existence, now impressed universally by the Spirit, provides the adequate object for human stereoscopic vision. The vertical is not reduced to the horizontal. The cry of the poor is bathed in the light of the Lord who hears them. Nor does the horizontal become transparent to our intentionality as we direct ourselves to God in our daily existence. The Spirit uses the forms of creation, including its dramatic struggles, to give God's address its incarnational contours. The Spirit remains transcendent and free, and so the vertical will never harden into an immanent principle of the moral horizon. Yet the Spirit will gently encourage creation, ever oriented to the covenant, to speak christological words. Creation will do so in its own native tongue. As Gerard M. Hopkins expressed it: "For Christ plays in ten thousand places, / Lovely in limbs, and lovely in eyes not his / To the Father through the features of men's faces."[1] The stars which moved Ignatius to tears will hardly be made by the Spirit to speak a word of divine indifference, nor will a hate crime against a brother or sister be made to speak a word of divine pleasure. It is not a matter of judging a drama or situation for ourselves and later projecting on it divine approval. The images and drama of the Christian community's word and sacrament first establish our bivalent vision and continue to tutor it.

This encounter of the Christ-form in earthly garments can be interpreted as a synthesis of the theological aesthetics of *The Glory of the Lord* and the dramatics of *Theo-Drama* into a "trinitarian dramatics." Christians behold the dramas of the world in light of the economy of salvation, where they experience the pull and appeal of appearing glory (theological aesthetics) and the openness of that drama to their own response (theo-drama); in seeing the scene, Christians see their response in it. Such a contemplation of the world in light of the gospel is a fundamental practice of Ignatius's *Spiritual Exercises*. Therefore, we might describe von Balthasar's ethics as an "Ignatian reconfiguration" of divine command ethics.

The appearance of divine glory within the church awakens in the Christian a surrender that is the total self-giving of faith. The christological shape of faith's object permanently marks this surrender with its own human/divine bivalence. It will be a contemplative "readiness" to "encounter God in what is human."[2] This surrendering response receives the particular finite form it will take in any given moment according to the way God approaches in the finite form.[3] Faith's surrender will thus take shape as a receptive wonder before the mystery of divine being in the glory of worldly forms. It will be a self-giving gratitude for the drama of the divine economy, which continues before us, an active laboring with God in that drama, and a trusting acceptance of events and happenings beyond our control even when painful and disappointing. Finally, it will involve a ready listening "daily and hourly to the call of God" in the voices of the world and a constant openness "to be touched and guided" by those voices.[4]

As we become actively receptive to God's approach to us in the forms of the world, God will deepen our attunement with Christ. This means we will come increasingly to have the character of Christ and to see the world as he does. In chapter 3, we examined what I consider to be the heart of von Balthasar's ethics, the christological mission. Like Christ, the Christian is sent by the Father on a task. The task will be "christological" inasmuch as it participates in and continues the mission of Christ. But the missioning word does not just arrive from on high, a bare vertical command. It grows out of earthly goods and values—for example, the goods and values at stake in our response to the neighbor, in our treatment of the environment, in the way we handle the various refugee crises, in the means we take to control crime, in the hope we bring to broken relationships—that are now "tuned" to the biblical narrative. Pondering these goods with a christological mind, reflecting on them, finding the Spirit's economic labor in them, and committing ourselves to them will increasingly attune our entire selves to them. A kind of christomorphic solidity will begin to mark our individual stories. We participate in Christ's mission not only by doing some action that can be considered "Christlike" but also by becoming true christological actors, that is, agents with the mind and heart of Christ.

Narrative ethicists and Thomists who emphasize the theological virtues could be read as saying something similar. Von Balthasar's contribution to this discussion is to make the bipolarity between human agency and earthly goods participate in and mediate vibrantly the encounter between the human person and the God who approaches us in Christ. The Christian becomes attuned to the world's goods because in them he experiences the Ancient Beauty revealed in Christ and is moved to give an answering word. When an interpersonal framework is allowed to interpret the moral horizon, we inject a permanent element of indeterminacy or "play" in the encounter of moral claim and response. The appropriate response to a moral situation will not be like the "solution" to a mathematical problem. It will rather involve the creative interplay of freedoms, divine and human. As we saw in chapter 3, the freedoms do not engage one another simply on the same plane, but God provides something like a christological stage which gives the Christian agent space for input and creativity. The encounter between God and the particular person will produce personalizing nuances to the Christ-mediated relationship that God has with all of humanity. Moral actors are not interchangeable; a discernment of what is fitting for one agent in a particular situation does not necessarily apply to other agents. The Christian will respond to God's approach not only according to what is required of all good people or all Christians but also according to "who" the Christian senses God calls him or her to be. That call will come objectively and subjectively —through neighbor-need, one's natural talents and gifts, one's life situation, the ways God gives one strength to do difficult tasks, the experience one has of one's identity, what biblical and ecclesial witnesses (or saints) one finds inspiring, one's own creative desires, and so on.

Von Balthasar introduces the "interpersonal" in the theological aesthetics of *The Glory of the Lord* and develops the same in his theo-dramatics. "Who" God calls the Christian to be is given through the role that God calls the Christian to occupy in the (immanently tragic) drama of fallen human existence. But here, in this theo-drama, we see the fluidity of divine–human interchange. The drama that the Christian occupies has been given a sovereign meaning, and that meaning is found in the cross. To it the Christian must submit. But creative room remains as to how the inner workings of this drama will embody its final and guaranteed meaning. God is moved by our response, not out of a weakness in the divine nature, but out of strength: triune love allowing in "reciprocity" "that which is not God to participate in all the treasures of his love" (*TD2* 127).

> Here, therefore, [in God's trinitarian salvific decision,] the whole intra-mundane dialogue of standpoints, world views and perspectives is over-taken by an ultimate dramatic dialogue, which, while it lets God have the first and last word in all things, acknowledges that this same God has determined to send his Word into the world and leave it there. Thus, not only can the world hear this "key word," this "cue": it is also prompted to respond to it, well or ill; the world is obliged to step forth from the wings and act, in freedom, on the stage. (*TD2* 128)

I showed in chapter 2 how von Balthasar uses the metaphor of a play as an image for the interplay between the ultimate divine governance of the moral life and the latitude that God allows the Christian "actor." The image is imperfect and can still seem to offer too little space for human creativity. Von Balthasar offers another image at one point that we can now use to supplement it: the extemporized play. He appeals to Herder's idea of open-ended and meaningful play that comes into existence through the spontaneous creativity of its actors (*TD1* 178–80). Apart from the Spirit, however, the creativity and autonomy imaged in such a play cannot work for the Christian; the play will fall into meaningless disarray. But such open-ended creativity and spontaneity in the Christian can be allowed once he has surrendered, through indifference, to pneumatological (and, therefore, christological and trinitarian) governance by committing himself to the Christian story and fully entering its rhythm. Yet, even lacking the full surrender of faith, the Christian can hope (not expect, but hope) that the Spirit's providential direction of the play will find ways to work his flawed response into the theo-drama's "production." The drama, because it has already included the response of human sin, allows that hope. How the drama of the divine–human interchange will unfold is left in part to human freedom (individual, ecclesial, social). The Spirit's governance is not punctual and occasional, but dramatic, in that the Spirit looks finally to impress the christological form, which is itself a dramatic form, onto the drama of the world's broken tragedy. There will, of course, be important junctures of transition where the Spirit's direction to the Christian agent will be more defined and pressing, but it will be for the sake of our own more complete entry into the Christian story and for that story's continuing inception in the various realms of earthly drama.

There are endless ways in which the ever-free and ever-greater Spirit of God can both speak God's address to each person in the idiom of the world and call forth something new, creative, and original in the drama of divine–human encounter. But that there are "endless ways" for the Spirit to direct the drama need not imply, and does not for von Balthasar, that creation is endlessly malleable. I argued in chapter 4 that the image of a christological "light," illumining and clarifying goods and values without overshadowing their immanent meaning, represents von Balthasar's understanding of how the Christ-event transforms the created order. Thus, even "natural" reflections about the ordering of earthly goods can be helpful.

> Thus, in this anteroom [of human freedom], prior to revealed Christology, man the agent can establish certain "general" norms of action, abstracted from human existence, and these may be relatively correct. But once the absolute norm has appeared on the scene, as we have said, they must be understood as rays emitted from it or approaches toward it. (*TD2* 85)

General "norms" (not moral absolutes) are appropriate guides for the Christian so long as breathing space is allowed to the Spirit to impress new christological forms in our world and call forth new responses. The Christian community can and should develop concrete norms that assist the Christian in discerning where the Spirit is leading.[5]

Garth Hallet correctly observes that a moral theory "need not be useful to be valid."[6] The moral theory proposed above is not primarily a method for ascertaining the good, but rather a description and explanation of the nature of Christian conduct. And so it is not a mortal blow to von Balthasar's theory to acknowledge that it does not easily produce clear answers to the perplexing ethical situations that confront the human agent. Indeed, that could be its strength. The temptation might be to simplify von Balthasar's ethics by pruning the vertical and focusing one's discernment energies entirely on the horizontal (interpreted, perhaps, through biblical themes and imagery), but that is not von Balthasar's path.

Here I think we can make a helpful parallel between von Balthasar's approach to Scripture and contemporary scholarship on the topic, on the one hand, and his approach to the moral life and the different philosophical and theological reflections on it, on the other. Von Balthasar's advocacy for a contemplative approach to Scripture (*GL1* 546) applies as well to the ethical encounter and for a similar reason. The issue at stake in both the ethical encounter and scriptural mediation is the covenantal approach of God, which cannot be frozen into any earthly form. Our contemplation of God, both in Scripture and in the moral horizon before us, will always include a receptive "hearing," because "what is beheld is the free and infinite Person who, from the depths of his freedom, can give himself in a way that is ever new, unsusceptible and unpredictable."[7] Further, von Balthasar's ambivalence toward biblical scholarship can be extended to the field of ethics. Von Balthasar believed contemporary biblical scholarship contributes to our knowledge of revelation, but its use must be subordinated to its ultimate purpose: to help us see the whole organic form of Scripture. Similarly in regard to ethics, we can say that good, practical insight can be gained from breaking down and studying the various component elements of the particular moral situation. We *should* gather and clarify the facts, figure out what values and goods are at stake, look to the consequences of the action, weigh different possibilities, and so on. Von Balthasar can initially allow a wide expanse of methological pluralism in ethics as well as in Scripture, I want to suggest. The many forms of ethical decision making available to us (consequentialism, utilitarianism, natural law, adherence to biblical injunctions, etc.) can all assist the Christian's discernment. Yet these remain assistants in any discernment process; they yield only "signposts" on the way to the final answer. The ultimate object of discernment is not simply the collection of all these considerations but the form of Christ that does, or can be allowed to, appear in the contingent circumstances of the ethical situation. What von Balthasar, following Newman, says about the perception of the Christ-form can be gently applied to ethical perception: in order that we "see" what God wishes to reveal to us, God provides a "convergence of the indicators" (*TD2* 132). We might call discernment so directed an aesthetic "rationalism"; it is a creative and imaginative process drawing together in moral insight the various (theological, empirical, affective, experiential) elements composing the situation. This discernment takes as its object a world whose meaning is transformed in light of the divine economy and the laboring presence of the Spirit. Like the discernment proposed by narrative ethicists, it will not have "the 'firmness' of some sciences, but it can exhibit the rationality of a good story."[8] We will be able to look into the thicket of relative goods and values and perceive God's path open before us in a way that is both a seeing and a hearing, an understanding and a trust.

The Christian moral life for von Balthasar is first a matter of holiness, not heroism; of contemplation, not self-sacrifice. Some might question von Balthasar's ethics on account of the fact that it presumes (and not just commends) a level of spiritual intensity rarely found in the church. That is, the prayerfulness, divine intimacy, and spiritual wisdom typically associated with the saints are not merely ideals of the Christian life. In von Balthasar's ethics, they act as operating principles without which his ethics will not "work." While we might wish for more, von Balthasar has some sympathy for the difficulty facing the typical Christian in hearing God's call.

> All our petty excuses—we simply can't do that kind of listening; we have no interest in it; we are not suited to it on account of our particular character, talents, occupation, or the multiplicity of our activities; our religious interests tend in a different direction; repeated attempts have failed to produce any result—all these little objections, *however correct they may be in their limited way,* do not affect the great fundamental fact that God, in giving us faith, has also given us the ability to hear.[9]

He also suggests that there is a pastoral danger for the church in holding the general body of believers accountable to the same moral expectations appropriate to fully committed members.[10] But von Balthasar, faithful to his theological aesthetics, begins not with the actual state of

Christian practice, but with the fullness of the Christ-form itself and the possibility of human response illuminated by it. It is in this center of glory that our moral lives find their full meaning. And that meaning is given in nothing less than the fact that God wants us to share in divine glory by entering into the self surrendering love of the triune Godhead. The moral lives of all Christians, saints and sinners, are viewed through this focal point; the "imperfect (the ethic for sinners) derives its inner form from the perfect" (*GL5* 66). For most of us, the fullness is "distantly" eschatological, experienced in privileged moments of grace only to be lost once again in the din of the world's voices. But blessed by the Spirit's presence, those fleeting encounters can be enough to enkindle Christian hope for the day of unwavering vision.

I argued that because God uses the forms of the world to address us and does so in a way meaningful to us, von Balthasar does have room for moral reasoning and tentative moral norms. Nonetheless, von Balthasar should allow more room for reason and could do so without undermining his project. Von Balthasar rarely, if ever, reflects at any length on difficult, concrete ethical situations.[11] One can wonder if von Balthasar's reluctance to ponder particular ethical dilemmas contributes not only to the ambivalent status of moral reasoning but also to the high and possibly excessive rhetoric with which he describes Christian love. We can easily fail to notice the important role that moral reasoning plays in helping us discern the good if we avoid perplexing and "messy" ethical situations. Von Balthasar complains that as the Christian draws away from the ideal, the command to love "disintegrates into a multiplicity of individual commandments that function separately according to the situation we find ourselves in."[12] And at another point, he tells us:

> The finite limits of human existence seem to be a permanent justification for the finite limits of love—and since life as a whole cannot be explained in terms of love, love withdraws into little islands of mutual sympathy: of eros, of friendship, of patriotism, even a certain universal love based on the nature common to all men . . .[13]

Oddly, von Balthasar states this as a criticism of one view of Christian love and seems to ignore the truth of the position: Christian love will always be a "compromised" love, not sinful or un-Christlike, but qualified by the finite limits of human existence and our incapacity to respond to all the needs before us. Our responses will sometimes lead to someone getting hurt—someone we want to help, who "deserves" our help, and who in an ideal world would receive our help. As Stanley Hauerwas states, "Our moral lives are not made up of situations where asking the question of love always makes ethical sense. . . . For the question is not 'to hurt or not to hurt,' but when to hurt with justice."[14] Choices have to be made, and sometimes at least, perhaps more often than von Balthasar's thought implies, Christians make those choices primarily, even solely, on a reasoned consideration of the situation before them.

Von Balthasar's ethics, I think, has resources to respond to this challenge without undermining its systematic commitments. I indicated some of those resources above. For example, we can say that von Balthasar advances an aesthetic "rationalism"—not so much discursive reasoning about the options at hand as a creative imagining of the situation in light of the considered goods and values at stake. In addition, there is a reasoning that takes place within the Christian community, united through the ministry of the church's leadership, as together the community discerns the Spirit's guidance.[15] There is room in von Balthasar for moral reasoning, but because of the almost total lack of discussion in von Balthasar's works of concrete issues, it is difficult to know exactly how von Balthasar might understand moral reasoning or how great a role he would allow it.

Perhaps this is the complaint of one whose vision is too earthbound. Yet I think von Balthasar's thought is committed to the idea that God approaches and seeks a response even from those (many) whose eyes still see dimly. They (we!) too are invited up to the stage, and their imperfect moral reasoning will *help* them know how to play their parts. Von Balthasar's eschatology emphasizes the "already" and not so much the "not yet," and perhaps this leads him to highlight the non-discursive (mystical) element of the Christian moral knowing.

This imbalance, if indeed it is an imbalance, does not strike a serious blow against von Balthasar's ethical framework or his fundamental interpretation of the moral life. His ethics is a profound and inspiring reading of the ethical life in the context of the Christian surrender of faith. It also offers, I have tried to argue, a decidedly Catholic approach to themes traditionally associated with other Christian communities, and thus can contribute to the complex ecumenical discussion of the nature of the Christian life

The theory of the Christian life that emerges in the above lacks the ordered tidiness associated with good theories. There is no formula which draws the vertical and horizontal together into a systematic relationship and which would then allow us to progress straightforwardly from the intrahorizontal claims of our finite existence to a claim about what the personal God of Jesus Christ is calling us to do in this moment. But von Balthasar's theological aesthetics proscribes just such a move. There can be no human anticipation of God's appearing glory; nor can there be a neat closure to our grasp of it. The principle applies to all the theological sciences. If we are right to inscribe the moral life within the faith response, then the principle must likewise govern our ethical reflections. The deeper justification, then, of the indeterminacy of the moral life is not anthropological (i.e., the ethical uniqueness of the person) but theological. Christian perception does not bring the God who irradiates our moral horizon into sharp "focus." Like the rest of the theological sciences, ethics too must put aside the goal of gaining a mastery of God's glory and approach the revealed mystery humbly and on bended knee.

Notes

◆━◆◆◆━◆

Introduction

1. Von Balthasar's major work is his trilogy, composed of *The Glory of the Lord: A Theological Aesthetics,* 7 vols. (San Francisco: Ignatius Press); *Theo-Drama: Theological Dramatic Theory,* 5 vols. (San Francisco: Ignatius Press), and *Theologik,* 3 vols. (Einsiedeln: Johannes Verlag). *The Glory of the Lord,* vol. 1, *Seeing the Form,* trans. Erasmo Leiva-Merikakis (1982); vol. 2, *Studies in Theological Style: Clerical Styles,* trans. Andrew Louth, Francis McDonagh, and Brian McNeil, C.R.V (1984); vol. 3, *Studies in Theological Styles: Lay Styles,* trans. Andrew Louth et al. (1986); vol. 4, *The Realm of Metaphysics in Antiquity,* trans. Brian McNeil, C.R.V., et al. (1989); vol. 5, *The Realm of Metaphysics in the Modern Age,* trans. Oliver Davies et al. (1991); vol. 6, *Theology: The Old Covenant,* trans. Brian McNeil, C.R.V., and Erasmo Leiva-Merikakis (1991); vol. 7, *Theology: The New Covenant,* trans. Brian McNeil, C.R.V. (1989). *Theo-Drama: Theological Dramatic Theory,* vol. 1, *Prolegomena,* trans. Graham Harrison (1988); vol. 2, *The Dramatis Personae: Man in God* (1990); vol. 3, *The Dramatis Personae: The Person in Christ,* trans. Graham Harrison (1992); vol. 4, *The Action,* trans. Graham Harrison (1994); vol. 5, *The Last Act* (1998). *Theologik,* vol. 1, *Wahrheit der Welt* (1985); vol. 2, *Wahrheit Gottes* (1985); vol. 3, *Der Geist der Wahrheit* (1987). References to *Glory of the Lord, Theo-Drama,* and *Theologik* will be made according to the list of abbreviations given on p. ix above.

2. "Special care should be given to the perfecting of moral theology. Its scientific presentation should draw more fully on the teaching of holy Scripture and should throw light upon the exalted vocation of the faithful in Christ and their obligation to bring forth fruit in charity for the life of the world" (*Optatam Totius* 16, in *Vatican Council II,* ed. Austin Flannery, O.P. [Northport, N.Y.: Costello Publishing, 1988], 720).

3. The reform has led, among other things, to a restoration of the *theological* component of Aquinas's ethics; greater reflection on religious affections

161

and the ways they lead to good action; a renewal in liturgical studies and the tie between liturgy and praxis; and an appreciation for the doxological dimension of Christian life. In different ways, as I hope to show, von Balthasar's moral theory resonates with these developments in Catholic ethics.

4. Karl Barth, *Church Dogmatics*, III/2, ed. G. W. Bromiley and T. F. Torrance, trans. Harold Knight et al. (Edinburgh: T&T Clark, 1960), 77; henceforth, *CD* III/2. The command of God "secretly fills every moment of our life" (Karl Barth, *Church Dogmatics* II/2, trans. G. W. Bromiley et al. [Edinburgh: T&T Clark, 1957], 610; henceforth, *CD* II/2). There is "no human action which does not stand under God's command" (*CD* II/2, 535).

5. "Christian life is not merely satisfying universal norms which are proclaimed by the official church. Rather in these norms and beyond them it is the always unique call of God which is mediated in a concrete and loving encounter with Jesus in a mysticism of love" (Karl Rahner, *Foundations of Christian Faith*, trans. William V. Dych [New York: Crossroad, 1989], 311).

6. See Karl Rahner, "On the Question of a Formal Existential Ethics," in *Theological Investigations*, vol. 2, trans. Karl-H. Kruger (New York: Crossroad, 1990), 225.

7. Rahner, *Foundations*, 307–8 (emphasis added).

8. Karl Rahner, "The Individual in the Church," in *Nature and Grace: Dilemmas in the Modern Church* (New York: Sheed & Ward, 1964), 19–20. Also: "It would be absurd for a God-regulated, theological morality to think that God's binding will could only be directed to the human action in so far as the latter is simply a realization of the universal norm" (Rahner, "On the Question of a Formal Existential Ethics," 227).

9. Rahner, of course, spent his entire life as a Jesuit; von Balthasar was a Jesuit from 1929 until 1950.

10. Rahner, "On the Question of a Formal Existential Ethics," 232. "Are we not entitled to say that in the *Exercises* Ignatius wrote lines which have not yet been transformed into the necessary pages in treatises of moral theology?" (Rahner, "The Logic of Concrete Individual Knowledge in Ignatius Loyola," in *The Dynamic Element in the Church* [New York: Herder & Herder, 1964], 170).

11. Hans Urs von Balthasar, *The Christian State of Life*, trans. Sister Mary Frances McCarthy (San Francisco: Ignatius Press, 1983), 391.

12. Rahner, "Ein brüderlicher Geburtstagbrief," in *"Gemeinsame Arbeit in brüderlicher Liebe": Hugo und Karl Rahner—Dokumente und Würdigung hirer Weggemeinschaft*, ed. Abraham Peter Kustermann and Karl H. Neufeld (Stuttgart: Akademie der Diozese Rottenburg, 1993), 72. Cited by Philip Endean, in "Moral Theology, Karl Rahner, and the Ignatian Spiritual Exercises," *The Way Supplement* 88 (1997): 63.

In regard to von Balthasar, note also his statement that the *Spiritual Exercises* of Ignatius "appear fresher and more relevant than ever; they have functioned far too little in these four hundred years as the charismatic kernel of a theology of revelation that could offer the unsurpassed answer to all the problems of our age that terrify Christians" (Hans Urs von Balthasar, *My Work: In Retrospect*, trans. John Saward and Brian McNeil [San Francisco: Ignatius Press, 1993], 21).

13. Hans Urs von Balthasar, in *Principles of Christian Morality*, trans. Graham Harrison (San Francisco: Ignatius Press, 1986), 75–104.

Chapter 1
Aesthetics and Human Response

1. Still, the two, the radiant beauty of creation and divine glory made manifest through God's grace, cannot be neatly separated in the real order of things. "We will never be able to determine exactly the extent to which this splendour, given with creation itself, coincides objectively with what Christian theology calls 'supernatural revelation'" (*GL1* 449).

2. The importance that the approach held for von Balthasar can be seen in that he intentionally aligns his trilogy—*The Glory of the Lord, Theo-Drama*, and *Theologik*—with the transcendentals of the beautiful, the good, and the true.

3. Jan A. Aertsen, *Medieval Philosophy and the Transcendentals: The Case of Thomas Aquinas* (Leiden: E. J. Brill, 1996), 20.

4. Scott MacDonald, "The Metaphysics of Goodness and the Doctrine of the Transcendentals," in *Being and Goodness*, ed. Scott MacDonald (Ithaca, N.Y.: Cornell University Press, 1991), 33.

5. Jan Aertsen argues that beauty never was a transcendental for Thomas (*Medieval Philosophy*, 337). Until recently little was done to clarify this "forgotten transcendental." For a description of contemporary attempts, see Aertsen, *Medieval Philosophy*, 335–59.

6. Etienne Gilson, *The Elements of Christian Philosophy* (New York: North American Library, 1963), 148.

7. John F. Wippel observes that Thomas, against most of his contemporaries, refused to include God within the subject of metaphysics. God does not fall under being in general, though he can "be studied by the metaphysician, but only as the principle or cause of *ens commune*" ("Thomas Aquinas and Participation," in *Studies in Medieval Philosophy*, vol. 17, ed. John Wippel [Washington, D.C.: Catholic University of America Press, 1987], 149).

8. "Therefore it must be said that these names are said of God and creatures in an analogous sense, that is, according to proportion" (*ST* I.13.6). For this and all references to Aquinas's *Summa Theologica*, I use the translation by the Fathers of the English Dominican Province (New York: Benziger Brothers, 1948).

9. Here von Balthasar's project converges with the concerns of *nouvelle théologie*, which similarly sought to correct the often desiccated and rational-

ist theology of neoscholasticism by a reintroduction of themes such as divine splendor and human desire.

10. Because the beautiful form "always expresses more in the most perfect and determined expression than what goes into the thing formed itself," it can as such be "available as a form of revelation" (*GL4* 34).

11. There are no "purely spiritual" revelations (*GL6* 34). In revelation God uses the thickness of the world to "a new depth" (*GL1* 29). The "word of God must be written into the word of Being" (*GL5* 631).

12. An excellent overview of Erich Przywara's thought and its influence on von Balthasar can be found in Edward T. Oakes, *Pattern of Redemption: The Theology of Hans Urs von Balthasar* (New York: Continuum, 1994), 15–44.

13. Erich Przywara, *Analogia entis Analogia entis: Metaphysik* (Munich: Josef Kosel & Friedrich Pustet, 1932), 152; cited by von Balthasar in *The Theology of Karl Barth: Exposition and Interpretation*, trans. Edward T. Oakes (San Francisco: Ignatius Press, 1992), 255.

14. Charles Taylor, for example, has called for fresh language and images that liberate our lived experience from the ways in which it has been "occluded" by the "regnant mechanistic construal," and that will restore "our vision of things" in order that the deep goods that inspire moral action will once again be made visible (Charles Taylor, *Sources of the Self: The Making of the Modern Identity* [Cambridge, Mass.: Harvard University Press, 1989], 460, 490, 513–21). On the theological side, H. Richard Niebuhr has recommended the use of narrative forms to illuminate our world and highlight the personal and historical dimensions of human agency (*The Responsible Self: An Essay in Christian Moral Philosophy* [New York: Harper & Row, 1963]). Contemporary ethicists such as Stanley Hauerwas, Charles Curran, William Spohn, and Philip Keane have in different ways used biblical imagery to interpret moral situations. See, e.g., Stanley Hauerwas, *The Peaceable Kingdom: A Primer in Christian Ethics* (Notre Dame, Ind.: University of Notre Dame Press, 1983); Charles Curran, "The Stance of Moral Theology" in *Directions in Fundamental Moral Theology* (Notre Dame, Ind.: University of Notre Dame Press, 1985); William Spohn, *Go and Do Likewise: Jesus and Ethics* (New York: Continuum, 1999); and Philip Keane, *Christian Ethics and Imagination: A Theological Inquiry* (New York: Paulist, 1984).

15. Iris Murdoch, "Vision and Choice in Morality," in *Existentialists and Mystics: Writings on Philosophy and Literature*, ed. Peter Conradi (New York: Penguin Press, 1998).

16. In this chapter we will focus primarily on von Balthasar's theory of the beautiful form as it is developed in the seven volumes of *The Glory of the Lord*.

17. Beauty is, von Balthasar tells us, "nothing other than the immediate emergence of the groundlessness of the ground" from all that exists, the transparency "of the mystery-filled background of Being" (*TL1* 253–54). See also: "The finite appearance is as such the walking-into-the-light of a certain infinity. . . . [The perceiver] truly grasps something, which will not escape him.

More importantly however remains perhaps the other teaching: that the truth of being will always be infinitely richer and larger than he is able to grasp" (*TL1* 90).

18. "A light shines through the form itself and the same light refers to the reality that shines in it and at the same time spreads it. In this duality of recumbent-in-itself luminous form and of the 'expelling-outward' of the form in a (real) nature illuminating itself in the form lies the inner polarity of the transcendental characteristic of being, beauty" (Hans Urs von Balthasar, *Epilog* [Einsiedeln: Johannes Verlag, 1987], 46).

19. Oakes, *Pattern of Redemption*, 148.

20. It is not excessive to say that for von Balthasar aesthetics makes metaphysics a viable human enterprise. Concrete particularity and metaphysical pointing co-appear in the beautiful form. Here he follows contemporary phenomenologists more than his scholastic, metaphysical language would suggest.

21. See Martin Heidegger, "On the Essence of Truth," trans. John Sallis, in *Martin Heidegger: Basic Writings*, ed. David Farrell Krell (New York: Harper & Row, 1977), 113–41. In one examination of Heidegger (*GL5* 430–50), von Balthasar lifts out images and themes from Heidegger's corpus that show just how multiple are the commonalities between himself and Heidegger—most importantly, Heidegger's ideas of the graciousness and glory of Being and the response of obedience to the voice of Being. However, there are also significant differences, principally over the question of Christianity's culpability in the modern era's loss of glory and the prognosis for a recovery of glory. See Cyril O'Regan, "Von Balthasar's Valorization and Critique of Heidegger's Genealogy of Modernity," in *Christian Spirituality and the Culture of Modernity: The Thought of Louis Dupré*, ed. George P. Schner, S.J., and Peter Casarrella (Grand Rapids: Eerdmans, 1998), 123–58.

22. Von Balthasar uses the image of a child wakening into consciousness through the presence of another to indicate that wonder before the world, and not self-awareness, is the original experience of human subjectivity. In the primal moment in which the child is "introduced" to the world by the inviting love of parents and others, the world discloses itself to the child as good and beautiful (*GL5* 616–17).

23. He argues this in his volume on the Old Testament. A similar argument appears in discussion of the New Testament. "Every living being, and above all the free person, achieves for itself a sphere of power in its own environment, so that in this it may exercise control, may make itself known and appear; this powerfulness or importance (*gravitas*) merges in the physical-moral sphere into esteem, acknowledgment and praise, and, in a world of beings that are both intellectual and sensual, this radiance is always both intellectual and perceptible to the senses" (*GL7* 241).

24. "If we see the seed develop itself, as it breaks through its hard bode, leaf after leaf, spread out and finally the unexpected wonder of flower arises,

... when ultimately this entire form, closed in itself, inclines to its end and precisely there, where we suspect the end, surprises us with the gift of fruit ... then no one will say, he has grasped nothing of the mystery of life" (*TL1* 88).

25. Von Balthasar explores this expressivist theme in his monograph on Bonaventure; see *GL2* 260–362.

26. The disengaged self is "capable of objectivizing not only the surrounding world but also his own emotions and inclinations, fears and compulsions, and [achieves] thereby a kind of distance and self-possession which allows him to act 'rationally'" (Taylor, *Sources,* 21).

Heidegger shares a similar concern, reflected in his distinction between the object as "present-at-hand" and "ready-at-hand." The former looks at the now-disengaged, self-standing object as "some naked thing," over which we throw some "signification." The latter is the more primordial way of knowing in which objects reveal themselves in their relatedness to ourselves and the world (Heidegger, *Being and Time,* trans. John Macquarrie and Edward Robinson [New York: Harper & Row, 1962], 188–90).

27. Heidegger, "Essence of Truth," 128. Also: "To let be—that is, to let beings be as the beings which they are—means to engage oneself with the open region and its openness into which every being comes to stand, bringing that openness, as it were, along with itself" (ibid., 127).

28. This balance in the subject/object relation continues in the realm of the ethical. The object makes its claim on the subject; human action unfolds in a responsiveness to and responsibility for the appearing form.

29. Hans Urs von Balthasar, *A Theological Anthropology* (New York: Sheed & Ward, 1967), 101.

30. *GL5* 363. Von Balthasar here is referring to Goethe's thought.

31. "For we can be sure of one thing: we can never again recapture the living totality of form once it has been dissected and sawed in pieces, no matter how informative the conclusions which this anatomy may bring to light" (*GL1* 31). "Whoever dissects the historical aspect of revelation by means of the 'historical-critical' method, in order to be left with the content that fills revelation as sole interior kernel, will in turn have no eyes to perceive the beauty and the evidence peculiar to this form" (*GL1* 209). As an example of the kind of nonreductive, aesthetic holism with which von Balthasar approaches the scriptural text, see his section on Jesus' recapitulation of Old Testament themes (*GL7* 31–76, esp. 54–76).

32. We regain self "only on account of having been communicated" (*GL1* 21). The spirit "in order to achieve itself [is] dependent on and compelled to the other" (*TL1* 79).

33. Also: "just as the Divine Persons are *themselves* only insofar as they go out to the Others (who are always Other), the created essences too are *themselves* only insofar as they go beyond themselves . . . [and] surrender themselves for their neighbor" (*TD5* 76).

34. A number of scholars have argued that receptivity can be an integral part of human freedom. See Margaret A. Farley, "Fragments of an Ethic of Commitment in Thomas Aquinas," *Journal of Religion* 2 (1978); W. Norris Clarke, S.J., *Person and Being* (Milwaukee: Marquette University Press, 1993). A discussion of the latter can be found in *Communio* 21 (spring 1994): 151–90.

35. The relationality that arises in this engagement, von Balthasar tells us, is the event of the good and is what confers on reality its worthiness. The encounter of communication "is understood as the original and elementary encounter of the good, because love confers its worth on Being" (*TL1* 252). Given that von Balthasar holds inwardness and relationality to be codeterminants of human subjectivity, it is not surprising that he suggests that the goodness of another—its worthiness of being striven for—manifests itself in the context of a relationship.

36. The truth of the Trinity revealed in Christ, that "'the Other' exists is *absolutely good*," by analogy "also applies to creation" (*TD5* 81).

37. Von Balthasar, *Epilog*, 51.

38. "For the moment the essential thing is to realize that, without aesthetic knowledge, neither theoretical nor practical reason can attain to their total completion. If the *verum* lacks that *splendor* which for Thomas is the distinctive mark of the beautiful, then the knowledge of truth remains both pragmatic and formalistic. The only concern of such knowledge will then merely be the verification of correct facts and law, whether the latter are laws of being or laws of thought, categories, and ideas. But if the *bonum* lacks the *voluptas* which for Augustine is the mark of its beauty, then the relationship to the good remains both utilitarian and hedonistic: in this case the good will involve merely the satisfaction of a need by means of some value or object, whether it is founded objectively on the thing itself giving satisfaction or subjectively on the person seeking it. Only the apprehension of an expressive form in the thing can give it that depth-dimension between its ground and its manifestation which, as the real *locus* of beauty, now also opens up allowing . . . him to achieve the spiritual distance that makes a beauty rich in form desirable in its being-in-itself (and not only its being-for-me), and only thus worth striving after" (*GL1* 152).

39. In his desire to unite without merging the subject and object, von Balthasar betrays a debt to Goethe. "The decisive characteristic of [Goethe's] world view that absolutely separates him from Kant is the fact that he seeks for the unity of the subject and objective principle, of nature and the spirit, *within the appearance itself*" (Georg Simmel, *Kant und Goethe: Zur Geschichte der modernen Weltanschauung* [Leipzig: Kurt Wolff Verlag], 20–21; cited in Oakes, *Pattern of Redemption*, 94). O'Regan argues that von Balthasar prefers Goethe over other interlocutors because he "never confounds Greek with Christian sensibilities." The lines between them are kept clearer and thus the danger of subverting Christian thought through alien discourse is less

(O'Regan, "Von Balthasar's Valorization and Critique of Heidegger's Genealogy of Modernity," 142).

40. This tie between gift and response lies at the foundation of von Balthasar's ethics and distinguishes his thought from that of Rahner, where the emphasis lies less on the character of *responsiveness* than on the transcendental *self*-realization of the subject. Still, the dimension of responsiveness is not at all absent from Rahner. See Josef Römelt, *Personales Gottesverständnis in Heutiger Moraltheologie: Auf dem Hintergrund der Theologien von K. Rahner und H. U. von Balthasar* (Innsbruck: Tyrolia-Verlag, 1988), 107–11.

41. Enda McDonagh, *Gift and Call: Towards a Christian Theology of Morality* (Dublin: Gill & Macmillan, 1975), 75, 86.

42. This epiphanic dimension is not absent from Kant. For example, in his *Critique of Practical Reason*, he speaks of admiration and awe before the "starry heavens above" and "the moral law within" (trans. Lewis White Beck [New York: Macmillan, 1956], 166). And in his *Religion Within the Limits of Reason*, he states that the "majesty of the moral law (like that on Sinai) instills awe" (trans. Theodore M. Greene and Hoyt H. Hudson [San Francisco: Harper & Row, 1960], 19n; cited in *GL5* 500). But the epiphanic dimension does little or no motivational, epistemological, or explanatory work for Kant. In what O'Regan calls a "reading conspicuous in its generosity," von Balthasar accents these moments of epiphanic sightings and allows them to situate Kant's overall work in the three *Critiques* (O'Regan, "Von Balthasar's Valorization and Critique of Heidegger's Genealogy of Modernity," 138).

43. Rowan Williams, "Balthasar and Rahner," in *The Analogy of Beauty*, ed. John Riches (Edinburgh: T&T Clark, 1986), 13–14.

44. By "the Lukan δεῖ," I am referring to the Greek term appearing frequently in Luke's Gospel, meaning "it is necessary" (or "fitting," "appropriate"). See, for example, Luke 9:22: "It is necessary [δεῖ] for the Son of Man to suffer many things." Anselm argued that considering the entire salvific narrative will help us see that it makes "sense," that is, that it is fitting (or that it evidences *rectitude*) that the Son should be born of a virgin, that the Son should die for us, and so on.

45. "The power of aesthetic expression is never an overwhelming power" (*TD2* 29).

46. No one "can really behold who has not also already been enraptured, and no one can be enraptured who has not already perceived" (*GL1* "Foreword").

47. It is "the creative power of God himself" to "read the world of forms" (*GL1* 424). "This logic of love will not be grasped by any observer who stands outside, any more than an act between husband and wife will be experienced by anyone other than the two who accomplish it" (*GL7* 113).

48. Cf. Margaret Farley: "But if love is a receiving of the beloved, it is not a purely passive receiving. For the reception which love is is an active recep-

tion, one which entails a willing of the beloved, a being with and a being for the beloved. There is no created love which is not awakened by receiving the beloved; but there is no receiving of the beloved as beloved which is not the active receiving which is loving. Receptivity and activity are not here two separable realities; they are two aspects of one and the same love; they coalesce into the reality which is the loving" ("Fragments of an Ethic of Commitment in Thomas Aquinas," 145). Also, Edward Vacek speaks of an "active readiness," a state of openness to the object of one's attention. As the process of love unfolds, he tells us, we first become aware of and directed toward the goodness and value in the object and then are realigned to that appearing goodness. See Edward Collins Vacek, S.J., *Love, Human and Divine: The Heart of Christian Ethics* (Washington, D.C.: Georgetown University Press, 1994), chapter 2. See also Aquinas, *ST* I-II.23.4, 26.1.

49. ". . . whoever does not summon up indifference and readiness, to receive and touch the object in such a manner as it wishes to give and show itself, lacks the most elemental presumptions of knowledge" (*TL1* 292).

50. "At the same time, the intellectual creature (upon whom a ray of the eternal glory rests: Ps 8.6) bears in itself something of this structure of absolute being: its free self-expression and self-giving is able to reveal itself and bestow itself, but always in such a manner that the coastlines of what is shown and expressed remains untouched—the inalienability of freedom, and thereby the inexhaustibility of the personal mystery" (*GL7* 266).

51. "To put this in religious language: the more spiritual and independent a being is, the more it is aware in itself of God and the more clearly does it point to God" (*GL4* 31).

52. Von Balthasar, "Forgetfulness of God and Christians," in *Creator Spirit*, vol. 3 of *Explorations in Theology*, trans. Brian McNeil, C.R.V. (San Francisco: Ignatius Press, 1993), 332.

53. In our "innermost constitution," we have been "designed for dialogue" with those to whom we can say "Thou" (Hans Urs von Balthasar, *Prayer*, trans. Graham Harrison [San Francisco: Ignatius Press, 1986], 22).

54. "Here we have to recall that God, the sea and abyss of Being, is not a being among others, hence not an 'object' that might be detached from a surrounding world, and especially not from the knowing subject" (Hans Urs von Balthasar, *The God Question and Modern Man* [New York: Seabury Press, 1967], 147). God "since he is the Absolute, is also the Non-other, more interior to me than I am to myself" (*TD2* 421).

55. Cf. von Balthasar: This openness of creation "contains . . . an indication of the 'wholly other' fulfillment, not far off but already present. . . . This openness really belongs to the world as such and must not be considered supernaturalized; it is the dwelling place of the 'gods' . . ." ("Revelation and the Beautiful," in *The Word Made Flesh*, vol. 1 of *Explorations in Theology* [San Francisco: Ignatius Press, 1989], 111–12). The openness of the finite form

helps von Balthasar maneuver between Barth and liberal Christianity. See
Jeffrey Ames Kay, *Theological Aesthetics: The Role of Aesthetics in the Theological Method of Hans Urs von Balthasar* (Frankfurt: Peter Lang, 1975), v.

56. Only a Christian—and, therefore, trinitarian—context can give rise to
the unity-in-difference of the dialogical encounter, where discrete interpersonal relationships are not ultimate (*GL7* 447), but rather occur within "the
global reality of the Lord" (*GL7* 458).

Chapter 2
The Trinitarian Horizon of Human Action

1. "Saying No to a work of art has relatively no consequences. But saying
No to God's definitive and meaning-full Word can turn into a judgment of
the individual who freely ignores it. Thus, again, the transition from aesthetics to dramatic theory is analogical" (*TD2* 29).

2. Karl Rahner, *The Trinity* (New York: Herder & Herder, 1970), 22. Still,
many theologians want to qualify the axiom in some way. Catherine Mowry
Lacugna surveys the different takes on the axiom in her *God For Us: The Trinity and Christian Life* (San Francisco: Harper, 1973), 209–32. Karl Barth has
strong reservations about the axiom, doubting whether it does justice to
God's freedom (*Church Dogmatics*, I/1, trans. G. T. Thomson [Edinburgh:
T&T Clark, 1960], 172; henceforth, *CD* I/1).

3. Von Balthasar criticizes Rahner for his hesitation on this point; see *TD3*
526.

4. "In God, radical reciprocal relationships of this kind can only be personal. That they really are such, however, we can only read from Jesus' attitude to the Father in the Spirit and from his attitude to the Spirit, whom
he—together with the Father—wishes to send from the Father" (*TD3* 511).
"As we penetrate the consciousness of Jesus—as it expresses itself in his words
and deeds, in his unique claim and his humble submission—we encounter the
radiance of the mystery of his own divinity and of God's self-subsistent tri-
personality" (*TD3* 515).

5. Walter Kasper criticizes Rahner's approach for just such a loss. In arguing that the term "person" can lead to heterodoxy and thus should be
avoided, Rahner and Barth assume a contemporary view of the term. But in
rejecting the contemporary usage of the term, they implicitly separate from
their trinitarian portrayal all the orthodox implications traditionally associated
with the term. We are left instead with terms such as "mode of being" or "distinct manner of subsisting," which do not fully convey the tradition's understanding of the hypostasis (Walter Kasper, *The God of Jesus Christ*, trans.
Matthew J. O'Connell [New York: Crossroad, 1992], 288).

6. Kasper, *God of Jesus Christ*, 289. Cf. von Balthasar: ". . . even if the three
Divine Persons are not also three centres of activity, but three manners of participating in the one, intellectual-personal center of activity of the absolute

Spirit, this shared possession is also a factor in the constitution of the Divine Person. And precisely the sovereignty of free disposing [speaking of the activity of the Spirit], indeed, of a differentiated act of choice and preference (e.g., in the distribution of the various charisms through one and the same Spirit, 1 Cor 12:4–11), allows the share in the possession of the divine center of activity to appear clearly" ("The Holy Spirit as Love," in *Creator Spirit*, vol. 3 of *Explorations in Theology*, trans. Brian McNeil, C.R.V. [San Francisco: Ignatius Press, 1993], 128–29 n. 11).

7. And because the relationship is interpersonal, it is also dramatic. "The dramatic dimension that is part of the definition of the person of Jesus does not belong exclusively to the worldly side of his being: its ultimate presuppositions lie in the divine life itself" (*TD3* 159).

8. Karl Rahner, "Remarks on the Dogmatic Treatise 'De Trinitate,'" trans. Kevin Smyth, in *Theological Investigations* (London: Darton, Longman & Todd, 1966), 81.

9. However, von Balthasar does employ the spatial and temporal language of distance, separation, and "super-time" as metaphors to underscore the kind of space that is within the Trinity for real interchange and dialogue. "Something like infinite 'duration' and infinite 'space' must be attributed to the acts of reciprocal love so that the life of the *communio*, of fellowship, can develop" (*TD2* 257). "God's 'abiding forever' must not be seen as a 'non-time' but as a super-time that is unique to him" (*TD5* 30).

10. The trinitarian theology of Richard of St. Victor as appropriated by Herbert Mühlen has a significant influence on von Balthasar. Developing the dialogical idea of a primordial word "I" which arises only in being addressed by a primordial word "Thou," Mühlen points to a primordial word "We" which is "not merely the sum of the 'I' and the 'Thou,'" but rather "expresses a new and higher level of being." See von Balthasar, "The Holy Spirit as Love," 126–28. Also: "Love is that which reconciles unity and multiplicity; it is the uniting unity in the threeness" (Kasper, *God of Jesus Christ*, 296). See also John R. Sachs, "Deus Semper Major—Ad Majorem Dei Gloriam: The Pneumatology and Spirituality of Hans Urs von Balthasar," *Gregorianum* 74, no. 4 (1993): 644 n. 44; John O'Donnell, "The Trinity as Divine Community: A Critical Reflection Upon Recent Theological Developments," *Gregorianum* 68, no. 1 (1998): 30–34; and William J. Hill, *The Three-Personed God* (Washington, D.C.: Catholic University of America Press, 1982), 232–36.

11. Thomas takes up the question in the context of his discussion of the equality of the divine persons. Against the argument that the Father is greater than the Son because of the testimony of Scripture (e.g., 1 Cor. 15:28: ". . . then the Son himself will be subjected to the One who subjected everything to him"), Thomas answers that these "words are to be understood of Christ's human nature, wherein He is less than the Father, and subject to Him; but in His divine nature He is equal to the Father" (*ST* I.42.4ad1). A similar reserve appears in Thomas's discussion of God the Father commanding the Son.

Thomas explains this command first as the Father giving the Son knowledge and will for action in his eternal begetting of the Son. In doing so Thomas effectively discards any genuinely analogous sense of "command" in the Father/Son relationship. His inclination to this direction is indicated by his closing statement on the issue: "Or, *better still*, this [the Father commanding the Son] may be referred to Christ in His human nature" (*ST* I.42.6.*ad* 2; emphasis mine).

12. Elizabeth A. Johnson, *She Who Is: The Mystery of God in Feminist Theological Discourse* (New York: Crossroad, 1992), 4.

13. "Father, Son, and Spirit are coequal because they *are* the same thing, namely, God. No person is prior to another person, no person is the reason for another's existence, and each person is equally interdependent on every other person" (Lacugna, *God For Us*, 273).

14. "'Father, if you are willing, take this cup away from me; still, not my will but yours be done'" (Luke 22:42). "My food is to do the will of him who sent me" (John 4:34). "I cannot do anything on my own; I judge as I hear, and my judgment is just, because I do not seek my own will but the will of the one who sent me" (John 5:30). ". . . because I came down from heaven not to do my own will but the will of the one who sent me" (John 6:38). Jesus does "everything the Father has commanded" (John 14:31). ". . . the Lord Jesus Christ, who gave himself for our sins that he might rescue us from the present evil age in accord with the will of our God and Father . . ." (Gal. 1:4).

15. Kasper, *God of Jesus Christ*, 290. Rahner similarly argues that we must avoid excluding too quickly from our understanding of the Son his earthly "obedience to the Father, his adoration, his submission to the Father's unfathomable will" (Rahner, *Trinity*, 62).

16. "When someone loves us, our proper response is not to obey them but to love them in return" (Edward Collins Vacek, "Divine-Command, Natural-Law, and Mutual-Love Ethics," *Theological Studies* 57, no. 4 [December 1996]: 646).

17. This is the approach that Vacek takes. "As friends we do not obey God, but we do want God's will to be fulfilled" ("Divine-Command, Natural-Law, and Mutual-Love Ethics," 646).

18. ". . . absolute obedience can become the economic form of the Son's absolute response to the Father" (*TD3* 530).

19. Christ's "mode of being here on earth will simply be the manifestation in the created sphere . . . of this heavenly form of existence: existence as receiving, as openness to the will of the Father, as subsistent fulfillment of that will in a continuous mission" (Hans Urs von Balthasar, *A Theology of History* [San Francisco: Ignatius Press, 1994], 31).

20. Thus, using von Balthasar's problematic gender images, there is something "feminine about the Father" since "in the action of begetting and breathing forth he allows himself to be determined by the Persons who thus

proceed from him" (*TD5* 91). See Gerard F. O'Hanlon, *The Immutability of God in the Theology of Hans Urs von Balthasar* (Cambridge: Cambridge University Press, 1990), 121–25.

21. Buried in a footnote is a rather astounding assertion that von Balthasar cites from the writings of Adrienne von Speyr: "Perhaps the Father would have had other suggestions, other ideas pertaining to redemption that would not have made the abandonment of the Cross necessary. But he does not express them; he leaves redemption up to the Son" (*TD5* 89 n. 19).

22. The "Son's *missio* is the economic form of his eternal *processio* from the Father" (*TD3* 201, citing Thomas Aquinas). Also: "The world can only be created within the Son's 'generation'; the world belongs to him and has him as its goal. . . . Accordingly, in whatever way the Son is sent into the world (*processio* here is seen to be *missio*, up to and including the Cross), it is an integral part of his 'co-original' thanksgiving for the world" (*TD4* 326).

23. Hans Urs von Balthasar, "Christian Universalism," in *The Word Made Flesh*, vol. 1 of *Explorations in Theology* (San Francisco: Ignatius Press, 1989), 246. Von Balthasar states that we are "indebted" to Origen and Barth for their exposition of this point.

24. "A statue can be placed anywhere; a symphony can be performed in any concert-hall. . . . The form of Jesus, however, cannot be detached from the place in space and time in which it stands" (*GL1* 198).

25. I borrow the term from the recent work of Aidan Nichols, O.P., *No Bloodless Myth: A Guide Through Balthasar's Dramatics* (Washington, D.C.: Catholic University of America Press, 2000).

26. "The suffering of Jesus Christ is more than a mere symbol by which one can discern God's reconciling will that had always been there but was only just now [in this symbol] clearly emerging into view; rather, it is the act of reconciliation itself" (Hans Urs von Balthasar, "On Vicarious Representation," in *Spirit and Institution*, vol. 4 of *Explorations in Theology*, trans. Edward T. Oakes, S.J. [San Francisco: Ignatius Press, 1995], 415).

27. "God himself is forsaken by God because of man's godlessness. Here the nub of the theo-drama must lie: God himself brings it to this point so delicately that, on the one hand, nothing godless is imported into God and, on the other hand, man's freedom is not overridden by a drama within the Godhead that seems to have nothing to do with him" (*TD2* 194).

28. Also: " . . . we are actually brought to participate, by grace, in the begetting of the Son from the Father . . ." (von Balthasar, *Prayer*, trans. Graham Harrison [San Francisco: Ignatius Press, 1986], 70). And: "In an infrangible unity with [Christ], we enter the place reserved for him in the heavens" (*TD5* 519, citing Adrienne von Speyr, *The Letter to the Ephesians* [San Francisco: Ignatius Press, 1996], 84).

29. See "Admirabile Commercium," *TD3* 237–45.

30. Athanasius, *C. Arian.* 3.34; cited by von Balthasar, *TD3* 238.

31. Von Balthasar, *A Theology of History*, 16–17.

32. For an excellent introduction to von Balthasar's soteriology, see John O'Donnell, S.J., *Hans Urs von Balthasar* (Collegeville, Minn.: Liturgical Press, 1992), 108–13.

33. Some typical examples: "there is no condemnation for those in Christ Jesus" (Rom. 8:1); "if anyone is in Christ he is a new creation" (2 Cor. 5:17); "you are all children of God in Christ Jesus" (Gal. 3:26).

34. See *TD3* 245–50. Von Balthasar's deployment of the theme is more extensive and developed than indicated in this short section.

35. Joseph A. Fitzmyer, "Pauline Theology," in *The New Jerome Biblical Commentary*, ed. Raymond E. Brown, Joseph A. Fitzmyer, and Roland E. Murphy (Englewood Cliffs, N.J.: Prentice Hall, 1990), 1409, §82.121.

36. Ernest Best notes that A. Deissmann "was the first to draw attention to the significance of the phrase." He cites Deissmann as stating that the formula is "the characteristic expression of his Christianity" and expresses "the most intimate possible fellowship of the Christian with the living spiritual Christ" (Ernest Best, *One Body in Christ: A Study in the Relationship of the Church to Christ in the Epistles of the Apostle Paul* [London: S.P.C.K., 1955], 8). He quotes from Deissmann's *Paul: A Study in Social and Religious History*, 142. Von Balthasar is familiar with the work (*TD3* 246 n. 56).

37. Fitzmyer, "Pauline Theology," 1409, §82.121.

38. Christ is the image of God (2 Cor. 4:4) and those who follow him "are being transformed into the same image" (2 Cor. 3:18).

39. Morna D. Hooker, "Interchange in Christ and Ethics," *Journal for the Study of the New Testament* 25 (1985): 10.

40. Some biblical scholars argue that Paul's writings do not support this idea of a "co-laboring" Christian. Ernest Best, for example, rejects the idea, both because of what he sees as a lack of biblical evidence and because of a concern to keep separate the unique and inimitable work of Christ and that of the church. See Morna D. Hooker, "A Partner in the Gospel: Paul's Understanding of His Ministry," in *Theology and Ethics in Paul and His Interpreters: Essays in Honor of Victor Paul Furnish*, ed. Eugene H. Lovering, Jr., and Jerry L. Sumney (Nashville: Abingdon Press, 1996), 87 n. 7. Morna Hooker, however, presents a persuasive counterargument. Her argument centers on the question of how to interpret Paul's description of himself as a "participant [συγκοινωνός] in the Gospel" (1 Cor. 9:23), specifically whether Paul is referring to his participating in the *benefits* (passively received) or in *work* (actively undertaken) of the Gospel. The former might seem to suggest that Paul is proudly declaring his egoistic motivation. The context, Hooker argues, indicates the latter. Paul does his work for the Gospel "so that others may share in its benefits" with him (thus "syn-koinōnos"). His work is not just to convey the Gospel message but to make it real through his ministry in the lives of others (Hooker, "Partner in the Gospel," 85).

41. Von Balthasar cites approvingly H. D. Betz: the imitator of Christ for

Paul is one who "lives *en Christōi*; he regards himself as involved with the life and work, not of the Jesus *of that time*, but of the Christ who is at work *here and now*, who is none other than the crucified Jesus" (*TD3* 127, citing Betz, *Nachfolge und Nachahmung Jesu Christi im Neuen Testament* [Tübingen: Mohr, 1967], 144; emphasis in original).

42. Hooker, "Partner in the Gospel," 100.

43. Kilian McDonnell complains that the Spirit is treated as an "extra, an addendum, a 'false' window to give symmetry and balance to theological design" ("The Determinative Doctrine of the Holy Spirit," *Theology Today* 39 [1982]: 142). Kasper observes that the Holy Spirit does not play an important role in our theological consciousness (*God of Jesus Christ*, 198). Lacugna similarly mourns that our theologies are "christomonistic" (*God For Us*, 235 n. 15).

44. Hans Urs von Balthasar, "Office in the Church," in *Spouse of the Word*, vol. 2 of *Explorations in Theology* (San Francisco: Ignatius Press, 1991), 107. Rahner also has some reserve in regard to the limitations placed on "appropriation," though his reservation does not so much concern our new relationship with God as how God acts in the world. He asks, "[M]ight it not derive from the peculiar nature of the second person (and respectively from that of the third person) that, when the one God communicates himself to the world, the peculiarity of this self-communication, insofar as it is determined by the peculiarity of the second person, consists in becoming a 'hypostatic union,' whereas such would not be the case if this self-communication were determined by the peculiarity of the third person?" (*Trinity*, 27).

45. Of course, this is the classic challenge for pneumatology, that is, how to speak of the Spirit's hypostatic density *and* how to do so vis-à-vis the hypostases of the Father and the Son.

46. Von Balthasar, "Holy Spirit as Love," 125. This "anonymous Spirit shows all the traits of the highest personal freedom and freedom of movement . . . he is the unfathomable, incomprehensible freedom of the love of God brought near to us" (ibid., 125–26).

47. "Wherever something new arises, whenever life is awakened and reality reaches ecstatically beyond itself, in all seeking and striving, in every ferment and birth, and even more in the beauty of creation, something of the activity and being of God's Spirit is manifested" (Kasper, *God of Jesus Christ*, 227).

48. The freedom of the Spirit "to blow where he wills" extends beyond the bounds of the visible church. The Spirit can thus "spread God's graces and secret revelations even outside the visible Church. The Church of the earliest period certainly knew all this, and it is humiliating for us to have to learn it anew after so many centuries of at least partial forgetting" (von Balthasar, "Council of the Holy Spirit," in *Creator Spirit*, 262–63).

49. Von Balthasar, *A Theological Anthropology* (New York: Sheed & Ward, 1967), 71.

50. The use of this aesthetic form to interpret and see the Christ-event does

not impose an arbitrary framework (a human a priori) on revelation. The principles of our theological aesthetics remain: the theological event, not human categories, must determine the form of revelation. However, once one recognizes that the divine has appeared in earthly form, it becomes appropriate to explore the nature of that form. And it is, von Balthasar argues, dramatic and tragic.

51. We will return to this relationship between the particular and absolute in chapter 3.

52. Thus in the suffering and death of Antigone, accompanied by the witness of the chorus and the subsequent destruction that befalls Creon, shine not only her valor but the light and favor of the gods.

53. Dramatic action "is ultimately only meaningful when seen against the background of a given, absolute meaning" (*TD1* 74).

54. Christianity, von Balthasar adds, follows the "trail that was lost ever since the demise of ancient tragedy," bringing "to light the significance and change of meaning of all intramundane tragedy" (*TD2* 49).

55. And thus, "all the dimensions and tensions of life remain present instead of being sublimated in the abstractions of a 'systematic' theology" (Rowan Williams, "Balthasar and Rahner," in *The Analogy of Beauty*, ed. John Riches [Edinburgh: T&T Clark, 1986], 226).

56. "[God] has already taken the drama of existence which plays on the world stage and inserted it into his quite different 'play' which, nonetheless, he wishes to play on our stage" (*TD1* 20).

57. He discusses the two triads at length in *TD1* 259–324, and then summarizes them in *TD3* 532–35.

58. As John McDade suggests, invoking a distinction of Northrop Frye, a "*sequential reading*" of the trinitarian narratives, "in which the flow of the narrative is followed from the beginning to end" without attending to the whole structure, must be complemented by a "*non-sequential*" reading, where the "coherent and single meaning" is permitted to emerge ("The Trinity and the Paschal Mystery," *Heythrop Journal* 29 [1988]: 181).

59. Rahner, *Trinity*, 109.

60. We need the doctrine of the Trinity to bring together the two truths: that God, to be God, cannot become entangled in worldly affairs, and that God, to be the approachable God of the covenant, *must* be involved in human affairs; see *TD3* 529–30.

61. The image of God "authoring" our play and assigning each person's christological role might seem to threaten human freedom. We will take up this concern in chapter 3.

62. "Surely the main function of all tragic episodes is to satisfy in certain ways our love both of beauty and of truth, of truth to life and about it" (F. L. Lucas, *Tragedy: Serious Drama in Relation to Aristotle's Poetics* [New York: Macmillan, 1958], 72).

63. Martha C. Nussbaum, *Love's Knowledge: Essays on Philosophy and Literature* (Oxford: Oxford University Press, 1990), 171.

64. "In his surrender to death, [Jesus] brings the deaths of all sinners with him; he envelops them in his uniquely definitive death and gives them a changed value, thereby changing the value of all life destined for a similar death" (*TD5* 327).

65. "Now, as before, the horizon within which the play is acted out is by no means an uninvolved background that relativizes the entire foreground play to the level of shadowy futility . . . [N]ow, with a dramatic dimension that bursts forth from the Absolute itself, [the horizon] comes to meet the human play and imparts to it an ultimate destination, acting alongside man, from within. The uniqueness of the Christian conception of the horizon must be acknowledged: in it, and in it alone, meaning breaks forth (in a hidden manner, discerned by faith, in and through the stumbling block of Christ's Cross) from the depth of the horizon and informs the whole foreground action of the world play" (*TD1* 319–20).

66. For von Balthasar this divine intention to open up an "acting area" of the human person within the trinitarian life was present from the beginning (*TD3* 43). See also "The Dramatic Aspect of Inclusion in Christ" and "The Acting Area," in *TD3* 33–56.

67. There are clear parallels here with narrative theology and ethics. See, for example, "[O]ur story is inadequate as well: The story of each and all is itself hungry for a greater story that overcomes our persistent self-deceit, redeems our common life, and provides a way for us to be a people among all earth's peoples without subtracting from the significance of others' peoplehood, their own stories, their lives" (James W. McClendon, *Ethics: Systematic Theology* [Nashville: Abingdon Press, 1986], 356). But von Balthasar's thought also departs in significant ways from most narrative ethicists, as I will attempt to show in chapter 5.

68. For a recent proposal of divine command ethics, see Robert M. Adams, "A Modified Divine Command Theory of Ethical Wrongness," in *The Virtue of Faith and Other Essays in Philosophical Theology* (New York: Oxford University Press, 1987). Two works by Philip L. Quinn are helpful: *Divine Command Theories and Moral Requirements* (Oxford: Clarendon Press, 1978), and "The Recent Revival of Divine Command Ethics," *Philosophical and Phenomenological Research*, vol. 1, Supplement (1990). Finally, see Richard J. Mouw, *The God Who Commands* (Notre Dame, Ind.: University of Notre Dame Press, 1990).

69. Barth, *CD* III/2 157; von Balthasar, *Theological Anthropology*, 232–33.

70. Barth, *Church Dogmatics* III/4, trans. A. T. Mackay et al. (Edinburgh: T&T Clark, 1961), 13; henceforth, *CD* III/4.

71. The word "command" itself indicates an encounter between persons because, unlike law, it represents a "momentary utterance issued directly by one person to another" (Nigel Biggar, *The Hastening That Waits: Karl Barth's Ethics* [Oxford: Clarendon Press, 1993], 14).

72. The "impersonal *nomos* . . . is replaced by the living and personal Lord" (*TD2* 198). If "God wills the finite as such, it follows that he also has a par-

ticular will for each finite subject" (*TD2* 302). "If the individual is unmade, indifferent, calmly receptive to the whole of God's will, he does not sink into the 'pathless' abyss of Godhead: the Father's infinite will fashions him in and according to his Son; thus he is given a path, which, as 'being in Christ' . . . is totally specific" (*TD2* 305).

Cf. Rahner: "there must be unique and personal relationship between Jesus Christ and each individual in his faith . . . which is not exhausted by abstract norms" (*Foundations of Christian Faith*, trans. William V. Dych [New York: Crossroad, 1989], 307). "Christian life is not merely satisfying universal norms which are proclaimed by the official church. Rather in these norms and beyond them it is the always unique call of God which is mediated in a concrete and loving encounter with Jesus in a mysticism of love" (ibid., 311). Also see his "On the Question of a Formal Existential Ethics," in *Theological Investigations*, vol. 2, trans. Karl-H. Kruger (New York: Crossroad, 1990).

73. Von Balthasar, "The Word, Scripture, and Tradition," in *Word Made Flesh*, 24.

74. For example: "But because it is the call of the living God, who as Person is always more than an abstract commandment and a universally applicable principle, this call, which is spoken at this moment and at every moment, must also be heard at this moment and every moment and must be obeyed because it is heard" (von Balthasar, *The Christian State of Life*, trans. Sister Mary Frances McCarthy (San Francisco: Ignatius Press, 1983), 391.

Cf. Barth: "absolutely nothing either outward or inward . . . is left to chance or to ourselves, . . . even in every visible or invisible detail. He wills of us precisely the one thing and nothing else" (*CD* II/2 664). Barth's own particular take on the person-constituting wholism effected by the concrete command can be seen on his reflections on character. "Character is the particular form in which each is commanded to be" (*CD* III/4 388). Ideas like these lead Nigel Biggar to propose that Barth's "divine command should be understood, in the end, in terms of personal vocation" (*Hastening*, 44).

75. Only "in the Bible is the [creaturely] image something which God himself has set up with bold freedom over against himself—something which is to know God, respond to him in freedom, and welcome him with love. The full light of revelation will show that such a feat of daring on God's part is possible only because in God himself there exists an eternal reciprocity of living love: in the final analysis the biblical doctrine of the image can be understood only in light of the divine Trinity" (*GL6* 87).

76. "Christ's mission opens up the 'acting area' to the characters who share the action, but this 'acting area' is not a mere fluid medium; it is a personal and personalizing area" (*TD3* 249).

77. The "word which God addresses to man is always, in addition, the gift of a sharing in God's nature, the individual who receives the word acquires a new quality: he becomes a *unique person*" (*TD2* 402).

78. "Within the drama of Christ, every human fate is deprivatized so that

its personal range may extend to the whole universe, depending on how far it is prepared to cooperate in being inserted into the normative drama of Christ's life, death, and Resurrection. Not only does this gather the unimaginable plurality of human destinies into a concrete, universal point of unity: it actually maintains their plurality within the unity, but as a function of this unity. This is the aim of an organic integration of all individual destinies in Christ (Eph 1:3–10), which is simultaneously the commissioning of the organic fullness of vocations and tasks by the organizing center (Eph 4:7–16)" (*TD2* 50).

79. "The statement 'God is one in three modes of being, Father, Son, and Holy Spirit' thus means that the one God, i.e., the one Lord, the one personal God, is what he is not in one mode only but . . . in the mode of the Father, in the mode of the Son, in the mode of the Holy Spirit" (*CD* I/1 413). Barth's modalist leanings can be seen in his Christology. "If the eternal Logos is the Word in which God speaks with Himself, thinks Himself and is conscious of Himself, then in its identity with the man Jesus it is the Word in which God thinks the cosmos, speaks with the cosmos and imparts to the cosmos the consciousness of its God" (Karl Barth, *Church Dogmatics*, III/2, ed. G. W. Bromiley and T. F. Torrance, trans. Harold Knight et al. [Edinburgh: T&T Clark, 1960], 147; henceforth, *CD* III/2). God "acts by speaking His Word" (*CD* III/2 182). The "man Jesus" is the very Word of God addressed to the world; he is the "embodiment of the divine will to save" (*CD* III/2 147). The image here of the Logos is that of an inner manifestation of God by which God is active, by which God expresses Self.

80. Barth, *CD* I/1 381.

81. Hill, *Three-Personed God*, 119.

82. When the triune God "produces a world out of himself and takes responsibility for it, this process, *corresponding to the archetype from which it springs*, is bound to be sublimely dramatic" (*TD3* 531; emphasis mine).

83. Compare the following statements of Barth and von Balthasar. "The Yes in which man answers the divine Yes . . . can never have more than the *force and reach of an echo*" (Barth, *CD* III/2 188; emphasis added). "When God speaks, He wants a partner. He wants one who is erect, who, hearing his voice, is yet able to stand upon his feet and answer . . . when he utters his personal word, he wants that word to be returned to him, *not as a dead echo*, but as a personal response from his creature, in an exchange that is genuinely a dialogue" (von Balthasar, *Christian State of Life*, 394; emphasis added).

Chapter 3
Divine Commands and Human Fulfillment

1. Josef Fuchs, "Our Image of God and the Morality of Innerworldly Behavior," trans. Brian McNeil, in *Christian Morality: The Word Becomes Flesh* (Washington, D.C.: Georgetown University Press, 1981), 44.

2. Ibid., 45–46.

3. Ibid., 45.

4. "Strange as it may seem, [the] general conception of ethics coincides exactly with the conception of sin" (Karl Barth, *CD* II/2 518). "What man manufactures in these areas [of justice, goodness, and freedom] is illusion and self-justification, a means of escaping judgment and grace" (Jacques Ellul, *The Ethics of Freedom*, trans. G. W. Bromiley [Grand Rapids: Eerdmans, 1976], 273). The latter is cited in Gene Outka, "Discontinuity in the Ethics of Jacques Ellul," in *Jacques Ellul: Interpretive Essays*, ed. Clifford G. Christians and Jay M. Van Hook (Chicago: University of Illinois Press, 1981), 178.

5. Norbert Rigali, S.J., "The Uniqueness and the Distinctiveness of Christian Ethics and Morality," in *Moral Theology: Challenges for the Future*, ed. Charles Curran (New York: Paulist, 1990), 79.

6. "God's remoteness does not actually lie in the fact that he is unknown, so much as in the incomprehensible fact that he, the only one (Isa. 43:10–12), who is absolutely free and sovereign, deigns to communicate himself to the others, to the many, permitting them to enter the sphere of his uniqueness and holiness. This grace is an unheard-of demand made of the creature, something that snatches it from its own dwelling in the land of servitude into a 'land' that belongs to God, and all the creature's concepts are transformed thereby: a ray of God's glory touches them all, and this makes them more beautiful, but also heavier. Everything is now measured against the standard of divine rightness . . ." (*GL6* 177).

7. Hans Urs von Balthasar, *Love Alone: The Way of Revelation* (New York: Herder & Herder, 1969), 47.

8. This is where moral philosophers who attempt to fashion arguments in favor of divine command ethics must begin, inevitably leading to an ancillary modification of the initially presumed, neutral concept of God. The God who commands, it is added, is *loving* and *good*. Note, for example, the definitions of Robert Adams: "I could say that by 'X is ethically wrong' I mean 'X is contrary to the commands of a *loving* God' (i.e., 'There is a *loving* God and X is contrary to his commands') and by 'X is ethically permitted' I mean 'X is in accord with the commands of a *loving* God' (i.e., 'There is a *loving* God and X is not contrary to his commands')" (Adams, "A Modified Divine Command Theory of Ethical Wrongness," in *The Virtue of Faith and Other Essays in Philosophical Theology* [New York: Oxford University Press, 1987], 101).

9. The two events are also distinguished, of course, by the fact that the first is in the realm of the mythical while the latter belongs to the realm of historical fact.

10. "This is the covenant history of the chosen people with God, a history with a greatness, a catastrophe and a self-transcendence that drives forward to a fulfillment that cannot be clearly seen or constructed: that which brings fulfilment can be understood only together with *what* it fulfils. It is essential today to insist as strongly as possible that Christianity cannot be understood

without the old covenant; every attempt to interpret the form, message and subsequent impact of Christ in the world necessarily fails unless it is able to assess it all precisely in its closeness to and its distance from the old covenant" (*GL6* 402–3).

Thus, for example, the three unsuccessful attempts of Judaic thought to reestablish God's lost glory—in the proclamation of a coming Messiah, in the anticipation of the apocalyptic destruction of the present age, in the contemplation of creation and salvation history (*GL6* 303)—serve to heighten the glory of Christ who dismantles only to fulfill and unite the three attempts (*GL7* 39).

11. The "boundless obedience of the Son" is revealed as the "boundless self-giving love of the Father" (*GL7* 283).

12. "If the theophany in the *kabod* in the old covenant was the prelude and signal of the coming revelation of the Word, then in the new covenant 'the epiphany itself' demands 'the decision,' because appearing and word fundamentally coincide" (*GL7* 276).

13. "Had [Jesus] not borne the whole history of Israel (and therein the world) with God in himself, then he could not have been the final word of the history of God with Israel (and therein with the world)" (*GL7* 55). See his study of Irenaeus, *GL2* 31–94.

14. Gerard Hughes, *Authority in Morals: An Essay in Christian Ethics* (London: Heythrop Monographs, 1978), 5.

15. Eric D'Arcy, "'Worthy of Worship': A Catholic Contribution," in *Religion and Morality*, ed. Gene Outka and John P. Reeder (Garden City, N.Y.: Doubleday Anchor, 1973).

16. The highest perfection for human existence is, according to Thomas, that our minds become "attached" to God (*Summa Contra Gentiles*, bk. 3, chapter 130).

17. Thomas's theory is not at all uncongenial to contemporary narrative ideas. On the contrary, his theory of virtue readily lends itself to being transformed into a narrative ethics. Contemporary approaches, like that of Hauerwas, are testimonies to the fruitfulness of this transformation. Particular virtues (courage, loyalty, mercy) both illuminate the plot of one's life and are themselves illuminated by being displayed in a narrative framework.

18. Stanley Hauerwas, "Story and Theology," *Religion in Life* 45 (autumn 1976): 344.

19. The seriousness and centrality of meaning for von Balthasar's understanding of human fulfillment can be seen in his (hyperbolic?) statement about those who reject the mission that God has in mind for them: ". . . they are compelled in the end to acknowledge that their lives have withered and—worst of all punishments!—lost their meaningfulness" (von Balthasar, *The Christian State of Life*, trans. Sister Mary Frances McCarthy [San Francisco: Ignatius Press, 1983], 503).

20. She yearns "to write the absolute on the relative, to put some ultimate

mark upon fleeting time" (*TD4* 83). The "yearning for the absolute is at the very heart of man" (*TD4* 73). "To the best of his ability, he will attempt to make present, in finite terms, his orientation to the absolute that transcends him; thus arise the temples and kingdoms that are symbols of the absolute. In the post-Christian era, the finite realities that have been thus divinized can be secularized but not the yearning that created them in the first place. For this yearning for the absolute is at the very heart of man; it is the source of his search for meaning as such, including the meaning that he tries to discern in horizontal history. However, none of the passing moments of the world of time can encapsulate that desired absolute meaning" (*TD4* 73).

I think there is a similarity here to Rahner's claim that the word "God" is an inescapable part of human vocabulary. If the word "God" were to disappear "without a trace and without an echo," then the human person "would no longer be brought face to face with the single whole of reality, nor with the single whole of his own existence" (Rahner, *Foundations of Christian Faith*, trans. William V. Dych [New York: Crossroad, 1989], 47).

21. Apart from this in-breaking of the vertical, humanity is left with a tendency to "attribute absolute significance to relative fragments of meaning in history" (*TD4* 72–73).

22. Von Balthasar finds traces of these ideas in contemporary psychology where the "I" is seen "as resting upon and oriented toward a vital substratum that governs and sustains it." All of the major schools of psychology (i.e., those led by Freud, Jung, and Adler) "advocate that man should come to accept what he is; they will see the ultimate goal of therapy as that of integrating man into the totality that embraces him" (*TD1* 505).

23. Platonism is the chief suspect here, though not irredeemably so. It enters Christian thought as a baptized form of Neoplatonism, enriching the Christianity of Augustine, Bonaventure, and Thomas. However, it nearly, if not in fact, subverts the theological enterprise of Meister Eckhart. Thus von Balthasar asks "whether [Eckhart's] radical dying of the 'I' in God . . . is not bound to cause its existence in time and space to seem inauthentic and alienated" (*TD1* 556).

German Idealism fails in this regard because it tends to dissolve the "empirical, personal 'I' in the 'essential,' the 'ideal'" (*TD1* 558). Even Aquinas is rebuked for not going far enough on this point, though it is done in an oblique fashion. "One can ask, however, whether *Thomas* . . . was in a position to lead the battle for the Christian dignity of the individual to a triumphant conclusion. For here the human person becomes an individual *ratione materiae*, and an entity is more intelligible the more it is abstracted from matter and generalized" (*TD1* 550–51). Von Balthasar likewise criticizes the piety of those Christians who would rather flee the present life in order to be with Christ in the next. "Ignatius of Loyola energetically restored the balance by saying that, in spite of his yearning for heaven, he would rather do Christ's work on earth" (*TD5* 338).

24. A good exploration of the two together though can be found in his essay "Eschatology in Outline," in *Spirit and Institution*, vol. 4 of *Explorations in Theology*, trans. Edward T. Oakes, S.J. (San Francisco: Ignatius Press, 1995), 423–67.

25. Romano Guardini proposes a similar idea. "My being 'I' consists essentially in this, that God is my 'Thou.' . . . The human person has absolute dignity. But this it can receive not from its own being, which is finite, but only from the absolute. And not from an abstract absolute, such as an idea, a value, a law, or the like. These could only determine the content of its concrete life, not its personality, which it derives from the fact that God has brought it into existence as a person. . . . God is the absolute 'Thou' of man" (Romano Guardini, *The World and The Person*, trans. Stella Lange [Chicago: Henry Regnery, 1965], 141–42).

26. We can see the beginnings of an Ignatian corrective in von Balthasar's careful interpretation of the "eros" theme as it appears in both classical Greek and Christian literature. Eros was, for the Greeks, von Balthasar points out, more than the self-centered grasping sketched by Anders Nygren (see Nygren, *Agape and Eros*, trans. Philip S. Watson [Philadelphia: Westminster Press, 1953], 92–95). Socrates, for example, criticizes an interpretation of eros that makes it essentially a yearning desire after something that is lacked. Instead, it is the movement of the *daimōn*, neither human nor divine, who provides interchange (and not one-directional movement) between the gods and humans (*GL4* 189). Similarly, a moment of descent from the gods to the realm of humanity is not at all absent from Plato's theme of ascent, encouraging von Balthasar to note the daring use of "the analogy of reciprocal love for the relationship to the Absolute" and the presence of a "personal 'sign from God'" in Plato's writings (*GL4* 192, 193). Both of these themes are taken over by Christianity: the ascent "theme of *erôs* as the fundamental yearning of the finite creature for transcendence in God as the primordial unity" and the "world affirming" descent theme which, von Balthasar argues, gains full justification within the Christian sphere in God's free love of creation (*GL4* 321–22).

For a helpful examination of von Balthasar's treatment of the *eros/agapē* debate, see Raymond Gawronski, *Word and Silence: Hans Urs von Balthasar and the Spiritual Encounter Between East and West* (Grand Rapids: Eerdmans, 1995), 132–40.

27. In Hans Urs von Balthasar, *Homo Creatus Est* (Einsiedeln: Johannes Verlag, 1986), 11–25. The translation of the text is my own.

28. In it, salvation is solitary. There are no "ecstases in pairs, let alone in groups" (*Homo Creatus Est*, 20). The dimension of co-humanity and human relationality is lost to view. Second, unity with God, the state in which salvation lies, is accomplished only by surmounting all that is dissimilar to God, that is, created reality itself. Finally, the Neoplatonic approach absolutizes the creaturely aspiration and makes the divine a means for its fulfillment. Rather

than a "secret egoism" driving the moral life, Christians must look to the witness of the Second Person, who "never sets himself as absolute, but rather as the one eternally turned to the bosom of the Father" (*Homo Creatus Est*, 24–25).

29. The "First Principle and Foundation" is an opening meditation in Ignatius of Loyola's *Spiritual Exercises*. It begins: "The human person was created to praise, reverence and serve God and by this means to save his soul." While the particular phrasing here (i.e., "and by this *means* . . .") might suggest that the praise of God has been made merely instrumental to human salvation, the meditations that follow in the text of the *Spiritual Exercises* support von Balthasar's interpretation of the prayer: there is a distinct priority given to the doxological element that is not due to its usefulness for human salvation.

30. It is unfortunate that this ordering is sometimes obscured, if not overturned to better suit the inclinations of the contemporary person. For example, David Fleming's paraphrase of the "First Principle and Foundation" reads: "The goal of our life is to live with God forever. / God, who loves us, gave us life. / Our own response of love allows God's life to flow into us without limit" (*Hearts on Fire: Praying with Jesuits*, ed. Michael Harter [St. Louis: Institute of Jesuit Sources, 1993], 9). Lost is the biblical corrective to Greek Neoplatonism, which von Balthasar believes was introduced into the spiritual tradition by Ignatius.

31. This movement is characteristic of Augustine's experiences in his *Confessions*. See the account of his mystical experience in *Confessions* 9.10.

32. Christian mysticism—which, properly understood, is for von Balthasar a normative part of all Christian life and praxis—is not simply "the movement of the person from below upwards to the absolute, in order possibly to disappear there, but rather as Ignatius of Loyola repeats with emphasis, the movement '*de arriba*,' from above downward, whereby God empties himself in order to fill the person with *his* loving self-giving" (*TL2* 258).

33. The divine persons "gazed on the whole surface or circuit of the world" and decided that the Son should become human to save the human race (Ignatius of Loyola, *The Spiritual Exercises of St. Ignatius*, trans. George E. Ganss, S.J. [Chicago: Loyola University Press, 1992], #102). Those who wish to follow the Son must give themselves in service, to hear and respond to the address of the king who calls the person to join him in the enterprise of saving the world (*Spiritual Exercises* #95).

34. So that one is able to desire "solely according to what God our Lord will move one's will to choose" (Ignatius of Loyola, *Spiritual Exercises* #155). Ignatius examines the conditions and considerations for making a choice in ##169–88. His rules for discernment are found in ## 313–36.

35. We say "complete" and "final" because neither Ignatius nor von Balthasar advocates a radical voluntarism, but rather that the divine decision to create did not exhaust divine freedom vis-à-vis creation.

36. See #23, #155.

37. Jacques Servais explores in detail the role of Ignatian indifference in von Balthasar's understanding of creaturely freedom. Servais also maintains that von Balthasar ties creaturely freedom to a love for the world which itself participates in triune love for the world (*Theologie Des Exercices spirituels: Hans Urs von Balthasar interprète Ignace* [Bruxelles: Culture et Vérité, 1996], 317–29).

38. In regard to the relation between God's will and human agency, von Balthasar will say that "only Ignatius of Loyola had the balance right" (*GL5* 132).

39. The "achievement of indifference" aims at this: "making the choosing by God *for me* my choice" (von Balthasar, *Homo Creatus Est*, 24).

40. Von Balthasar traces various literary appearances of the theme of the "holy fool" (e.g., Erasmus's *In Praise of Folly*, Cervantes' *Don Quixote*, Dostoevsky's *Idiot* [*GL5* 141–204]). The "holy fool" as a literary device is used to convey a sense of the disruption of practical reasoning that can follow upon being touched by the grace of God. It does this by creating internal to the story a sort of rational distance between the outlook of a saintly figure and the widespread, and even benevolent, wisdom of the majority.

41. Von Balthasar, *Christian State of Life*, 216–17; emphasis in text.

42. The person knows that he is "begotten in grace along with the absolute Son," as "someone to whom it has been '*granted* to have life in himself.' Thus, when man acknowledges his indebtedness, no alienating compulsion is involved: there wells up within him, spontaneously, a sense of privilege in handing himself over to his origin" (*TD3* 35–36).

43. Von Balthasar, "Eschatology in Outline," 435.

44. "An imperative to which I owe absolute obedience must necessarily come in the most radical sense from [without], in order that it may claim me most radically within. A command which transcends our actions cannot in the last analysis be merely a command which I have given myself on the basis of what I myself have seen and experienced and felt and judged of the good and the true and the beautiful. *It must come to me as something alien, as the command of another, demanding as such that I should make its content the law of my life*" (*CD* II/2 651).

45. "Power as power does not have any divine claim, no matter how imposing or effective it might be" (*CD* II/2 553).

46. The decision to be a God of election is also a decision about the meaning of human existence; to be human now means to be in fellowship with God Our lives are "to be the witness of this event" (*CD* III/2 145). Thus Barth can say that the ethical command "is only the form of the Gospel of God" (*CD* II/2 588). The decision to be *for* sinful humanity sums up the Gospel and is the "content of the good news which is Jesus Christ" (*CD* II/2 10).

47. It "is not possible for us," Barth declares, "to see God's gracious dealing and work in Jesus Christ without recognizing that it is good for man" (*CD* II/2 581).

48. God's word does not come to believers in such a way as to make them "marionettes who move only at his will" (Karl Barth, *Christian Life*, vol. IV/4 of *Church Dogmatics*, trans. Geoffrey W. Bromiley [Grand Rapids: Eerdmans, 1981], 102). Rather, it is "permission" (*Church Dogmatics*, III/4, ed. G. W. Bromiley and T. F. Torrance, trans. A. T. Mackay et al. [Edinburgh: T&T Clark, 1961], 14). It liberates us (*CD* II/2 586). And it is something to which we respond in gratitude (*CD* III/2 166).

49. Karl Barth, *Church Dogmatics*, *CD* II/1, ed. G. W. Bromiley and T. F. Torrance, trans. T. H. L. Parker et al. (Edinburgh: T&T Clark, 1980), 650–52.

50. Ibid., 655.

51. Ibid., 653.

52. Ibid., 659.

53. Ibid., 653.

54. Ibid., 652.

55. Which, of course, is related to the proper status of beauty since one concern that both *analogia entis* and beauty raise for Barth is the proper Christian justification for attributing creaturely qualities to God: either narrowly and exclusively through the permission granted by particular revelation or through an appeal that allows general revelation at least an ancillary role.

56. "Autonomy asserts that man as the bearer of universal reason . . . is his own law. Heteronomy asserts that man, being unable to act according to universal reason must be subjected to a law, strange and superior to him. Theonomy asserts that the superior law is at the same time, the innermost law of man himself, rooted in the divine ground which is man's own ground" (Paul Tillich, *The Protestant Era*, trans. James Luther Adams [Chicago: University of Chicago Press, 1948], 56–57).

The kind of autonomy familiar to the contemporary person, Tillich goes on to suggest, arose as modern culture lost its "ultimate reference" (*Protestant Era*, 58). It is, however, a false autonomy, for it suppresses the human orientation toward an "ultimate concern."

57. The "form established by God bears its evidential force in itself and is able of itself to show this to the eyes of faith: but it is precisely this power to assert oneself, to demonstrate oneself, and to achieve acceptance for oneself, that belongs to the most original meaning of the biblical glory of God (as Karl Barth has shown above)" (*GL7* 28).

58. Cf. Barth: God's glory "is not a presence which leaves blind eyes blind" (*CD* II/1 647).

59. ". . . glory would not be glory if it merely sent forth an external radiance without affecting internally the being that is the recipient of grace" (*GL6* 146).

60. Von Balthasar, *Christian State of Life*, 400–401. Also: "Anyone who asks in the Spirit of Christ, that is, in a trinitarian context, will infallibly be heard" (*TD5* 123). This is how von Balthasar would want to interpret Vacek's reminder that "we can and should also engage in quasi-independent, innova-

tive self-determination" (Edward Collins Vacek, "Divine-Command, Natural-Law, and Mutual-Love Ethics," *Theological Studies* 57, no. 4 [December
1996]: 643). Such creative self-fashioning must ultimately remain within the
vertical stream of divine willing, and thus assumes the acceptance of one's mission.

61. Thus the paradox of human autonomy within divine choice "is ultimately resolved only in the mystery of trinitarian love between Father and
Son, which, in the genuine mutuality of an exchange that does not destroy the
personal freedom of the Son . . . , allows the unity of divine will to exist and
to have its origin in the unity of the Holy Spirit" (von Balthasar, *Christian
State of Life*, 401–2).

62. "The divine freedom is so all-encompassing that it makes room, with
its single Truth, for countless aspects; thus it does not override or infringe the
area of mystery of each individual's creaturely spontaneity. . . . God's will,
embracing the entire, infinitely diversified heaven, is so generous that it draws
into itself all the fullness of redeemed human freedoms, pride of place being
given to that of the incarnate Son; and even though it is the originating will,
providing the (analytic) norm for all freedom, it nonetheless desires to be
simultaneously the (synthetic) will that is the resultant of all the others" (*TD5*
485–86).

63. It "is the creature's freedom that causes him to be termed the 'image
and likeness of God'" (*TD2* 123). "Here [in the Second Adam] the possibility emerges, most importantly, of defining 'image' of God in man as finite
freedom" (*TD2* 326–27). "[T]he 'image of God' in the creature consists deci-
sively in its *autexousion*, in the created mirroring of uncreated freedom" (*TD2*
397).

64. Hans Urs von Balthasar, "The Unknown Lying Beyond the Word," in
Creator Spirit, vol. 3 of *Explorations in Theology*, trans. Brian McNeil, C.R.V.
(San Francisco: Ignatius Press, 1993), 107.

65. Hans Urs von Balthasar, *A Theology of History* (San Francisco: Ignatius
Press, 1994), 102.

66. Thus in *GL1*, it is the Spirit who gives us the (subjective) capacity to
see the Christ-form ("Spiritual Senses," 365–424, 551, 553), and in *GL7* it is
in the sphere of Spirit that Christians live out their christological vocation.
The work of the Holy Spirit "makes the life of love well up, not in front of us
nor above us, but in us" (*GL7* 389). Von Balthasar closely ties the new subjectivity of the Christian to the economic work of the Holy Spirit: "the dialogue [with God] is not between our spirit and the *Pneuma*, but between our
spirit, borne by the *Pneuma*, and the Father" (*GL7* 405).

67. "In creation, God fashions a genuine creaturely freedom and sets it
over against his own, thus in some sense binding himself. . . . [God] has
endowed man with a freedom that, in responding to the divine freedom,
depends on nothing but itself" (*TD4* 328).

68. This convergence offers another example of how the human is "reca-

pitulated" in Christ and one more indication of the aesthetic "rightness" of the event.

69. "To offer an account of the act whereby man responds and corresponds to the divine revelation . . . excludes two extremes. The first extreme is to portray this act as a paradox or a dialectical contradiction which destroys all human intellectual modes and in which the only valid guide is the *credo quia absurdum*. . . . The other excluded extreme would be to make man's ultimate attitude intelligible in terms of worldly and natural thought-categories . . ." (*GL1* 142).

70. Von Balthasar, "Eschatology in Outline," 428.

71. "What is a person without a life-form, that is to say, without a form which he has chosen for his life, a form into which and through which to pour out his life, so that his life becomes the soul of the form and the form becomes the expression of his soul? For this is no extraneous form, but rather so intimate a one that it is greatly rewarding to identify oneself with it. Nor is it a forcibly imposed form, rather one which has been bestowed from within and has been freely chosen. Nor, finally, is it an arbitrary form, rather that uniquely personal one which constitutes the very law of the individual. . . . We are not speaking here of isolated little 'acts' by which, as with a needle, a person can pierce through the desolation of his everyday life, of his sham existence, to reach the Absolute. . . . This will not salvage his lost dignity. We speak, rather of a life-form which is determined—and, therefore, able—to bestow nobility upon a person's everyday life itself" (*GL1* 24). He goes on to speak of this form as one that "unites God and man in an unimaginable intimacy" (*GL1* 25).

72. Part of the fruitfulness of the *Spiritual Exercises* of Ignatius is due to its ability to unlock the power of the Christian biblical drama for the individual.

73. Hans Urs von Balthasar, "Nine Propositions on Christian Ethics," trans. Graham Harrison, in *Principles of Christian Morality* (San Francisco: Ignatius Press, 1986), 89–90.

Chapter 4
Creation and Covenant

1. Hans Urs von Balthasar, "Immediacy to God," in *Creator Spirit*, vol. 3 of *Explorations in Theology*, trans. Brian McNeil, C.R.V. (San Francisco: Ignatius Press, 1993), 350.

2. For a helpful overview of the characteristic differences between Protestant and Catholic ethics, see James Gustafson's *Protestant and Roman Catholic Ethics: Prospects for Rapprochement* (Chicago: University of Chicago Press, 1978).

3. *Gaudium et Spes*, in *Vatican Council II*, ed. Austin Flannery, O.P. (Northport, N.Y.: Costello Publishing, 1988), #36.

4. Proportionalism, in short, is an ethical approach which emphasizes that the good act is one which maximizes those goods and values at stake in one's ethical choice. Since proportionalists maintain that we cannot decide what is good until we consider all the relevant values and disvalues, they, in general, support only the idea of "virtually exceptionless" norms, not the type of moral absolutism found in official Catholic Church pronouncements.

5. Hans Urs von Balthasar, *A Theology of History* (San Francisco: Ignatius Press, 1994), 18.

6. Vincent MacNamara provides an excellent summary of the debate over "faith ethics." See his *Faith and Ethics: Recent Roman Catholicism* (Washington, D.C.: Georgetown University Press, 1985), 1–66.

7. For a helpful overview of the nature/grace debate during the first part of last century, see Stephen J. Duffy, *The Graced Horizon: Nature and Grace in Modern Catholic Thought* (Collegeville, Minn.: Liturgical Press, 1992).

8. The gospel message "is in harmony with the most secret desires of the human heart" (*Gaudium et Spes* in *Vatican Council II*, ed. Flannery), 922.

9. De Lubac makes this argument in his *The Mystery of the Supernatural*, trans. Rosemary Sheed (New York: Herder & Herder, 1965); see in particular pp. 181–216.

10. Because Suarez's approach was so influential on Catholic theology, Rahner described the division between nature and grace as the "mortal sin of Jesuit theology" (Karl Rahner, "Nature and Grace," in *Theological Investigations*, vol. IV [London: Darton, Longman & Todd, 1966], 167).

11. *Commentaria in Primam Partem, Opera Omnia of St. Thomas, I, q. 12, a.1 comment. IX* (cited in Peter Ryan, "Moral Action and the Ultimate End of Man: The Significance of the Debate Between Henri de Lubac and His Critics" [diss., Rome: Gregorian University, 1996], 100).

12. Ambroise Gardeil, "Le désir naturel de voir Dieu," *Revue thomiste* (1926): 385–86; cited by de Lubac, *Mystery of the Supernatural*, 194.

13. Karl Rahner, *Faith in a Wintry Season: Conversations and Interviews with Karl Rahner in the Last Years of His Life*, ed. Paul Imhof and Hubert Biallowons, trans. Harvey D. Egan (New York: Crossroad, 1991), 49.

14. De Lubac, *Mystery of the Supernatural*, xi.

15. "To obtain the end of human life, it is necessary that man also observe the laws *of the natural order*, for the supernatural end does not exclude the natural end but subordinates it and completes it" (H. Noldin, *Summa Theologiae Moralis*, vol. 1, *De Principiis* [Freiburg: Herder, 1962], 4; cited in Ryan, "Moral Action," 169).

16. Henry Davis, *Human Acts, Law, Sin, Virtue*, vol. 1 of *Moral and Pastoral Theology* (New York: Sheed & Ward, 1943), 46–50.

17. Gérard Gilleman, *The Primacy of Charity in Moral Theology*, trans. William F. Ryan and André Vachon (Westminster, Md.: Newman Press, 1959), xxix.

18. *Optatam Totius* #16 in *Vatican Council II*, ed. Flannery, 720.

19. De Lubac, *Mystery of the Supernatural*, 299.

20. John P. Galvin, "The Invitation of Grace," in *A World of Grace: An Introduction to the Themes and Foundations of Karl Rahner's Theology*, ed. Leo J. O'Donovan (New York: Crossroad, 1984), 72.

21. Richard McCormick, "Does Faith Add to Ethical Perception?" in *The Distinctiveness of Christian Ethics*, vol. 2 of *Readings in Moral Theology*, ed. Charles E. Curran and Richard A. McCormick (New York: Paulist, 1980), 162.

22. Gerard J. Hughes, *Authority in Morals: An Essay in Christian Ethics* (London: Heythrop Monographs, 1978), 7.

23. Charles E. Curran, *Moral Theology: A Continuing Journey* (Notre Dame, Ind.: University of Notre Dame Press, 1982), 42.

24. David Hollenbach, "Fundamental Theology and the Christian Moral Life," in *Faithful Witness: Foundations of Theology for Today's Church*, ed. Leo J. O'Donovan and T. Howland Sanks (New York: Crossroad, 1989), 171.

25. John Milbank, *Theology and Social Theory: Beyond Secular Reason* (Oxford: Blackwell, 1990), 220.

26. Karl Rahner, "Concerning the Relationship Between Nature and Grace," in *Theological Investigations*, vol. 1 (London: Darton, Longman & Todd, 1961), 300.

27. Karl Rahner, *Foundations of Christian Faith*, trans. William V. Dych (New York: Crossroad, 1989), 309.

28. Karl Rahner, "The Ignatian Mysticism of Joy in the World," in *Theological Investigations*, vol. 3 (London: Darton, Longman & Todd, 1967), 285–86.

29. Clearly the acceptance of philosophical arguments against "moral universalism" is more prevalent among scholars in the field of moral theology than in the teaching of the magisterium.

30. And thus not leading to the "disastrous" results feared by some: "Balthasar . . . rejects the traditional concept of 'pure nature' . . . [T]his attitude has been disastrous. In the first place it made any real dialogue between the Christian and his millions of non-Christian fellows . . . impossible" (Noel Dermot O'Donoghue, "Do We Get Beyond Plato?" in *The Beauty of Christ*, ed. Bede McGregor and Thomas Norris [Edinburgh: T&T Clark, 1994], 258 n. 2).

31. Hans Urs von Balthasar, *The Theology of Karl Barth: Exposition and Interpretation*, trans. Edward T. Oakes (San Francisco: Ignatius Press, 1992).

32. Barth, *CD* III/2 204.

33. The "idea of what it means to be human as such cannot be derived or deduced from the Incarnation of Christ but can only be *presupposed* in it" (von Balthasar, *Theology of Karl Barth*, 119). "For if revelation is centered in Jesus Christ, there must be by definition a periphery to this center. Thus, as we say, the order of the Incarnation presupposes the order of creation, which is not

identical with it. And, because the order of creation is oriented to the order of the Incarnation, it is structured in view of the Incarnation: it contains images, analogies, as it were, dispositions, which in a true sense are the presuppositions of the Incarnation" (*Theology of Karl Barth*, 163).

34. Hans Urs von Balthasar, "The Implications of the Word," in *The Word Made Flesh*, vol. 1 of *Explorations in Theology* (San Francisco: Ignatius Press, 1989), 48. Christ is the "one and only criterion," "by which we measure the relations between . . . grace and nature" ("Characteristics of Christianity," in *Word Made Flesh*, 162).

35. Von Balthasar, *Theology of Karl Barth*, 161.

36. Von Balthasar, "Nine Propositions."

37. Von Balthasar, *Theology of Karl Barth*, 91.

38. Ibid., 105.

39. "It is only because he is not God, because he comes to meet God as the unalterably not-God, that he shares in the independence, unity, personality and freedom of his Creator. . . . To undertake any movement of love at all, the lover must proceed from the sure state of his own existence" (Hans Urs von Balthasar, *The Christian State of Life*, trans. Sister Mary Frances McCarthy [San Francisco: Ignatius Press, 1983], 68).

40. Von Balthasar, *Theology of Karl Barth*, 126.

41. Ibid., 130. He cites Barth: God can "let Himself be conditioned by faith in Him" (". . . *sich durch den Glauben an ihn bestimmen zu lassen*"; *CD* II/1 512 [*KD* II/1 575]).

42. Von Balthasar, *Theology of Karl Barth*, 135.

43. Ibid., 153.

44. Barth, *CD* III/2 402.

45. Von Balthasar, *Theology of Karl Barth*, 143ff.

46. Von Balthasar, *Christian State of Life*, 438, 451.

47. Von Balthasar, *Theology of Karl Barth*, 103.

48. Ibid., 280.

49. Ibid., 242.

50. Ibid., 300, discussing Rahner. "The Incarnation demands that there be a relatively solid content of meaning that cannot be totally robbed of its substance when we provisionally abstract from our supernatural goal" (von Balthasar, *Theology of Karl Barth*, 362; see also von Balthasar, *A Theology of History*, 114).

51. In saying "general" pattern, I mean to indicate that the modes of Ignatian discernment of God's will are more complex than described here. Ignatius offered three different ways in which the Christian might find himself making a choice about his life; the third is itself further divided into two "methods." See *Spiritual Exercises* ##175–88. There is a vibrant debate in Ignatian circles about how the three relate to one another. See Jules J. Toner, S.J., *Discerning God's Will: Ignatius of Loyola's Teaching on Christian Decision Making* (St. Louis: Institute of Jesuit Sources, 1991), especially the appendices, 316–28.

52. Von Balthasar says at one point in his discussion of the balance Ignatius strikes between contemplation and action that "Ignatius had it right" (*GL5* 132). Although in the context he is not referring to our issue of the noetic element of the moral life, it is a verdict that, I believe, extends to this element as well.

53. The church historian John O'Malley writes: "But of such [descriptions of the infant Society of Jesus] none occurs more frequently in Jesuit documentation—on practically every page—than 'to help souls.' . . . By 'soul' Jesuits meant the whole person. Thus they could help souls in a number of ways, for instance, by providing food for the body or learning for the mind. That is why their list of ministries was so long, why at first glance it seems to be without limits. *No doubt, however, the Jesuits primarily wanted to help the person achieve an ever better relationship with God.* They sought to be mediators of an immediate experience of God that would lead to an inner change of heart or a deepening of religious sensibilities already present" (John W. O'Malley, S.J., *The First Jesuits* [Cambridge, Mass.: Harvard University Press, 1993], 18–19; emphasis added).

54. Thus, in making a decision about how to proceed, he exhorts the Christian: "I should beg God our Lord to be pleased to move my will and to put in my mind what I ought to do in regard to the matter proposed, so that it will be more to his praise and glory. I should beg to accomplish this by reasoning well and faithfully with my intellect, and by choosing in conformity with his most holy will and good pleasure" (*Spiritual Exercises* #180).

55. In the christological obedience of the Christian, God's "glory finds a receptacle. . . . [This] is a receptacle in which it can stand out clearly as the real glory of the Lord, the manifestation of absolute sovereignty" (*GL5* 107).

56. See also Hans Urs von Balthasar, *Prayer*, trans. Graham Harrison (San Francisco: Ignatius Press, 1986), 19.

57. Hans Urs von Balthasar, *The Moment of Christian Witness*, trans. Richard Beckley (San Francisco: Ignatius Press, 1994), 55. "In concentric rings around the nondeducible and sovereignly free fact of the Son's Incarnation-Cross-Resurrection, we can discern, according to the laws of theology, all the events of salvation history and world history, and of nature too, since ultimately everything exists for the sake of this center" (*TD2* 281).

58. Von Balthasar, *A Theology of History*, 20.

59. Von Balthasar rarely discusses concrete ethical issues, and so it is difficult to say whether this meaning transformation will also lead to clear material changes in what constitutes normative practices. In his discussion of *Humanae Vitae*, he comes close to suggesting that there are such material changes: "From all this we have gained one general insight: for the Christian husband and for the Christian wife, the norm of their sexual relationship is a *theological* one, namely, the relationship between Christ and the Church. We could say that this holds true for all *non*-Christians as well, only they know nothing of this norm and therefore cannot consciously pattern themselves

after it" (445). Then several pages later, virtually dismissing the natural law appeal of Paul VI's opening comments, he states, "I think that only Christians can understand the challenge posed by *Humanae Vitae*" (450) ("A Word on *Humanae Vitae*," *Communio* 20 [summer 1993]).

60. Von Balthasar, *Christian State of Life*, 82.

61. Ibid., 420.

62. Ibid., 391.

63. Von Balthasar, "Nine Propositions," 100.

64. Similar to von Balthasar, Barth speaks of "conditional imperatives" and "signposts" that offer a preliminary indication of God's will yet wait ultimately for God's personal address (Karl Barth, *The Humanity of God*, trans. John Newton Thomas and Thomas Wieser [Richmond, Va.: John Knox Press, 1969], 86–88). But there is also an important difference in his and von Balthasar's understanding of the way the "natural" order guides us, and it is a difference which underscores von Balthasar's commitment to the relative solidity of the created order. Barth is much more circumspect than von Balthasar in allowing the natural order itself as an expression of the divine will. As a result, God's call can seem to hover apart from it, sometimes using it, sometimes overturning it.

65. Hans Urs von Balthasar, *Two Sisters in the Spirit: Thérèse of Lisieux and Elizabeth of the Trinity*, trans. Donald Nichols and Anne Elizabeth England (San Francisco: Ignatius Press, 1992), 302.

66. Even on a natural level, the encounter of human freedoms is "the center from which the cosmos as a whole, with all its wonders, laws and terrors becomes theophanous" (von Balthasar, "Encountering God in Today's World," in *Creator Spirit*, 315). And thus von Balthasar describes the "polarity of two human beings" as "the authentic, basic and indestructible *imago dei*" (von Balthasar, *Theology of Karl Barth*, 126). Furthermore, this *imago* provides the creaturely "point of contact" for the divine/human encounter (von Balthasar, *Theology of Karl Barth*, 89). "One can ask himself whether the natural 'point of contact' for revelation does not lie [in the interdependent service to the other]: that in such a view of co-human person . . . true joy lies in the self-forgetting service to [the neighbor] and thus something like blessedness" (von Balthasar, *Homo Creatus Est*, 20).

67. See Barth, *CD* III/4. Barth's formed references act as a *preparation* for hearing a command that is itself not given by them, whereas von Balthasar is more willing to allow that the ethical situation, christologically interpreted, is itself a revelation of God's command. "The demands of the particular situation will show [the Christian] what Christ's word means in all its truth" (von Balthasar, *Prayer*, 215).

68. Our neighbor is not "Christ in disguise" but the "sacrament of Christ." Christ "infallibly communicates his presence under these signs [of our neighbor]; thus he can be genuinely found and encountered. For the believer, the myriad forms of relationships between human beings" are "ways of encoun-

tering Christ, each one new, original and surprising" (von Balthasar, *Prayer*, 215).

69. "To the extent that Jesus wills to share and take to himself this experience of the sin of all, he secretly enters each person's solitariness and isolation; he is there as a silent, unknown companion who in that way interrupts the total alienation of sin" (Mark A. McIntosh, *Christology from Within: Spirituality and Incarnation in Hans Urs von Balthasar* [Notre Dame, Ind.: University of Notre Dame Press, 1996], 112).

70. See Hans Urs von Balthasar, *Mysterium Paschale*, trans. Aidan Nichols O.P. (Grand Rapids: Eerdmans, 1993), 148–88.

71. He cites Adrienne von Speyr, *Johannes*, vol. 1 (Einsiedeln: Johannes Verlag), 272. Also, the "doctrine of God's triune life," the loving interchange between the Father and the Son in the unity of the Spirit, enters creation as the "doctrine of God's absolute act by which henceforth God will see the world's sin in the light of the undergirding death of his Son" (*TD5* 329). The solidarity extends to all creation, and thus, even plants and animals are included in the work of Christ (*TD5* 421).

72. And thus, "all the Old Testament rejoicing at the punishment of the wicked, all eschatological delight at their torment, must fall silent" (*TD5* 278; also *TD5* 178).

73. "I too live in God through the power of Christ's death for me, and must therefore interpret all things according to the prescriptions of this love" (von Balthasar, *Love Alone: The Way of Revelation* [New York: Herder & Herder, 1969], 93). The "eyes of Christian love" have a "luminosity which discovers and lights up a supernatural depth in whatever and whomever they fasten upon" (von Balthasar, *Prayer*, 216).

74. Von Balthasar, "Secular Piety?" in *Creator Spirit*, 360.

75. Ibid. Also: "It follows that everything that human endeavour achieves in respect of the commission given at creation—the struggle against injustice, hunger, sickness, need and depravity, and the struggle for better conditions of life, education, wages, etc.—acquires a positive significance in view of what God has done in Christ and of the help of the Holy Spirit, and that nothing of this will be lost ultimately" (*GL7* 519).

Von Balthasar's idea here is not Rahner's "anonymous Christianity." For von Balthasar, one's encounter with the Christ-form is decisive and transformative, and it alone opens the individual to Christian faith. "Thematization" as a description of one's coming to full faith *might* be adequate in Rahner's understanding of Christian faith; it cannot, however, do justice to von Balthasar's. Nonetheless, von Balthasar allows that there can be an "implicit faith" in the non-Christian, and so Rahner's idea is not rejected altogether: "Of course this is not to deny Karl Rahner's legitimate notion that there is a *fides implicita* and a corresponding supernatural love outside the sphere of Christianity (see Lk 21:1–4) and of the Bible (see Mt 15:21–28), as well as with those who are theoretically atheists (Rom 2:14–16)" (von Balthasar,

Moment of Christian Witness, 113 n. 42). For a more critical response to Rahner, however, see Hans Urs von Balthasar, *My Work: In Retrospect,* trans. John
Saward and Brian McNeil (San Francisco: Ignatius Press, 1993), 53–57.
Other differences appear in the context of their respective ideas about the tie
between the love of God and love of neighbor. See the next paragraphs.

76. Hans Urs von Balthasar, *The God Question and Modern Man* (New
York: Seabury Press, 1967), 147.

77. Karl Rahner, "Reflections on the Unity of the Love of Neighbour and
the Love of God," in *Theological Investigations,* vol. 6 (London: Darton,
Longman & Todd, 1974), 246.

78. Von Balthasar, *Moment of Christian Witness,* 113. The absence of an
explicit vertical act is also what moves von Balthasar to reject the approach in
some traditional texts which implies that the commandment to love neighbor
is given by natural morality while the commandment to love God is fulfilled
when the former is done by one in the state of grace. See von Balthasar,
Moment of Christian Witness, 110–11.

79. Rahner, "Reflections on the Unity of the Love of Neighbour and the
Love of God," 246.

80. As he puts it, Jesus Christ effects the "absolutely creative" synthesis
between the commandments to love God and neighbor; and he does so in a
way that "prevents the dissolution of the vertical dimension into the horizontal through the dissolution of the love of God into the love of neighbor."
Christ "refuses to let the act of adoration in spirit and in truth . . . be dissolved
into the equally demanding act of doing the whole will of the Father in the
whole of the mission" (*GL7* 441).

81. Ultimately, the difference between the two Catholic theologians might
be construed as contrary phenomenological accounts: the position, on the
one hand, that the act of neighbor love is a love which follows, grows out of,
and mediates an explicit, christologically specified love for God (von Balthasar), and the view, on the other hand, that an explicit love for God is pre-
ceded by and comes to fruition within the act of neighbor love in which the
response to the divine is already unthematically present (Rahner). The two
views need not be sharply contrasted or seen as opposed to one another. Perhaps attending to the complex process of coming to faith would reveal the
truth of both and the coherence between them. Nonetheless, the two reflect
different emphases that are played out throughout the thought of both.

82. "'Activity and passivity,' however, together constitute 'the original
unity of action and contemplation,' and this applies both 'within the divine
nature and in creation'" (*TD5* 90). Von Balthasar cites Adrienne von Speyr's
Die Welt des Gebetes. There is even something receptive ("super-feminine")
about the Father "since . . . in the action of begetting and breathing forth he
allows himself to be determined by the Persons who thus proceed from him"
(*TD5* 91). The Father, too, "owes his Fatherhood to the Son who allows himself to be generated, and he also owes his power of 'spiration' . . . to the

Spirit" (*TD5* 245). Jesus' earthly ministry witnesses to the divine dynamic: his "main achievement cannot be called simply ethical: it consists in his *allowing* something to happen, in *letting* himself be plundered and shared out in Passion and Eucharist" (*TD3* 29).

83. L. Gregory Jones, *Embodying Forgiveness: A Theological Analysis* (Grand Rapids: Eerdmans, 1995), 47.

84. Von Balthasar, "Characteristics of Christianity, in *The Word Made Flesh*, vol. 1 of *Explorations in Theology* (San Francisco: Ignatius Press, 1989), 176.

85. "Can we say . . . that there is anxiety and anguish in the heart of God, producing not 'certainty of salvation,' but something far more, namely the flower of hope?" (*TD5* 290). He cites Charles Péguy. See also von Balthasar's *Dare We Hope "That All Men Be Saved?"* trans. David Kipp and Lothar Krauth (San Francisco: Ignatius Press, 1988).

86. Von Balthasar, *The God Question and Modern Man*, 149.

87. "It only is by virtue of this divine relationship [between the Father and the Son] that we need never be discouraged or tempted to break off relations with our neighbour, when it seems that there is nothing more to be done for him" (von Balthasar, *Love Alone*, 93–94). Christian hope receives "mysterious awakening powers which co-operate in the upward flight of the brother [and sister]" (von Balthasar, *The God Question and Modern Man*, 149). Christian hope recognizes that all brothers and sisters, "not only those filled with love but the very [ones] who are empty and destitute of love, are images and sacraments of the Son of God on the cross, forsaken by his Father" (von Balthasar, *Prayer*, 289).

88. Von Balthasar, *Mysterium Paschale*, 265.

89. Von Balthasar, "Forgetfulness of God and Christians," 332.

90. See von Balthasar's exploration of how Christian literature has portrayed the extravagant glory of Christ's love by veiling it within the "holy fool" ("Folly and Glory," in *GL5* 141–204).

91. Divine love "*out of love* takes upon itself the sins of the world" (*GL7* 207).

92. See *TD5* 383; *Homo Creatus Est*, 21; and *The God Question and Modern Man*, 151. The text is from Origen, *Homily 7 in Lev.*

93. "The divine love which is bestowed vertically by God on sinful men is glorified 'horizontally' in the love of human fellowship" (*GL7* 433). "In brotherly love, the created world is permitted to enter the divine world" (*GL7* 517).

94. The love which communes with the sinner is one part of the foolishness of Christian love which von Balthasar believes is exemplified in Myshkin, the central character of Dostoevsky's *The Idiot*. Love in its deepest sense is "communication with the sinner, as communion with his guilt without the will to distinguish oneself from him" (*GL5* 199).

95. Von Balthasar describes "reciprocal recognition through the word of acknowledgment and reconciliation" as "the highest ethical act" (*TD1* 589).

96. Von Balthasar, "Nine Propositions," 102; and *The God Question and Modern Man*, 37.

97. In what follows I am relying on ideas presented by Gene Outka in his article "Universal Love and Impartiality," in *The Love Commandments: Essays in Christian Ethics and Moral Philosophy*, ed. Edmund N. Santurri and William Werpehowski (Washington, D.C.: Georgetown University Press, 1992), 1–103. There he describes four asymmetries that mark the relationship between the Christian love for neighbor and the Christian love for self. I adapt two of these asymmetries: (1) "one's obedient willing before and for God . . . means that I should value my particular identity and projects," and not simply forgo them whenever they conflict with opportunities for neighbor love; (2) there is a "fixed and structural difference between what I can do for another and what I can do for myself" (Outka, "Universal Love," 5).

98. Von Balthasar, *Who Is a Christian?* (London: Burnes & Oates, 1968), 12.

99. This love is an active receptivity, as we have seen—we lovingly receive into being the other—and is an "*imago trinitatis*, since in God each Hypostasis can only be itself insofar as it 'lets' the others 'be' in equal concreteness" (*TD5* 75).

100. And it must also include, I think, a resistance to those forces which seek to undermine basic agency (e.g., individual criminal pursuits, oppressive regimes), though this "dark" Christian love—that is, one that is directly and actively *opposed* to the neighbor—is not given much attention in von Balthasar's works.

101. Von Balthasar, "Immediacy to God," 336–37. He gives the example of the U.N. Declaration of Human Rights.

102. Von Balthasar, "The Word and History," in *The Word Made Flesh*, 38.

103. Von Balthasar, *Theology of Karl Barth*, 363; emphasis added.

104. "When grace is bestowed on Israel, it receives thereby access to God, a place beside him and the right to dwell there. But the primary meaning of grace *must be, not that God bestows on the creature . . . a new 'quality,' but rather that he bends down to the earth and raises man up to himself*" (*GL6* 149; emphasis added).

105. Thus von Balthasar states that God's address does not override but "presupposes a realm, an (ante-)room in which human freedom makes decisions about values according to criteria that are largely drawn from the world itself." Within this "anteroom," the human person can "establish certain 'general' norms of action, abstracted from human existence, and these may be relatively correct," though the final norm must be, as it was for Ignatius, that which best serves divine glory (*TD2* 85). Also, the Christian must bring "a loving appreciation of the existing values" of the world in his fidelity to Christ's mission, and yet show that "they are genuinely fulfilled only in the message of Christ" (*TD4* 465).

106. "Therefore, in this act of faith that is demanded here [of the non-

believer], it is *also* a question of the natural activity of human reason. It is precisely human reason that is summoned not only to know God but to acknowledge him in its logical thinking" (von Balthasar, *Theology of Karl Barth*, 315).

Chapter 5
Contemplation and Action

1. Iris Murdoch, *Metaphysics as a Guide to Morals* (New York: Penguin Books, 1992), 177. We must use "suitable metaphors" and invent "suitable concepts" to make certain features of our existence "visible" (Iris Murdoch, *The Sovereignty of Good* [London: Routledge & Kegan Paul, 1970], 75). "The development of consciousness in human beings is inseparably connected with the use of metaphor. Metaphors are not merely peripheral decorations or even useful models, they are fundamental forms of our awareness of our condition: metaphors of space, metaphors of movement, metaphors of vision" (Murdoch, *Sovereignty*, 77).

2. Similarly, Stanley Hauerwas argues that the language and metaphors of Christianity help us see the world as it truly is (*Vision and Virtue: Essays in Christian Ethical Reflection* [Notre Dame, Ind.: Fides Publishers, 1974], 46).

3. Murdoch, *Metaphysics as Guide*, 25.

4. "Value goes right down to the bottom of the cognitive situation" (Murdoch, *Metaphysics as Guide*, 384).

5. Charles Taylor, whose ethical theory grants a significant role to language in the articulation of a moral vision, offers a similar defense for secondary moral concepts. We "will come to see a certain vocabulary as the most realistic and insightful for the things of this domain [of human affairs]. What these terms pick out will be what to us is real here, and it cannot and should not be otherwise. If we cannot deliberate effectively, or understand and explain people's action illuminatingly, without such terms as 'courage' or 'generosity,' then these are real features of our world" (*Sources of the Self: The Making of the Modern Identity* [Cambridge, Mass.: Harvard University Press, 1989], 69).

6. Valuing "is not a specialized activity of the will, but an apprehension of the world" (Murdoch, *Metaphysics as Guide*, 265). Value "is a light in which the world is revealed" (ibid., 39).

7. Ibid., 168.

8. "What does seem to make perfect sense in the Platonic myth is the idea of the Good as the source of light which reveals to us all things as they really are" (Murdoch, *Sovereignty*, 70). The Good "fosters our sense of reality" (Murdoch, *Metaphysics as Guide*, 399).

9. Murdoch, *Sovereignty*, 41.

10. Murdoch, *Metaphysics as Guide*, 25.

11. Ibid., 52, 54.

12. Iris Murdoch, *The Fire and the Sun: Why Plato Banished the Artists* (New York: Viking Penguin, 1977), 46–47.

13. Iris Murdoch, "The Sublime and the Good," in *Existentialists and Mystics*, ed. Peter Conradi (New York: Penguin Press, 1998), 215.

14. There are different opinions about how much Plato's dialogues exclude any tragic element. Drew Hyland surveys several views and then argues that there is a strong connection between Plato's philosophy and tragedy ("Philosophy and Tragedy in the Platonic Dialogues," in *Tragedy and Philosophy*, ed. N. Georgopoulos [New York: St. Martin's Press, Inc., 1993], 123–38).

15. Murdoch, *Metaphysics as Guide*, 108.

16. Murdoch, *Fire and the Sun*, 80.

17. For example: "Truth contemplated and received is also active, and this in two respects: first, as the immanent act of the spirit, both in the process of discursive reasoning and in intellectual vision—there can be no intellect without will, will and intellect presuppose each other—secondly, . . . truth must be acted upon as well as perceived. This is the true sense of the existential character of truth; we only really possess it, when we do it; it has not only to be grasped and seen in concepts, but expressed in the whole of one's being and life" (Hans Urs von Balthasar, "Action and Contemplation," in *The Word Made Flesh*, vol. 1 of *Explorations in Theology* [San Francisco: Ignatius Press, 1989], 233).

18. In "The Idea of Perfection," Murdoch argues that our attempts to embody secondary moral concepts always seem imperfect, a fact that speaks of "an ideal [or transcendent] limit" to which these concepts point (Murdoch, *Sovereignty*, 28).

19. "If the magnetic field [of our vision] is right our movements within it will tend to be right" (Murdoch, "The Darkness of Practical Reason," in *Existentialists and Mystics*, 201). "When moments of decision arrive we see and are attracted by the world we have already (partly) made" (ibid., 200).

20. Something like an "obedience" ensues upon a "patient, loving regard, directed upon a person, a thing, a situation" (Murdoch, *Sovereignty*, 40).

21. "When a person is struck by something truly significant . . . an arrow pierces his heart, at his most personal level. The issue is one that concerns *him*. '*You* must change your life,' you must henceforth live in response to this unique and genuine revelation. . . . [W]here the aesthetic fails to reveal the ethical that lies within it, such a rapture is degraded to a prettifying excuse ('*ravissant*'). Where a thing of beauty is really and radically beheld, freedom too is radically opened up, and decision can take place" (*TD2* 30–31).

22. "While the Christian life ostensibly consists in alternate periods of action and contemplation, its aim should be to make the two interpenetrate more and more. With the saints they were no longer distinguishable" (von Balthasar, "Action and Contemplation," in *Word Made Flesh*, 237–38). Also: "And so we conclude that action and contemplation are indissolubly linked to each other in a variety of ways" ("Beyond Action and Contemplation?" in *Spirit and Institution*, vol. 4 of *Explorations in Theology*, trans. Edward T. Oakes, S.J. [San Francisco: Ignatius Press, 1995], 307).

23. Von Balthasar, "Action and Contemplation," 238.

24. "The Spiritual Senses," in *GL1* 365–425.

25. The contrast between the two and von Balthasar's desire to plot a path between them recurs throughout his writings. See, for example, his earlier discussion in *Glory of the Lord*, vol. 1, where he rejects both the view that the signs miracles of Jesus are empirical anomalies which, qua miraculous, point to his supernatural status and the approach that makes the signs transparent instruments for an immediate vision of the divine (*GL1* 147–55).

26. Von Balthasar cites a passage from Augustine's *Confessions* as an example of this sensory faith. "But what do I love, O God, when I love Thee? Not the beauty of a body nor the rhythm of moving time. Not the splendour of the light, which is so dear to the eyes. . . . And yet I do love a light and a sound and a fragrance and a delicacy and an embrace, when I love my God" (*GL1* 379, citing *Confessions* 10.6).

27. Karl Rahner, "Experience of the Holy Spirit," in *Theological Investigations*, vol. 18, trans. Edward Quinn (New York: Crossroad, 1983), 205–6. See also his articles on the "spiritual senses": "The 'Spiritual Senses' According to Origen" and "The Doctrine of the 'Spiritual Senses' in the Middle Ages," in *Theological Investigations*, vol. 16 (New York: Seabury Press, 1979), 81–134.

28. "Whatever happens in the sphere of the revelation of the living God takes place in an arena which has been opened by God and has been made accessible to man beyond any claims of his mere 'nature'" (*GL6* 13).

29. Hans Urs von Balthasar, "Revelation and the Beautiful," in *The Word Made Flesh*, vol. 1 of *Explorations in Theology* (San Francisco: Ignatius Press, 1989), 109; *GL4* 14; *GL5* 47. Von Balthasar does not exclude all extramural arguments in principle. For example, he believes that in the human person, even secular thinkers confront a phenomenon that they generally recognize to be more than a collection of facts. But such appeals are generally unpersuasive (von Balthasar, "Forgetfulness of God and Christians," 332).

30. Von Balthasar seems to sense the skepticism with which his position will be greeted by some. Though the "adaptation of the Christian senses . . . to the mysteries of the kingdom of God remains for us a mystery," he suggests, "it must not be dismissed *a priori* as being impossible" (*GL1* 415).

31. *GL1* 382; citing *CD* III/2 252.

32. "First and last and all the time [human] perception has properly only one object, of which everything else gives positive or negative witness. . . . God is the object and content in virtue of which and in relation to which [human] nature is a rational nature" (*GL1* 387, citing Barth, *CD* III/2 402).

33. The "inconceivability of the fact that God has loved us so much" is the "ungraspability of God" that shows itself in divine revelation (*GL1* 461).

34. Hans Urs von Balthasar, *Love Alone: The Way of Revelation* (New York: Herder & Herder, 1969), 83.

35. Cyril O'Regan, "Newman and von Balthasar: The Christological Contexting of the Numinous," *Église et Théologie* 26 (1995): 193.

36. Von Balthasar cites Barth approvingly on this point: "God does not usually meet [the individual] immediately but mediately in His works, deeds and ordinances. . . . [T]he history of God's traffic with him takes place in the sphere of the created world and of the world of objects distinct from God" (Barth, *CD* III/2 402, cited in von Balthasar, *The Theology of Karl Barth: Exposition and Interpretation*, trans. Edward T. Oakes [San Francisco: Ignatius Press, 1992], 153).

37. Von Balthasar, *The Christian State of Life*, trans. Sister Mary Frances McCarthy (San Francisco: Ignatius Press, 1983), 456. And since feeling is an important part of this undivided agency, it too can be used by God to texture our experience of God. It is not a self-standing component but rather an integral part of the person's total disposition toward and encounter with God—neither the privileged indicator of that encounter nor an additional "condiment" to it.

38. "The expression the 'centre of the form of revelation' does not refer to a particular section of this form however central which, in order to be read as form, would then essentially need to be filled out by other more peripheral aspects. What the phrase is intended to denote is, rather, the reality which lends the form its total coherence and comprehensibility, the 'wherefore' to which *all particular aspects have to be referred if they are to be understood*" (*GL1* 463; emphasis added).

39. Gene Outka detects an ambiguity in Hauerwas on this point. In general, Hauerwas sees his argument for the particularity of Christian ethics only as an extension of the thesis that "all moral schemes depend on given narratives." However, on a few occasions Hauerwas moves not from the narrative-dependency of all moral systems but from the particularity of Christian revelation (Stanley Hauerwas, "Character, Vision, and Narrative," *Religious Studies Review* 6, no. 2 [1980]: 117).

Thomas Ogletree raises a different challenge. Hauerwas's concern, he suggests, is not at all how "Christian convictions *form* lives," but rather how are we to "*understand* and *interpret* human character and its bearing on the moral life in light of Christian faith?" If Hauerwas *were* to make the former his question, he would have been forced to include the non-narrative forces he can seem eager to ignore (Thomas Ogletree, "Character and Narrative: Stanley Hauerwas' Studies of the Christian Life," *Religious Studies Review* 6, no. 1 [1980]: 26). One path available to Hauerwas in addressing the first question is that offered by von Balthasar's image of our play (with all its relative autonomy) playing within God's play.

40. George A. Lindbeck, *The Nature of Doctrine: Religion and Theology in a Postliberal Age* (Philadelphia: Westminster Press, 1984), 117.

41. Von Balthasar does not specifically identify Scripture with one of the five domains of divine–human encounter, but Scripture is clearly for him an inseparable part of the experience of the *ecclesia* and of the contemplative encounter that takes place within it.

42. Von Balthasar maintains that infant baptism "is inadequate as a model for the sacramental event." The idea that "the entrance into God's kingdom occurs unconsciously . . . is a fact so conspicuously alien to Scripture . . . that it must without question be regarded as an exception" (*GL1* 579).

43. See "The Mediation of the Form," *GL1* 527–604.

44. "The mere symbolism of the world of signs does not simply compel the event" (*GL1* 418). The Lord of the church "remains free, if it so pleases him, to manifest himself . . . to man even through the aesthetic symbols and the ostensive images of the world" (*GL1* 423).

45. "Positive mystery" is a term used by Cyril O'Regan, "Newman and von Balthasar," 188.

46. Rudolph Otto, *The Idea of the Holy*, trans. John W. Harvey (New York: Oxford University Press, 1958).

47. See O'Regan, "Newman and von Balthasar," 189.

48. All things must be seen "as the vessel and expression of the eternal activity of the eternal life" (von Balthasar, "Characteristics of Christianity," in *The Word Made Flesh*, vol. 1 of *Explorations in Theology* [San Francisco: Ignatius Press, 1989], 176–77).

49. Also, "Christians imitate Jesus . . . in the ability to discern and in the *de facto* active work of discerning the spirits" (*GL7* 126).

50. Hans Urs von Balthasar, "Reflections on the Discernment of Spirits," *Communio* 7 (1980): 207. See also "Unterscheidung der Geister," *TL3* 355–75. The U.S. Catholic bishops' letter on the use of nuclear weapons offers an example of such an ecclesial discernment of where God labors in our midst (National Conference of Catholic Bishops, *The Challenge of Peace: God's Promise and Our Response* [Washington, D.C.: United States Catholic Conference, 1983]).

51. H. Richard Niebuhr, *The Responsible Self: An Essay in Christian Moral Philosophy* (New York: Harper & Row, 1963), 126.

52. "Ignatius tacitly presupposes a philosophy of human existence in which a moral decision in its individuality is not merely an instance of general ethical normative principles" (Rahner, "The Logic of Concrete Individual Knowledge in Ignatius Loyola," in *The Dynamic Element in the Church* [New York: Herder & Herder, 1964], 110).

53. Stephen Fields, "Balthasar and Rahner on the Spiritual Senses," *Theological Studies* 57, no. 2 (1996): 232–34, 240–41.

54. Rahner, "Logic of Concrete Individual Knowledge," 124.

55. Karl Rahner, "Dialogue with God?" in *Theological Investigations,* vol. 18 (New York: Crossroad, 1983), 127.

56. Ibid., 131.

57. Von Balthasar, *Christian State of Life,* 420.

58. Von Balthasar, *Prayer,* 204.

59. Murdoch, *Metaphysics as Guide,* 106–8.

60. "Suffering remains but accompanied by a kind of passion, a high Eros, or purified joy, which is the vision of good itself which comes about when, or brings it about that, selfish desires, and the distress involved in their frustration, are removed" (Murdoch, *Metaphysics as Guide,* 109).

61. Murdoch, *Fire and the Sun,* 84.

62. Her original reads, "Man is a creature who makes a picture of himself and then comes to resemble the picture" (Murdoch, "Metaphysics and Ethics," in *Existentialists and Mystics,* 75). "This is metaphysics, which sets up a picture which it then offers as an appeal to us all to see if we cannot find just this in our deepest experience" (*Metaphysics as Guide,* 507).

63. "Morality has to do with not imposing form, except appropriately and cautiously and carefully and with attention to appropriate detail" (Iris Murdoch, cited in Michael O. Bellamy, "An Interview with Iris Murdoch," in *Contemporary Literature* [Madison: University of Wisconsin Press, 1977], 135).

64. Murdoch, *Metaphysics as Guide,* 109.

65. Martha Nussbaum, *The Fragility of Goodness: Luck and Ethics in Greek Tragedy and Philosophy* (Cambridge: Cambridge University Press, 1986), 153.

66. In 1699 Pope Innocent XII condemned as "offensive" the idea that there "is a habitual state of love for God, which is pure charity without admixture of the motive of self-interest" (Heinrich Denziger, *Enchiridion symbolorum, definitionum, et declarationum de rebus fidei et morum* [Freiburg: Herder, 1911] par. 1327, cited in Robert M. Adams, *The Virtue of Faith and Other Essays in Philosophical Theology* [New York: Oxford University Press, 1987], 174).

67. Murdoch, *Metaphysics as Guide,* 106.

68. Von Balthasar, *Theology of Karl Barth,* 53.

69. Spiritual senses "presuppose devout bodily senses which are capable of undergoing Christian transformation by coming to resemble the sensibility of Christ and Mary" (*GL1* 378).

70. Von Balthasar, "Nine Propositions on Christian Ethics," trans. Graham Harrison, in *Principles of Christian Morality* (San Francisco: Ignatius Press, 1986), 98; emphasis added. Also, Christian perfection "is inseparable from man's organic nature . . . [which] must be acknowledged" ("The Implications of the Word," in *The Word Made Flesh,* vol. 1 of *Explorations in Theology* [San Francisco: Ignatius Press, 1989], 63).

71. Don E. Saliers, "Liturgy and Ethics: Some New Beginnings," in *Liturgy and the Moral Self: Humanity at Full Stretch Before God,* ed. E. Byron Anderson and Bruce T. Morrill (Collegeville, Minn.: Liturgical Press, 1998), 24; reprinted from Don E. Saliers, "Liturgy and Ethics: Some New Beginnings," *Journal of Religious Ethics* 7, no. 2 (1979). See also William C. Spohn, *Go and Do Likewise: Jesus and Ethics* (New York: Continuum, 1999); and Philip S. Keane, *Christian Ethics and Imagination: A Theological Inquiry* (New York: Paulist, 1984).

Conclusion
In Praise of Glory

1. Gerard Manley Hopkins, "As Kingfishers Catch Fire," in *The Poems of Gerard Manley Hopkins*, ed. W. H. Gardner and N. H. MacKenzie (Oxford: Oxford University Press, 1970), 90.

2. Hans Urs von Balthasar, "The Place of Theology," in *The Word Made Flesh*, vol. 1 of *Explorations in Theology* (San Francisco: Ignatius Press, 1995), 150.

3. Thus, for example, one's surrender to the human Thou can be equated with one's surrender to the divine mission (von Balthasar, *The Christian State of Life*, trans. Sister Mary Frances McCarthy [San Francisco: Ignatius Press, 1983], 418).

4. Ibid., 435. "To be a recipient of revelation means more and more the act of renunciation which gives God the space in which to become incarnate and to offer himself as he will" (*GL1* 418). The Spirit "whispers and breathes right through everything that exists in the world, all intramundane values; and, without depriving the things of this world of their meaning and value, it lends them a bottomless dimension" (von Balthasar, *Prayer*, trans. Graham Harrison [San Francisco: Ignatius Press, 1986], 39).

5. "This does not mean that the Church, on the basis of the understanding vouchsafed her, cannot set up certain normative affirmations as signposts for our understanding, affirmations which will never prove to have been will-o'-the-wisps. But a signpost only sets us on the right path . . ." (*TD2* 74). Von Balthasar here is speaking of theological doctrines, but I think his comments apply as well to ethical teachings. See also Hans Urs von Balthasar, *Truth Is Symphonic: Aspects of Christian Pluralism*, trans. Graham Harrison (San Francisco: Ignatius Press, 1987), 81–85.

6. Garth L. Hallet, *Greater Good: The Case for Proportionalism* (Washington, D.C.: Georgetown University Press, 1995), 71.

7. Von Balthasar, *Prayer*, 24.

8. David Burrell and Stanley Hauerwas, "From System to Story: An Alternative Pattern to Rationality in Ethics," in *The Roots of Ethics*, ed. Daniel Callahan and H. Tristram Engelhardt (New York: Plenum Press, 1976), 85.

9. Von Balthasar, *Prayer*, 33; emphasis added. Cf. Barth: "The objection is obviously futile that God has not really given, and does not and will not give, His command with such wholeness, clarity and definiteness that it only remains for us to be obedient or disobedient" (Barth, *CD* II/2 669).

10. Von Balthasar, *Truth Is Symphonic*, 81–85.

11. I am only aware of two such discussions, though it is a stretch to describe them as "concrete": his brief study of *Humanae Vitae* and its prohibition of artificial contraceptives (von Balthasar, "A Word on 'Humanae Vitae,'" and his reflection on private ownership in *Christian State of Life*, 103–20).

12. Von Balthasar, *Christian State of Life*, 33. Also: "As love cools, the glowing lava of its immense spontaneity hardens into the fixed and narrow molds of individual commandments" (ibid., 30).

13. Hans Urs von Balthasar, *Love Alone: The Way of Revelation* (New York: Herder & Herder, 1969), 56.

14. Stanley Hauerwas, "Love's Not All You Need," in *Vision and Virtue: Essays in Christian Ethical Reflection* (Notre Dame, Ind.: Fides Publishing, 1974), 118.

15. But a note of caution can be added here: von Balthasar does not give absolute authority to the institutional leadership of the church. In his description of the service of the church leadership and its right to receive ecclesial obedience, von Balthasar states that, in light of the "persistent weaknesses and frequent failures of those exercising [church] authority," the ideal of an ecclesial obedience that is also christological (i.e., obedience *to* Christ) is "an approximation toward a never-attainable ideal" (Von Balthasar, "Christology and Ecclesial Obedience," in *Spirit and Institution*, vol. 4 of *Explorations in Theology*, trans. Edward T. Oakes, S.J. [San Francisco: Ignatius Press, 1995], 159). "There is no requirement that we overemphasize the directive that we 'are to see Christ' in the bearers of office in the Church, for every Christian can—and should—direct his gaze at Christ *immediately* . . ." (ibid., 160).

Bibliography

———

Works by Hans Urs von Balthasar
Books

von Balthasar, Hans Urs. *The Action*. Volume 4 of *Theo-Drama: Theological Dramatic Theory*. Translated by Graham Harrison. San Francisco: Ignatius Press, 1994.

———. *The Christian State of Life*. Translated by Sister Mary Frances McCarthy. San Francisco: Ignatius Press, 1983.

———. *Dare We Hope "That All Men Be Saved?"* Translated by David Kipp and Lothar Krauth. San Francisco: Ignatius Press, 1988.

———. *The Dramatis Personae: Man in God*. Volume 2 of *Theo-Drama: Theological Dramatic Theory*. Translated by Graham Harrison. San Francisco: Ignatius Press, 1990.

———. *The Dramatis Personae: The Person in Christ*. Volume 3 of *Theo-Drama: Theological Dramatic Theory*. Translated by Graham Harrison. San Francisco: Ignatius Press, 1992.

———. *Epilog*. Einsiedeln: Johannes Verlag, 1987.

———. *Der Geist Der Wahrheit*. Volume 3 of *Theologik*. Einsiedeln: Johannes Verlag, 1987.

———. *The God Question and Modern Man*. New York: Seabury Press, 1967.

———. *Homo Creatus Est*. Einsiedeln: Johannes Verlag, 1986.

———. *Love Alone: The Way of Revelation*. New York: Herder & Herder, 1969.

———. *The Moment of Christian Witness*. Translated by Richard Beckley. San Francisco: Ignatius Press, 1994.

———. *My Work: In Retrospect*. Translated by Brian McNeil, C.R.V. San Francisco: Communio Books, Ignatius Press, 1993.

———. *Mysterium Paschale*. Translated by Aidan Nichols, O.P. Grand Rapids: Eerdmans, 1993.

———. *Prayer*. Translated by Graham Harrison. San Francisco: Ignatius, 1986.

———. *Prolegomena*. Volume 1 of *Theo-Drama: Theological Dramatic Theory*. Translated by Graham Harrison. San Francisco: Ignatius Press, 1988.

———. *The Realm of Metaphysics in Antiquity*. Volume 4 of *The Glory of the Lord: A Theological Aesthetics*. Translated by Brian McNeil, C.R.V., et al. San Francisco: Ignatius Press, 1989.

———. *The Realm of Metaphysics in the Modern Age*. Volume 5 of *The Glory of the Lord: A Theological Aesthetics*. Translated by Oliver Davies et al. San Francisco: Ignatius Press, 1991.

———. *Seeing the Form*. Volume 1 of *The Glory of the Lord: A Theological Aesthetics*. Translated by Erasmo Leiva-Merikakis. San Francisco: Ignatius Press, 1982.

———. *Studies in Theological Style: Clerical Styles*. Volume 2 of *The Glory of the Lord: A Theological Aesthetics*. Translated by Andrew Louth, Francis McDonagh, and Brian McNeil, C.R.V. San Francisco: Ignatius Press, 1984.

———. *Studies in Theological Styles: Lay Styles*. Volume 3 of *The Glory of the Lord: A Theological Aesthetics*. Translated by Andrew Louth et al. San Francisco: Ignatius Press, 1986.

———. *A Theological Anthropology*. New York: Sheed & Ward, 1967.

———. *A Theology of History*. San Francisco: Ignatius Press, 1994.

———. *The Theology of Karl Barth: Exposition and Interpretation*. Translated by Edward T. Oakes. San Francisco: Ignatius Press, 1992.

———. *Theology: The New Covenant*. Volume 7 of *The Glory of the Lord: A Theological Aesthetics*. Translated by Brian McNeil, C.R.V. San Francisco: Ignatius Press, 1989.

———. *Theology: The Old Covenant*. Volume 6 of *The Glory of the Lord: A Theological Aesthetics*. Translated by Brian McNeil, C.R.V., and Erasmo Leiva-Merikakis. San Francisco: Ignatius Press, 1991.

———. *Truth Is Symphonic: Aspects of Christian Pluralism*. Translated by Graham Harrison. San Francisco: Ignatius Press, 1987.

———. *Two Sisters in the Spirit: Thérèse of Lisieux and Elizabeth of the Trinity*. Translated by Donald Nichols and Anne Elizabeth England. San Francisco: Ignatius Press, 1992.

———. *Wahrheit der Welt*. Volume 1 of *Theologik*. Einsiedeln: Johannes Verlag, 1985.

———. *Wahrheit Gottes*. Volume 2 of *Theologik*. Einsiedeln: Johannes Verlag, 1985.

———. *Who Is a Christian?* London: Burnes & Oates, 1968.

Articles

von Balthasar, Hans Urs. "Action and Contemplation." In *The Word Made Flesh*. Volume 1 of *Explorations in Theology*. San Francisco: Ignatius Press, 1989.

———. "Beyond Action and Contemplation?" In *Spirit and Institution*. Volume 4 of *Explorations in Theology*. San Francisco: Ignatius Press, 1995.

———. "Characteristics of Christianity." In *The Word Made Flesh*. Volume 1 of *Explorations in Theology*. San Francisco: Ignatius Press, 1989.

———. "Christian Universalism." In *The Word Made Flesh*. Volume 1 of *Explorations in Theology*. San Francisco: Ignatius Press, 1989.

———. "Christology and Ecclesial Obedience." In *Spirit and Institution*. Volume 4 of *Explorations in Theology*. San Francisco: Ignatius Press, 1995.

———. "The Council of the Holy Spirit." In *Creator Spirit*. Volume 3 of *Explorations in Theology*. San Francisco: Ignatius Press, 1993.

———. "Encountering God in Today's World." In *Creator Spirit*. Volume 3 of *Explorations in Theology*. San Francisco: Ignatius Press, 1993.

———. "Eschatology in Outline." In *Spirit and Institution*. Volume 4 of *Explorations in Theology*. San Francisco: Ignatius Press, 1995.

———. "Forgetfulness of God and Christians." In *Creator Spirit*. Volume 3 of *Explorations in Theology*. San Francisco: Ignatius Press, 1993.

———. "The Holy Spirit as Love." In *Creator Spirit*. Volume 3 of *Explorations in Theology*. San Francisco: Ignatius Press, 1993.

———. "Immediacy to God." In *Creator Spirit*. Volume 3 of *Explorations in Theology*. San Francisco: Ignatius Press, 1993.

———. "The Implications of the Word." In *The Word Made Flesh*. Volume 1 of *Explorations in Theology*. San Francisco: Ignatius Press, 1989.

———. "Nine Propositions on Christian Ethics." Translated by Graham Harrison. In *Principles of Christian Morality*. San Francisco: Ignatius Press, 1986.

———. "Office in the Church." In *Spouse of the Word*. Volume 2 of *Explorations in Theology*. San Francisco: Ignatius Press, 1991.

———. "On Vicarious Representation." In *Spirit and Institution*. Volume 4 of *Explorations in Theology*. San Francisco: Ignatius Press, 1995.

———. "The Place of Theology." In *The Word Made Flesh*. Volume 1 of *Explorations in Theology*. San Francisco: Ignatius Press, 1989.

———. "Reflections on the Discernment of Spirits." *Communio* 7 (1980).

———. "Revelation and the Beautiful." In *The Word Made Flesh*. Volume 1 of *Explorations in Theology*. San Francisco: Ignatius Press, 1989.

———. "Secular Piety?" In *Creator Spirit*. Volume 3 of *Explorations in Theology*. San Francisco: Ignatius Press, 1993.

———. "The Unknown Lying Beyond the Word." In *Creator Spirit*. Volume 3 of *Explorations in Theology*. San Francisco: Ignatius Press, 1993.

———. "The Word and History." In *The Word Made Flesh*. Volume 1 of *Explorations in Theology*. San Francisco: Ignatius Press, 1989.

———. "A Word on 'Humanae Vitae.'" *Communio* 20 (summer 1993).

———. "The Word, Scripture, and Tradition." In *The Word Made Flesh*. Volume 1 of *Explorations in Theology*. San Francisco: Ignatius Press, 1989.

Other Works Cited

Adams, Robert M. "A Modified Divine Command Theory of Ethical Wrongness." In *The Virtue of Faith and Other Essays in Philosophical Theology*. Oxford: Oxford University Press, 1987.

Aertsen, Jan A. *Medieval Philosophy and the Transcendentals: The Case of Thomas Aquinas*. Leiden: E. J. Brill, 1996.

Aquinas, Thomas. *Summa Contra Gentiles*. Translated by Anton C. Pegis. Vol. 4. Notre Dame, Ind.: University of Notre Dame Press, 1975.

———. *Summa Theologica*. Translated by the Fathers of the English Dominican Province. New York: Benziger Brothers, 1948.

Augustine. *The Confessions of St. Augustine*. Translated by Rex Warner. New York: Mentor, New American Library, 1963.

Barth, Karl. *Christian Life*. Vol. IV/4 of *Church Dogmatics*. Translated by Geoffrey W. Bromiley. Grand Rapids: Eerdmans, 1981.

———. *Church Dogmatics*, I/1. Translated by G. T. Thomson. Edinburgh: T&T Clark, 1960.

———. *Church Dogmatics*, I/2. Translated by G. W. Bromiley. Edinburgh: T&T Clark, 1975.

———. *Church Dogmatics*, II/1. Translated by T. H. L. Parker et al. Edinburgh: T&T Clark, 1980.

———. *Church Dogmatics*, II/2. Translated by G. W. Bromiley et al. Edinburgh: T&T Clark, 1957.

———. *Church Dogmatics*, III/2. Translated by Harold Knight et al. Edinburgh: T&T Clark, 1960.

———. *Church Dogmatics*, III/4. Translated by A. T. Mackay et al. Edinburgh: T&T Clark, 1961.

———. *The Humanity of God*. Translated by John Newton Thomas et al. Richmond, Va.: John Knox Press, 1969.

Bellamy, Michael O. "An Interview with Iris Murdoch." *Contemporary Literature*. Madison: University of Wisconsin Press, 1977.

Best, Ernest. *One Body in Christ: A Study in the Relationship of the Church to Christ in the Epistles of the Apostle Paul*. London: S.P.C.K., 1955.

Biggar, Nigel. *The Hastening That Waits: Karl Barth's Ethics*. Oxford: Clarendon Press, 1993.

Burrell, David, and Stanley Hauerwas. "From System to Story: An Alternative Pattern to Rationality in Ethics." In *The Roots of Ethics*, edited by Daniel Callahan and H. Tristram Engelhardt. New York: Plenum Press, 1976.

Casarella, Peter. "The Expression and Form of the Word: Trinitarian

Hermeneutics and the Sacramentality of Language in Hans Urs von Balthasar's Theology." *Renascence* 48 (winter 1996).

Clarke, W. Norris, S.J. *Person and Being*. Milwaukee: Marquette University Press, 1993.

Curran, Charles E. *Moral Theology: A Continuing Journey*. Notre Dame, Ind.: University of Notre Dame Press, 1982.

———. "The Stance of Moral Theology." In *Directions in Fundamental Moral Theology*. Notre Dame, Ind.: University of Notre Dame Press, 1985.

D'Arcy, Eric. "'Worthy of Worship': A Catholic Contribution." In *Religion and Morality*, edited by Gene Outka and John P. Reeder. Garden City, N.Y.: Doubleday Anchor, 1973.

Davis, Henry. *Human Acts, Law, Sin, Virtue*. Volume 1 of *Moral and Pastoral Theology*. New York: Sheed & Ward, 1943.

De Lubac, Henri. *The Mystery of the Supernatural*. Translated by Rosemary Sheed. New York: Herder & Herder, 1965.

Duffy, Stephen J. *The Graced Horizon: Nature and Grace in Modern Catholic Thought*. Collegeville, Minn.: Liturgical Press, 1992.

Ellul, Jacques. *The Ethics of Freedom*. Translated by G. W. Bromiley. Grand Rapids: Eerdmans, 1976.

Endean, Philip. "Moral Theology, Karl Rahner, and the Ignatian Spiritual Exercises." *The Way Supplement* 88 (1997).

Farley, Margaret A. "Fragments of an Ethic of Commitment in Thomas Aquinas." *Journal of Religion* 2 (1978).

Fields, Stephen. "Balthasar and Rahner on the Spiritual Senses." *Theological Studies* 57, no. 2 (1996).

Fitzmyer, Joseph A. "Pauline Theology." In *The New Jerome Biblical Commentary*, edited by Raymond E. Brown, Joseph A. Fitzmyer, and Roland E. Murphy. Englewood Cliffs, N.J.: Prentice Hall, 1990.

Frei, Hans W. *The Eclipse of the Biblical Narrative*. New Haven: Yale University Press, 1974.

Fuchs, Josef. "Our Image of God and the Morality of Innerworldly Behavior." In *Christian Morality: The Word Becomes Flesh*. Washington, D.C.: Georgetown University Press, 1981.

Galvin, John P. "The Invitation of Grace." In *A World of Grace: An Introduction to the Themes and Foundations of Karl Rahner's Theology*, edited by Leo J. O'Donovan. New York: Crossroad, 1984.

Gawronski, Raymond. *Word and Silence: Hans Urs von Balthasar and the Spiritual Encounter Between East and West*. Grand Rapids: Eerdmans, 1995.

Gilleman, Gérard. *The Primacy of Charity*. Translated by William F. Ryan and André Vachon. Westminster, Md.: Newman Press, 1959.

Gilson, Etienne. *The Elements of Christian Philosophy*. New York: North American Library, 1963.

Guardini, Romano. *The World and The Person*. Translated by Stella Lange. Chicago: Henry Regnery, 1965.

Gustafson, James. *Protestant and Roman Catholic Ethics: Prospects for Rapprochement*. Chicago: University of Chicago Press, 1978.

Hallet, Garth L. *Greater Good: The Case for Proportionalism*. Washington, D.C.: Georgetown University Press, 1995.

Häring, Bernard. *The Law of Christ*. Translated by Edwin G. Kaiser. Westminster, Md.: Newman Press, 1963.

Hauerwas, Stanley. *The Peaceable Kingdom*. Notre Dame, Ind.: University of Notre Dame Press, 1983.

———. "Story and Theology." *Religion in Life* 45 (autumn 1976).

———. *Vision and Virtue: Essays in Christian Ethical Reflection*. Notre Dame, Ind.: Fides Publishers, 1974.

Hearts on Fire: Praying with Jesuits. Edited by Michael Harter. St. Louis, Mo.: Institute of Jesuit Sources, 1993.

Heidegger, Martin. *Being and Time*. Translated by John Macquarrie and Edward Robinson. New York: Harper & Row, 1962.

———. "On the Essence of Truth." In *Martin Heidegger: Basic Writings*, edited by David Farrell Krell. New York: Harper & Row, 1977.

Hill, William J. *The Three-Personed God*. Washington, D.C.: Catholic University of America Press, 1982.

Hollenbach, David. "Fundamental Theology and the Christian Moral Life." In *Faithful Witness: Foundations of Theology for Today's Church*, edited by Leo J. O'Donovan and T. Howland Sanks. New York: Crossroad, 1989.

Hooker, Morna D. "Interchange in Christ and Ethics." *Journal for the Study of the New Testament* 25 (1985).

———. "A Partner in the Gospel: Paul's Understanding of His Ministry." In *Theology and Ethics in Paul and His Interpreters: Essays in Honor of Victor Paul Furnish*, edited by Eugene H. Lovering, Jr., and Jerry L. Sumney. Nashville: Abingdon Press, 1996.

Hopkins, Gerard Manley. "As Kingfishers Catch Fire." In *The Poems of Gerard Manley Hopkins*, edited by W. H. Gardner and N. H. MacKenzie. Oxford: Oxford University Press, 1970.

Hughes, Gerard J. *Authority in Morals: An Essay in Christian Ethics*. London: Heythrop Monographs, 1978.

Hyland, Drew A. "Philosophy and Tragedy in the Platonic Dialogues." In *Tragedy and Philosophy*, edited by N. Georgopoulos. New York: St. Martin's Press, Inc., 1993.

Ignatius of Loyola. *The Spiritual Exercises of Ignatius of Loyola*. Translated by George E. Ganss. Chicago: Loyola University Press, 1992.

Johnson, Elizabeth A. *She Who Is: The Mystery of God in Feminist Theological Discourse*. New York: Crossroad, 1992.

Jones, L. Gregory. *Embodying Forgiveness: A Theological Analysis*. Grand Rapids: Eerdmans, 1995.

Kant, Immanuel. *Critique of Practical Reason*. Translated by Lewis Whit Beck. New York: Macmillan, 1956.

————. *Religion Within the Limits of Reason*. Translated by Theodore M. Greene and H. Hudson Hoyt. San Francisco: Harper & Row, 1960.

Kasper, Walter. *The God of Jesus Christ*. Translated by Matthew J. O'Connell. New York: Crossroad, 1992.

Kay, Jeffrey Ames. *Theological Aesthetics: The Role of Aesthetics in the Theological Method of Hans Urs von Balthasar*. Frankfurt: Peter Lang, 1975.

Keane, Philip S. *Christian Ethics and Imagination: A Theological Inquiry*. New York: Paulist, 1984.

Killian, McDonnell. "A Trinitarian Theology of the Holy Spirit?" *Theological Studies* 46 (1985).

Lacugna, Catherine Mowry. *God For Us: The Trinity and Christian Life*. San Francisco: Harper, 1973.

Lindbeck, George A. *The Nature of Doctrine: Religion and Theology in a Post-Liberal Age*. Philadelphia: Wesminster Press, 1984.

Lucas, F. L. *Tragedy: Serious Drama in Relation to Aristotle's Poetics*. New York: Macmillan, 1958.

MacDonald, Scott. "The Metaphysics of Goodness and the Doctrine of the Transcendentals." In *Being and Goodness,* edited by Scott MacDonald. Ithaca, N.Y.: Cornell University Press, 1991.

MacNamara, Vincent. *Faith and Ethics: Recent Roman Catholicism*. Washington, D.C.: Georgetown University Press, 1985.

McClendon, James W. *Ethics: Systematic Theology*. Nashville: Abingdon Press, 1986.

McCormick, Richard. "Does Faith Add to Ethical Perception." In *The Distinctiveness of Christian Ethics*. Volume 2 of *Readings in Moral Theology,* edited by Charles E. Curran and Richard A. McCormick. New York: Paulist, 1980.

McDade, John. "The Trinity and the Paschal Mystery." *Heythrop Journal* 29 (1988).

McDonagh, Enda. *Gift and Call: Towards a Christian Theology of Morality*. Dublin: Gill & Macmillan, 1975.

McDonnell, Kilian. "The Determinative Doctrine of the Holy Spirit." *Theology Today* 39 (1982).

McIntosh, Mark A. *Christology from Within: Spirituality and Incarnation in Hans Urs von Balthasar*. Notre Dame, Ind.: University of Notre Dame Press, 1996.

Milbank, John. *Theology and Social Theory: Beyond Secular Reason*. Oxford: Blackwell, 1990.

Mouw, Richard J. *The God Who Commands*. Notre Dame, Ind.: University of Notre Dame Press, 1990.

Murdoch, Iris. "Against Dryness." In *Existentialists and Mystics: Writings on Philosophy and Literature,* edited by Peter Conradi. New York: Penguin Press, 1998.

————. "The Darkness of Practical Reason." In *Existentialists and Mystics:*

Writings on Philosophy and Literature, edited by Peter Conradi. New York: Penguin Press, 1998.
———. *The Fire and the Sun: Why Plato Banished the Artists.* New York: Viking Penguin, 1977.
———. "Metaphysics and Ethics." In *Existentialists and Mystics: Writings on Philosophy and Literature,* edited by Peter Conradi. New York: Penguin Press, 1998.
———. *Metaphysics as a Guide to Morals.* New York: Penguin Books, 1992.
———. *The Sovereignty of Good.* London: Routledge & Kegan Paul, 1970.
———. "The Sublime and the Beautiful Revisted." In *Existentialists and Mystics: Writings on Philosophy and Literature,* edited by Peter Conradi. New York: Penguin Press, 1998.
———. "The Sublime and the Good." In *Existentialists and Mystics: Writings on Philosophy and Literature,* edited by Peter Conradi. New York: Penguin Press, 1998.
———. "Vision and Choice in Morality." In *Existentialists and Mystics: Writings on Philosophy and Literature,* edited by Peter Conradi. New York: Penguin Press, 1998.
National Conference of Catholic Bishops. *The Challenge of Peace: God's Promise and Our Response.* Washington, D.C.: United States Catholic Conference, 1983.
Nelson, Paul. *Narrative and Morality: A Theological Inquiry.* University Park, Pa.: Pennsylvania State University Press, 1987.
Nichols, Aidan, O.P. *No Bloodless Myth: A Guide Through Balthasar's Dramatics.* Washington, D.C.: Catholic University of America Press, 2000.
Niebuhr, H. Richard. *The Responsible Self: An Essay in Christian Moral Philosophy.* New York: Harper & Row, 1963.
Noldin, H. *De Principiis.* Volume 1 of *Summa Theologiae Moralis.* Freiburg: Herder, 1962.
Nussbaum, Martha C. *The Fragility of Goodness: Luck and Ethics in Greek Tragedy and Philosophy.* Cambridge: Cambridge University Press, 1986.
———. *Love's Knowledge: Essays on Philosophy and Literature.* Oxford: Oxford University Press, 1990.
Nygren, Anders. *Agape and Eros.* Translated by Philip S. Watson. Philadelphia: Westminster Press, 1953.
Oakes, Edward T. *Pattern of Redemption: The Theology of Hans Urs von Balthasar.* New York: Continuum, 1994.
Ogletree, Thomas. "Character and Narrative: Stanley Hauerwas' Studies of the Christian Life." *Religious Studies Review* 6, no. 1 (1980).
Otto, Rudolph. *The Idea of the Holy.* Translated by John W. Harvey. New York: Oxford University Press, 1958.
Outka, Gene. "Character, Vision, and Narrative." *Religious Studies Review* 6, no. 2 (1980).
———. "Discontinuity in the Ethics of Jacques Ellul." In *Jacques Ellul: Inter-*

pretive Essays, edited by Clifford G. Christians and Jay M. Van Hook. Chicago: University of Illinois Press, 1981.

———. "Universal Love and Impartiality." In *The Love Commandments: Essays in Christian Ethics and Moral Philosophy*, edited by Edmund N. Santurri and William Werpehowski. Washington, D.C.: Georgetown University Press, 1992.

O'Donnell, John, S.J. *Hans Urs von Balthasar*. Collegeville, Minn.: Liturgical Press, 1992.

———. "The Trinity as Divine Community: A Critical Reflection Upon Recent Theological Developments." *Gregorianum* 68, no. 1 (1988).

O'Donoghue, Noel Dermot. "Do We Get Beyond Plato? A Critical Appreciation of the Theological Aesthetics." In *The Beauty of Christ*, edited by Bede McGregor and Thomas Norris. Edinburgh: T&T Clark, 1994.

O'Hanlon, Gerard F. *The Immutability of God in the Theology of Hans Urs von Balthasar*. Cambridge: Cambridge University Press, 1990.

O'Malley, John W. *The First Jesuits*. Cambridge, Mass.: Harvard University Press, 1993.

O'Regan, Cyril. "Newman and von Balthasar: The Christological Contexting of the Numinous." *Église et Théologie* 26 (1995).

———. "Von Balthasar's Valorization and Critique of Heidegger's Genealogy of Modernity." In *Christian Spirituality and the Culture of Modernity: The Thought of Louis Dupré*, edited by George P. Schner and Peter Casarella. Grand Rapids: Eerdmans, 1988.

Przywara, Erich. *Analogia entis: Metaphysik*. Munich: Josef Kösel & Friedrich Pustet, 1932.

Quinn, Phillip L. *Divine Command Theories and Moral Requirements*. Oxford: Clarendon Press, 1978.

———. "The Recent Revival of Divine Command Ethics." *Philosophical and Phenomenological Research*. vol. 1, Supplement (1990).

Rahner, Hugo, and Karl Rahner. "Ein Brüderlicher Geburtstagbrief." In *"Gemeinsame Arbeit in Brüderlicher Liebe": Hugo und Karl Rahner— Dokumente und Würdigung Hirer Weggemeinschaft*, edited by Abraham Peter Kustermann and Karl H. Neufeld. Stuttgart.

Rahner, Karl. "Concerning the Relationship Between Nature and Grace." In *Theological Investigations*. Volume 1. London: Darton, Longman & Todd, 1966.

———. "Dialogue with God?" In *Theological Investigations*. Volume 18. New York: Crossroad, 1983.

———. "Experience of the Holy Spirit." In *Theological Investigations*. Volume 18. New York: Crossroad, 1983.

———. *Faith in a Wintry Season: Conversations and Interviews with Karl Rahner in the Last Years of His Life*. Edited by Paul Imhof and Hubert Biallowons. Translated by Harvey D. Egan. New York: Crossroad, 1991.

———. *Foundations of Christian Faith*. Translated by William V. Dych. New York: Crossroad, 1989.

———. "The Ignatian Mysticism of Joy in the World." In *Theological Investigations*. Volume 3 London: Darton, Longman & Todd, 1967.

———. "The Individual in the Church." In *Nature and Grace: Dilemmas in the Modern Church*. New York: Sheed & Ward, 1964.

———. *Karl Rahner in Dialogue: Conversations and Interviews, 1965–1982*. Edited by Paul Imhof and Hubert Biallowons. New York: Crossroad, 1986.

———. "The Logic of Concrete Individual Knowledge in Ignatius Loyola." In *The Dynamic Element in the Church*. New York: Herder & Herder, 1964.

———. "Nature and Grace." In *Theological Investigations*. Volume 4. London: Darton, Longman & Todd, 1966.

———. "On the Question of a Formal Existential Ethics." In *Man in the Church*. In *Theological Investigations*. Volume 2.

———. "Reflections on the Unity of the Love of Neighbour and the Love of God." In *Theological Investigations*. Volume 6. London: Darton, Longman & Todd, 1974.

———. "Remarks on the Dogmatic Treatise 'De Trinitate.'" In *Theological Investigations*. London: Darton, Longman & Todd, 1966.

———. *The Trinity*. New York: Herder & Herder, 1970.

———. "The 'Commandment' of Love in Relation to the Other Commandments." In *Theological Investigations*. London: Darton, Longman & Todd, 1966.

Rigali, Norbert. "The Uniqueness and the Distinctiveness of Christian Ethics and Morality." In *Moral Theology: Challenges for the Future,* edited by Charles Curran. New York: Paulist, 1990.

Römelt, Josef. *Personales Gottesverständnis in Heutiger Moraltheologie: Auf dem Hintergrund der Theologien von K. Rahner und H. U. von Balthasar*. Innsbruck: Tyrolia-Verlag, 1988.

Ryan, Peter. "Moral Action and the Ultimate End of Man: The Significance of the Debate Between Henri de Lubac and His Critics." Diss., Gregorian University, Rome, 1996.

Sachs, John R. "Deus Semper Major—Ad Majorem Dei Gloriam: The Pneumatology and Spirituality of Hans Urs von Balthasar." *Gregorianum* 74, no. 4 (1993).

Saliers, Don E. "Liturgy and Ethics: Some New Beginnings." In *Liturgy and the Moral Self: Humanity at Full Stretch Before God*, edited by E. Byron Anderson and Bruce T. Morrill. Collegeville, Minn.: Liturgical Press, 1998.

Servais, Jacques. *Theologie Des Exercices Spirituels: Hans Urs von Balthasar Interprète Ignace*. Bruxelles: Culture et Vérité, 1996.

Simmel, Georg. *Kant und Goethe: Zur Geschichte der Modernen Weltanschauung*. Leipzig: Kurt Wolff Verlag.

Spohn, William C. *Go and Do Likewise: Jesus and Ethics.* New York: Continuum, 1999.

Taylor, Charles. *Sources of the Self: The Making of the Modern Identity.* Cambridge, Mass.: Harvard University Press, 1989.

Tillich, Paul. *The Protestant Era.* Translated by James Luther Adams. Chicago: University of Chicago Press, 1948.

Toner, Jules J. *Discerning God's Will: Ignatius of Loyola's Teaching on Christian Decision Making.* St. Louis: Institute of Jesuit Sources, 1991.

Vacek, Edward Collins. "Divine-Command, Natural-Law, and Mutual-Love Ethics." *Theological Studies* 57, no. 4 (December 1996).

———. *Love, Human and Divine: The Heart of Christian Ethics.* Washington, D.C.: Georgetown University Press, 1994.

Vatican Council II: The Conciliar and Post Conciliar Documents. Edited by Austin Flannery. Northport, N.Y.: Costello Publishing Company, 1988.

Williams, Rowan. "Balthasar and Rahner." In *The Analogy of Beauty,* edited by John Riches. Edinburgh: T&T Clark, 1986.

Wippel, John F. "Thomas Aquinas and Participation." In *Studies in Medieval Philosophy,* edited by John Wippel. Volume 17. Washington, D.C.: Catholic University of America Press, 1987.

Index

absolute, the
and contingency, 76
and meaningful existence, 73–77
and narrative identity, 76
Adams, Robert M., 177n. 68, 180n. 8, 203n. 66
Aertsen, Jan A., 163nn. 3, 5
agapē (kenotic love), 78
aesthetic ethics, 124–28
aesthetic holism, 166n. 31
aesthetic rationality, 94, 159
aesthetics
and beautiful form, 16–19
iconic, 6, 53, 86, 146
and metaphysics, 165n. 20
two meanings of, 16–17
theological, 1, 5, 16, 77, 81, 123, 128, 134, 152, 154
agency, human, 63, 102
integrity of, 64
and obedience, 72
analogy of being, 11, 13, 82, 186n. 55
Anselm, 10, 26, 168n. 44
appropriation, principle of, 49
Aristotle, 11
Athanasius, 45, 173n. 30
attunement, 127–28, 145–49, 153
Augustine, 10, 92, 167n. 38, 184n. 31
Neoplatonism of, 182n. 23
thought of, on love, 77, 93

autonomy
human, 63, 81, 83, 186n. 55, 187n. 61
of created order, 95
and Holy Spirit, 85
and obedience, 72

Bañez, Domingo, 97
baptism, 135
See also church; sacraments
Barth, Karl, 2, 4, 63, 162n. 4, 170n. 2, 173n. 23, 177n. 70, 178n. 74, 179nn. 79, 80; 179n. 83, 185nn. 46, 47; 186nn. 48, 49, 55, 57, 58; 190n. 32, 191nn. 41, 44; 193nn. 64, 67; 204n. 9
and beauty, 82
and covenantal relationship, 2–3
and divine command theory, 59–61
ethics of, 81
and "formed references," 112
von Balthasar's critical interpretation of, 103–8, 145
beauty, 164nn. 17, 18; 186n. 55
as address, 21–22
of Christ, 9
and connection between truth and goodness, 12
of creation, 163n. 1
divine, 8, 12, 66
and divine glory, 7–8, 9, 150

beauty (*cont.*)
    and gift and gratitude, 22–27
    and gospel, 10
    as heuristic lens, 77
    and human agency, 20–28
    meaning of, for von Balthasar, 8
    in von Balthasar's theological
        reflection, 9–14
    See also glory
Bellamy, Michael O., 203n. 63
Best, Ernest, 174nn. 36, 40
Betz, H. D., 174n. 41
biblical narrative, 133, 134
    See also divine–human encounter;
        Scripture
Biggar, Nigel, 177n. 71, 178n. 74
Blondel, Maurice, 96
Bonaventure, 182n. 23
Bouillard, Henri, 96
Burrell, David, 204n. 8

Cahill, Lisa Sowle, 96
Cajetan, Cardinal, 97
Catholic ethics, 94–95
    presuppositions of, 95
Catholic moral theory, 5
Christ
    sacrifice of, 86
    See also Jesus
Christ-event, 19, 89, 130, 133, 175n.
    50
    as drama, 55–56
    and economy of salvation, 70–71
Christ-form, 17, 19–20, 26, 70
    appearance of, 134, 150
    and beauty, 19
    and discontinuity, 80
    dramatic, 54–58
    glory of, 6
    kenotic movement of, 132
    mediation of, 134–36
    as ultimate moral object, 128–29
    visibility of, 20
Christian, as image of Christ, 47
Christian particularism. *See* particular-
    ism, Christian
Christian perception, 18, 128–45, 146
    subject and object of, 131–34

Christian response, 85–86
Christology
    and beauty, 11–12
church
    appearance of divine glory in, 152
    as mediator of Christ-form, 135–36
    ministry of, and glory of God, 1
Clarke, W. Norris, S.J., 167n. 34
Congar, Yves, 96
contemplation, 141, 156
    and action, 147, 192n. 52
    and moral life, 157
contingency, 141
    and the absolute, 76
    and human identity, 73
covenant
    between God and humans, 67–68,
        94
    and creation, 109
    and obedience, 69
    presuppositions of, 102–7
covenantal relationship, 2, 151
    and divine command ethics, 60
creation, 187n. 67
    agency in, 107
    and analogy of being, 13
    and covenant, 109
    God's call perceived in, 107
    and human fulfillment, 79–80
    as mediator of Christ-form, 134–35
    openness of, 169n. 55
    theological doctrine of, 103
Curran, Charles, 96, 100, 164n. 14,
    190n. 23

D'Arcy, Eric, 181n. 15
Davis, Henry, 98, 189n. 16
de Lubac, Henri, 96, 189nn. 9, 12,
    14; 190n. 19
    on nature and grace, 97–99
Deissmann, A., 174n. 36
Denziger, Heinrich, 203n. 66
discontinuity, 72–73, 79, 82
    and the Christ-form, 80
divine beauty. *See* beauty
divine command ethics, 1–2, 58–61,
    84, 123
    and covenantal relationship, 60

Ignatian reconfiguration of, 152
    particularist view of, 95
    as philosophical theory, 65
    and theological aesthetics, 81, 123
divine command theory, 6, 59
    and Karl Barth, 59
    motifs of, 2
divine glory
    and beauty, 7–8
    and human response, 30–32
    See also glory; God
divine–human encounter, 33, 133, 154
    as an encounter of freedoms, 33
    prayer and, 136
    Scripture and, 133–34, 201n. 41
divine–human relationship, 59
divine Other, 82
divine will
    ethics and, 2
doxa (glory), 17, 19
    See also glory
drama of salvation, 64
dramatic aesthetics, 6, 53, 86
    See also theo-dramatic aesthetics
dramatic form, 34, 50–58, 141–45
    and divine–human encounter, 33
    and interpersonal encounter, 32–33
    of tragedy, 142
Duffy, Stephen J., 189n. 7

Eckhart, Meister, 182n. 23
economy of salvation
    and Christ-event, 70
    church and, 135
    and God's glory, 123
    and obedience, 67–71
    and prophetic witness, 70
egoism, 141
Ellul, Jacques, 63, 180n. 4
En Christōi, 46–48
Endean, Philip, 162n. 12
eros-love, 77, 183n. 26
eschatology, realized, 129
esotericism, 6
ethics
    christological foundation of, 1
    grounding of, 9

narrative, 74, 133, 181n. 17
    teleological, 72–74
    theonomous, 82
    trinitarian, 87
Eucharist, 45, 149
existence, meaningful
    and the absolute, 73–77

faith
    as creaturely obedience, 80
    Spirit and, 48
    as total human response, 132, 150
Farley, Margaret A., 167n. 34, 168n. 48
Fields, Stephen, 202n. 53
Finnis, John, 96
Fitzmyer, Joseph A., S.J., 174nn. 35, 37
Fleming, David, 184n. 30
form
    and light, 16
    meaning of, 15
    See also form, beautiful
form, beautiful, 9, 14–20
    and aesthetics, 16–19
    and creation, 13
    Mozart's *Magic Flute* as example of, 24
    and splendor, 14–16
freedom
    Christian, 69
    creaturely, 185nn. 37, 63
    divine, 105, 187n. 62
    God as, 37
    and Holy Spirit, 85
    human, 63, 83, 105, 167n. 34
    and identity, 76
    and obedience, 72
    two poles of, 76
Frye, Northrop, 176n. 58
Fuchs, Josef, 62, 63, 87, 179n. 1
fulfillment
    human, 63, 64, 87–91
    question of, 72–80

Galvin, John P., 190n. 20
Gardeil, Ambroise, 189n. 12
Gawronski, Raymond, 183n. 26

German idealism, 182n. 23
gift
     and beauty and gratitude, 22–27
     and response, 168n. 40
Gilleman, Gérard, 1, 189n. 17
Gilson, Etienne, 11, 163n. 6
glory, 17, 19
     faith as response to, 132, 150
     meaning of, for von Balthasar, 8–9
     See also beauty
God
     as absolute Thou, 138–41
     as active presence, 138
     covenantal, encounter with,
          137–41
     as Father, 39
     as freedom, 37
     glory of, 1, 69, 81, 123, 130,
          163n. 1
     as mystery, 137–38
     as Son, 39
     transcendental experience of, 139
     triune personal, 36–39, 140
Godhead
     relation of Son to Father in, 39–43
     unity of, 38
Goethe, 167n. 39
Good, the, 125
     as ultimate moral object for Mur-
          doch, 128–29, 141
grace. See nature and grace
gratitude, 22–27
Grisez, Germain, 96
Guardini, Romano, 183n. 25
Gustafson, James, 188n. 2

Hallet, Garth, 156, 204n. 6
Häring, Bernard, 1, 96
Hauerwas, Stanley, 74, 159, 164n. 14,
          181nn. 17, 18; 198n. 2, 201n.
          39, 204n. 8, 205n. 14
Heidegger, Martin, 165n. 21, 166nn.
          26, 27
     idea of truth of, 17
heteronomy, 186n. 56
Hill, William J., 171n. 10, 179n. 81
Hollenbach, David, 100–101, 190n.
          24

holy fool, 185n. 40
Holy Spirit. See Spirit
Hooker, Morna D., 47, 174nn. 39,
          40; 175n. 42
hope
     christological, 116
     eschatological, 116–17
     theological, 117
Hopkins, Gerard Manley, 10, 152,
          204n. 1
horizontal order, 94
horizontal time, 116
Hughes, Gerard, 72, 83, 100, 181n.
          14, 190n. 22
human agency. See agency, human
human fulfillment, 63, 64, 77, 181n.
          19
     bipolarity of, 77
     and creation, 79–80
     desire for, 72–73
     as eschatological, 87
     and God's call, 72
     and identity
     and moral life, 72
     and obedience, 72–91
     two teleologies of, 76–77
     and trinitarian ethics, 87–91
human relationships, 22–23
Hyland, Drew, 199n. 14
hypostases, 37

iconic aesthetics, 6, 53, 86, 146
idealism. See German idealism
identity, 154
     and finite roles, 75–76
     and freedom, 76
     and fulfillment, 73
     and mission, 89
     narrative, 74–75
Ignatian ideal, 16, 149
Ignatian movements of love, 77–80,
          86, 93, 113, 149
Ignatian template of contemplation
          and action, 107–8, 192n. 52
Ignatius of Loyola, 94, 111, 152,
          162n. 12, 182n. 23, 184nn. 29,
          32, 33, 34, 35; 185n. 38, 188n.
          72, 191n. 51, 192n. 54, 202n.
          52

and bipolarity of human fulfillment, 77
influence of, 4, 5
images
and moral imagination, 13
Incarnation, 190n. 33
kenosis of, 41, 46
incorporation into Christ, 43–50
the Spirit and, 49
individual
and beauty of Christ, 9
uniqueness of, 4
Innocent XII (pope), 203n. 66
interpersonal encounter, 28–33
and dramatic form, 32–33
and love of neighbor, 112–21
See also neighbor
Irenaeus, 10, 181n. 13
idea of recapitulation of, 70

Jesus
glorification of, 70
relation of, to Father, 39–40
sacrifice of, on the cross, 70
as Word of God, 70
See also Christ
John Paul II (pope)
Veritatis Splendor, 96
Johnson, Elizabeth A., 172n. 12
Jones, L. Gregory, 196n. 83

kābôd (glory), 17, 19, 181n. 12
See also glory
kalokagathia, 125
Kant, Immanuel, 25, 168n. 42
Kasper, Walter, 170nn. 5, 6; 171n. 10, 172n. 15, 175nn. 43, 47
Kay, Jeffrey Ames, 170n. 55
Keane, Philip S., 164n. 14, 203n. 71
kenosis, 132
and Christ's love, 77
of crucifixion, 138
of Incarnation, 138
Kierkegaard, Søren, 9
knowledge, 20

Lacugna, Catherine Mowry, 170n. 2, 172n. 13, 175n. 43

light
and form, 16
as Platonic metaphor, 15
Lindbeck, George, 133, 201n. 40
love, 158–59
as answer, 115–16
divine, 196nn. 91, 93
eucharistic, 117–18
as free and obedient, 27–28
Ignatian movements of, 77–80
as moral response, 64
as moved by christological hope for the neighbor, 116–17
of neighbor, 112–21, 123
Neoplatonic idea of, 77
seeking communion with the other, 118–19
teleology of, 119
See also neighbor
Lucas, F. L., 176n. 62

MacDonald, Scott, 163n. 4
MacNamara, Vincent, 189n. 6
McClendon, James W., 177n. 67
McCormick, Richard, 96, 100, 190n. 21
McDade, John, 176n. 58
McDonagh, Enda, 24, 168n. 41
McDonnell, Kilian, 48, 175n. 43
McIntosh, Mark A., 194n. 69
mediators of Christ, 134–36
metaphors
and moral imagination, 13
metaphysics
aesthetics and, 165n. 20
Milbank, John, 190n. 25
mission, 64, 91
Christian, 6, 110–11, 123, 133
christological, 74, 88, 114, 151, 153, 173n. 22
as gift of the Father, 42–43
and identity, 89–90
as intersection of horizontal and vertical, 92
and Jesus, 36, 42
and the Trinity, 83, 87–88
Moltmann, Jürgen, 117
moral absolutism, 96, 189n. 4

moral action, 20
moral agent
    and encounter with the Good, 125
moral choices, 110
moral imagination
    metaphors and images and, 13
moral law, 25
moral life
    according to Roman Catholic tradi-
        tion, 72, 77
    and contemplation, 157
    and eros-love, 77
    holiness and, 157
    and human fulfillment, 72
    as objective and rational, 95
    and response to God, 65–67
    and self-realization, 77
    as "universal," 95
moral reasoning, 102, 158
    creation and, 103
moral universalism, 190n. 29
Mouw, Richard J., 177n. 68
Mozart
    Magic Flute, 24, 25
Mühlen, Herbert, 171n. 10
Murdoch, Iris, 14, 124, 134, 164n.
        15, 198nn. 1, 3, 4, 6, 8–13;
        199nn. 15–16, 18–20; 202n.
        59, 203nn. 60–64, 67
    aesthetics of, 126
    and dramatic form, 141
    and integration of good and beau-
        tiful, 125–26
    moral agency in, 127
    moral task in, 142–45
    purified joy in, 142–44
    and the vision of the good,
        124–28, 146
mystery
    Christian experience of, 138
    God as, 137–38
mysticism, Christian, 184n. 32
myth, 52–53

natural law, 63, 193n. 64
nature and grace, 97–102, 189n. 7,
    191n. 34

neighbor, 193n. 68
    encounter with, 135–36
    love of, 112–21, 195nn. 78, 80
    as mediator of Christ, 136
    as mediator of God's call, 113–14
Neoplatonism, 182n. 23, 183n. 28,
    184n. 30
neoscholasticism, 164n. 9
Newman, John Henry, 157
Nichols, Aidan, O.P., 173n. 25
Niebuhr, H. Richard, 138, 164n. 14,
    202n. 51
Noldin, H., 189n. 15
nouvelle théologie, 163n. 9
Nussbaum, Martha, 143, 176n. 63,
    203n. 65
Nygren, Anders, 183n. 26

Oakes, Edward T., 164n. 12, 165n.
    19, 167n. 39
obedience, 63, 64, 192n. 55
    of Christ, 71
    and covenant, 69
    creaturely, 80–83, 93, 151
    divine, 83–87, 93, 151
    and human autonomy, 72
    and human fulfillment, 72–91
    of the prophets, 68–71, 85–86
obedience, Christian, 64–71
    and economy of salvation, 67–71
O'Donnell, John, 171n. 10, 174n. 32
O'Donoghue, Dermot, 190n. 30
Ogletree, Thomas, 201n. 39
O'Hanlon, Gerard F., 173n. 20
O'Malley, John W., S.J., 192n. 53
O'Regan, Cyril, 165n. 21, 167n. 39,
    168n. 42, 200n. 35, 202nn. 45,
    47
Origen, 173n. 23, 196n. 92
Otto, Rudolph, 137, 202n. 46
Outka, Gene, 180n. 4, 197n. 97,
    201n. 39

particularism
    Christian, 94–102
    ethical, 95
Pascal, 10

Paul VI (pope)
  Humanae Vitae, 192–93n. 59,
    204n. 11
Péguy, Charles, 196n. 85
personhood
  call to, 140
phenomenological tradition, 18
Plato, 126, 142–43, 183n. 26, 199n.
    14
Platonism, 182n. 23
pleasure-seeking, 9
  and Christian ethics, 9
prayer
  and divine–human encounter, 136
processions
  of the Trinity, 39–40
prophets
  and obedience, 67–69, 85–86
proportionalism, 96, 189n. 4
Przywara, Erich, 13, 164nn. 12, 13
  and analogy of being, 13

Quinn, Philip L., 177n. 68

Rahner, Karl, 2, 3–4, 162nn. 5–10,
    12; 168n. 40; 170nn. 2, 3, 5;
    171n. 8, 175n. 44, 176n. 59,
    178n. 72, 182n. 20, 189n. 13,
    190nn. 26, 27, 28; 191n. 50,
    195nn. 77, 79, 81; 200n. 27,
    202nn. 52, 54, 55
  and "anonymous Christian," 100,
    194n. 75
  on influence of Ignatius of Loyola,
    5, 139
  on love of neighbor, 114–15
  on nature and grace, 97, 99–102,
    189n. 10
  on prayer, 139
  transcendental subjectivity of, 139
  on the Trinity, 36, 38, 40, 56,
    172n. 15
reason, use of
  and obedience, 72
reductionism, 18
relationality
  as basic to human existence, 21

relationships, human. *See* human rela-
    tionships
Richard of St. Victor, 171n. 10
Rigali, Norbert, S.J., 180n. 5
Römelt, Josef, 168n. 40
Ryan, Peter, 189nn. 11, 15

Sachs, John R., 171n. 10
sacraments
  pointing to events of the economy
    of salvation, 135
  See also church
Saliers, Don E., 203n. 71
salvation history, 43–44
  prophets and, 69
Scripture, 133–34, 165n. 23, 201n.
    41
  and the church, 135, 136
  contemplative approach to, 156–57
  and glory of God, 1
  See also biblical narrative
secondary moral concepts, 125
Servais, Jacques, 185n. 37
sin, 67, 141
solidarity
  of Christ with humanity, 113
Spirit, 175n. 45, 204n. 4, 48–50,
    155–56
  and autonomy, 85
  experience of, 129
  and freedom, 85
  as gift of God's presence, 85
  "liquefying" Christ, 49–50, 89,
    113, 132–33
spiritual senses, 129–30, 203n. 69
splendor
  meaning of, 15
  See also form, beautiful
Spohn, William, 164n. 14, 203n. 71
soteriology, 46
Suarez, Francisco, 97, 189n. 10
subordinationism, 39

Taylor, Charles, 17, 164n. 14, 166n.
    26, 198n. 5
Teilhard de Chardin, 96
teleology
  narrative, 76
  of freedom, 76

theo-drama, 53, 58
theo-dramatic aesthetics. 34
theological aesthetics. *See* aesthetics,
     theological
theological voluntarism, 2, 4, 65, 84
theonomy, 186n. 56
theory of beauty
     and aesthetics, 16
     See also theory of perception
theory of perception
     and aesthetics, 16–17
Thomas Aquinas, 5, 10–11, 39, 73,
     74, 92, 163n. 5, 167n. 38,
     169n. 48, 173n. 22, 181nn. 16,
     17
     and attunement, 148–49
     ethics and, 161n. 3
     highest act for, 75
     and metaphysics, 163nn. 7, 8
     on nature and grace, 97
     Neoplatonism of, 182n. 23
     on the Trinity, 171n. 11
Tillich, Paul, 82, 186n. 56
Toner, Jules J., S.J., 191n. 51
transcendentals, 10–11
Trinity, 167n. 36, 171nn. 9, 10; 194n.
     71
     as ground for relationality, 21
     and mission, 83

obedience and, 83
processions of, 39–40
von Balthasar's understanding of,
     35
truth
     as disclosure, for Heidegger, 17
     as event, 17
     and scientific conclusions, 12
     von Balthasar's idea of, 17

universalism
     ethical, 95–96
     moral, 190n. 29
     and moral order, 95–96

Vacek, Edward Collins, S.J., 169n. 48,
     172nn. 16, 17; 186n. 60
Vatican II, 1, 97, 161n. 2, 188n. 3,
     189n. 8, 190n. 18
     on moral theology, 98
vertical time, 116
von Speyr, Adrienne, 173nn. 21, 28;
     194n. 71, 195n. 82

Williams, Rowan, 168n. 43, 176n. 55
Wippel, John F., 163n. 7
Word of God, 82
world, engagement with, 137